PARALLEL SYSTEMS
IN THE DATA WAREHOUSE

ISBN 0-13-680604-X

9 780136 806042

90000

THE DATA WAREHOUSING INSTITUTE SERIES FROM PRENTICE HALL PTR

Parallel Systems in the Data Warehouse
   by Morse and Isaac

Planning and Designing the Data Warehouse
   by Barquin and Edelstein

Building, Using, and Managing the Data Warehouse
   by Barquin and Edelstein

Data Mining: A Hand's On Approach for Business Professionals by Groth

Decision Support in the Data Warehouse
   by Watson and Gray

Solving Data Mining Problems Through Pattern Recognition by Kennedy et al.

PARALLEL SYSTEMS IN THE DATA WAREHOUSE

Stephen Morse
David Isaac

To join a Prentice Hall PTR
Internet mailing list, point to
http://www.prenhall.com/mail_lists/

Prentice Hall PTR, Upper Saddle River, New Jersey 07458

Library of Congress Cataloging in Publication Data

Morse, Stephen.
    Parallel systems in the data warehouse / Stephen Morse, David
Isaac.
        p. cm. -- (The Data Warehousing Institute series from
Prentice Hall PTR ; 3)
    Includes bibliographical references and index.
    ISBN 0-13-680604-X
    1. Data warehousing. 2. Parallel processing (Electronic
computers) I. Isaac, David.   II. Title.   III. Series.
QA76.9.D37M67   1998
005.75'6--dc21
                                                                97-34527
                                                                CIP

Acquisitions editor: *Mark L. Taub*
Editorial assistant: *Tara Ruggiero*
Production supervision: *Kerry Reardon*
Cover design: *Anthony Gemmellaro*
Cover design director: *Jerry Votta*
Page layout: *Mary Strunk*
Manufacturing manager: *Alexis R. Heydt*
Marketing manager: *Dan Rush*

© 1998 by Prentice Hall PTR
Prentice-Hall, Inc.
A Simon & Schuster Company
Upper Saddle River, New Jersey 07458

Prentice Hall books are widely used by corporations and government
agencies for training, marketing, and resale.

The publisher offers discounts on this book when ordered in bulk
quantities. For more information, contact Corporate Sales Department,
Prentice Hall PTR, One Lake Street, Upper Saddle River, NJ 07458.
Phone: 800-382-3419; Fax: 201-236-7141; e-mail: corpsales@prenhall.com

All product names mentioned herein are the trademarks of their respective owners.

Printed in the United States of America
10 9 8 7 6 5 4 3 2 1

ISBN 0-13-680604-X

Prentice-Hall International (UK) Limited, *London*
Prentice-Hall of Australia Pty. Limited, *Sydney*
Prentice-Hall Canada Inc., *Toronto*
Prentice-Hall Hispanoamericana, S.A., *Mexico*
Prentice-Hall of India Private Limited, *New Delhi*
Prentice-Hall of Japan, Inc., *Tokyo*
Simon & Schuster Asia Pte. Ltd., *Singapore*
Editora Prentice-Hall do Brasil, Ltda., *Rio de Janeiro*

Dedicated to Our Wives,

Debbie and Mary

Verweile doch! Du bist so schön!
-- Goethe, *Faust*

Contents

Series Foreword

Parallelism has now been with us for several decades, and yet it has only been in the last few years that we have started to see in earnest what it has brought to the information technology world. I can recall my days in graduate school when real parallel processing was still a gleam in most professors' eyes. We dabbled with tools such as Petri nets, and with other techniques that were building blocks to asynchronous processing. In the blink of an eye effective and practical parallelism was upon us.

There have been several important breakthroughs that have enabled the application of data warehousing to solve enterprise problems. Certainly the emergence of very fast processors, the enhancement of indexing techniques in most popular relational DBMS, the development of proprietary multidimensional database engines, the utilization of innovative schemas such as the star, and the expansion of 64 bit processors have all played a significant role. Yet parallelism stands out as being among the truly most important.

What could we do with some of the current generation of data warehouses without parallel systems? If we were given a one terabyte data warehouse just a few years ago, there really wasn't much that we could accomplish in terms of timely response to queries or other on-line analytical processing (OLAP). Yet today, we have several multiple terabyte data warehouses, including Wal*Mart's going from 8 to 24 terabytes, that are actually achieving real business objectives with reasonable response times.

Without a doubt, parallel query databases have become the bread and butter of very large data warehouses. But because parallel query algorithms execute on data that sits in either local or remote memory or disk, the issue of architecture and scalability looms very large.

Symmetric multiprocessors (SMP) access only local memory and local disk. But massively parallel processors (MPP) have to access both local and remote data in both disk and memory and complexity starts to hit in a significant manner.

There was a time when even bright young programmers dreaded having to deal with MPP and its intricacies. Well, no longer; and one of the reasons is this book by Stephen Morse and David Isaac.

Morse and Isaac are very well positioned to write this book. They have been in the thick of parallelism—parallel databases, parallel processors, parallel systems—for years and have been dealing with very large databases as a result of work they *and their MRJ colleagues* have done for *the intelligence and law enforcement communities, as well as a number of commercial projects*. I have the pleasure of knowing both Stephen and David personally and professionally and think very highly of their technical capabilities. In this volume they have tackled a difficult area, and one that is central to data warehousing. And they have gone a long way toward demystifying parallelism, that is, taking it out of the black box and explaining the mechanics.

When I laid *out* the framework for the Prentice-Hall Data Warehousing Series of the Data Warehouse Institute, it was not clear in my mind where in the sequence we needed to tackle parallelism. After reading the Morse and Isaac book, I am convinced that this is where it belongs. Join us in going behind the covers and understanding better the world of parallel systems, and its meaning for data warehousing.

Dr. Ramon C. Barquin, Series Editor
President, Barquin and Associates, Inc.
Chair, Advisory Board, The Data Warehousing Institute

Preface

A TALE OF TWO TECHNOLOGIES

The time is 1991, and the topic is large-scale parallel processing. Several vendors have large systems that have already passed traditional vector processors for world speed records on scientific applications. Sales to the national labs and academic accounts are so-so, but it is becoming clear that these sales alone cannot sustain the R&D efforts required to keep the technology afloat, much less actually make a profit. The proponents of venture capital and federal funding for these various products are starting to get nervous: When will this technology begin to be able to pay its own way? What commercial application might demand the computing horsepower and I/O bandwidth that these architectures are able to deliver?

The time is still 1991, but now attention turns to the IT shops of many large corporations. It is becoming clear that buried in the transaction logs of the OLTP systems (accounting, inventory, point of sales, insurance claims, and so on) is information that could be of great strategic value to the business. The problem is that the schemas associated with OLTP (according to the consultants engaged to diagnose the problem) are not suitable for the types of queries that need to be processed. When submitted to the database system, these queries may run for days or weeks and can affect the ongoing production transaction stream. What is needed is a separate system that incorporates data from previously disparate organizations within the enterprise, with schemas and operational characteristics quite different from those of traditional production OLTP systems. The terms *data warehouse* and *decision support* are starting to turn up with increasing frequency in the IT journals and conferences. However, as soon as a requirements study is done, the I/O and processing requirements turn into truly unacceptable numbers of mainframes. Even if the data can be collected, cleaned, and organized into an acceptable design, where is the technology going to come from to process the complex queries against monster tables in acceptable time and at acceptable cost?

The reader will sense in the preceding paragraphs a "marriage made in heaven," and the way this union has developed—large parallel processing systems executing complex relational queries against very large decision support databases—is one of the most interesting and instructive stories in commercial computing over the past seven years. It is the *thesis* of this book that in its role of providing cost-effective platforms for data warehouses, parallel computing has at last come of age and entered the mainstream of commercial computing. It is the *purpose* of this book to provide the essential technical background to allow the reader to decide for herself whether the thesis is correct. A secondary benefit (perhaps primary in the minds of some) is to enable the reader to engage on more-or-less equal terms with representatives from the various vendors of parallel hardware and database software. What are the right questions to ask? What isn't being included in the sales pitch? Why aren't the good benchmark numbers an adequate summary of what the eventual experience with the deployed system will be? The attentive reader will come away from the book able to play "I'm from Missouri" about large parallel database systems with a sound technical underpinning.

ORGANIZATION, ASSUMPTIONS, AND LEVEL OF PRESENTATION

To impose some order on this large topic, we have divided the material into four parts, of four chapters each, as follows.

Part I: Hardware. A tutorial introduction to the three major parallel hardware architectures currently on the market: symmetric multiprocessors (SMP); distributed memory (DM) machines, sometimes called massively parallel processors (MPP); and distributed shared memory (DSM) machines, also referred to as nonuniform memory access (NUMA). A discussion is also provided in Chapter 4 of how parallel systems achieve very high I/O bandwidth against single tables.

Part II: Software. A tutorial introduction to parallel relational database software. How can a single large query be decomposed into many (hundreds) separate independent instruction streams so as to execute large complex queries at interactive rates? The three principal approaches—shared everything, shared disk, and shared nothing—are presented and compared. In Chapter 8 we then take up the question of sorting data in parallel and describe its importance for data mining algorithms.

Part III: Examples of Commercial Practice. Four hardware/software combinations from the commercial world are examined in some detail to illustrate in concrete terms the principles introduced in Parts I and II.

Part IV: Applications and Implementations. Chapters are provided for OLAP, data mining, object-relational databases (called universal database servers), and a capstone chapter on implementation considerations.

Two assumptions have influenced the selection and presentation of this material. First, we have focused exclusively on Unix systems. This is not because we think Unix is better than other operating systems (although it is now very good indeed) but because (1) it is an open industry standard, (2) we wish to avoid proprietary implementations, and (3) it is what we know best. Similarly, when we talk about databases, we will always mean relational databases, and we will use SQL terminology from time to time to illustrate key points. A further assumption, implicit in the title, is a focus on decision support systems (DSS). This type of processing is very different from on-line transaction processing (OLTP); and while parallel processing has been shown to be effective for OLTP, that will not be our interest.

The level of presentation is somewhat informal, reflecting our desire not to intimidate readers new to the material. There is an extensive glossary, and when new topics are introduced, the discussion is leisurely and full of examples. Although we do not compromise on technical accuracy, our primary concern is to convey useful information in a complete and accessible manner. Readers with a strong technical background can, we hope, rapidly skim introductory material and locate the next level of detail without undue difficulty.

THEMES

Two subthemes recur frequently and reflect our bias. The first concerns data mining. Our view is that data summaries at varying levels of detail—the "data cube" of OLAP products—is only the beginning of the utility of large decision support systems. The ability to extract unexpected patterns and relationships from very large databases is, we feel, of equal (or greater) value for many organizations. The algorithms to accomplish this type of knowledge extraction may not be easily expressed in SQL, so that an interface between the data mining application and the parallel database is required. At appropriate points we take up the question of what that interface ought to be. Similarly, sorting of very large flat files is a key component of many data mining algorithms, and the issues associated with sorting therefore receive special emphasis.

A second theme concerns the importance of sustained high-bandwidth I/O against single tables. For complex decision support queries, the traditional techniques for improving performance (indexing, high degrees of normalization) will not succeed. Rather, achieving very fast scan rates is the key to good performance in a data warehouse. Chief among techniques to achieve this goal is the need to partition the data over multiple disks, controllers, and I/O channels. Various approaches to data partitioning, and their respective strengths and weaknesses, thus receive considerable attention, since they are likely to be a key aspect of parallel design and tuning.

Finally, we pause briefly to mention our division of labor in writing the book. This has been a joint effort throughout, but primary responsibility for various chapters fell on one or another of our shoulders. David Isaac was the principal author for Chapter 10 and Chapters 13 to 15; Steve Morse was the principal author for the remainder of the book.

Acknowledgments

Although many people contributed to this book, the person most directly responsible for its success is the president of MRJ Technology Solutions, Dr. Robert M. Farrell. Bob took this project under his personal supervision and refused to allow any obstacles to prevent its successful completion. On the technical side, his vision and technical direction are evident throughout the book. He insisted on a difficult combination of the highest technical accuracy coupled with clarity and imagination in the presentation. In addition to a detailed technical review of the book, he spent many hours with us discussing difficult points, clarifying ambiguities, suggesting strategies, and selecting appropriate areas for emphasis. On the management side, Bob made available the resources—time and money—for us to pursue the project and smoothed the way through a forest of administrative difficulties. On a personal note it has been a wonderful experience to work closely with Bob throughout this process, and we are grateful for his insight and support.

The editor of this series on data warehouses is Ramon Barquin. We are grateful for his confidence in this project, and for his generous Foreword. We also thank Scott Miller, the director of the High Performance Computing division at MRJ, for making time available from other projects for writing.

In Part III we present a number of examples of commercial practice, both parallel hardware platforms and parallel relational database systems. To assemble this material required extensive direct support from technically knowledgeable employees of these companies. These people spent considerable time educating us about their products, providing background documentation, and reviewing our book for technical accuracy. We are glad, therefore, to acknowledge the assistance and support of the following people and their companies:

Dan Holle, White Cross Systems

Doug Heying, White Cross Systems

Glen Sheffield, IBM

Brad Carlile, Sun Microsystems

Pete McDonald, Hewlett-Packard

Ted Buis, Hewlett-Packard

Mike Tinius, Informix

A number of people at MRJ Technology Solutions also contributed in various ways to this project. Randy Crawford is MRJ's I/O guru, and his technical breadth and insight provided an invaluable resource. Chapter 4, in particular, owes much to Randy's gentle but insistent suggestions and corrections. George Wilson has been doing high-end parallel data mining at MRJ for a number of years and has a wealth of both practical experience and theoretical insight. His thorough technical review of Parts I and II provided a badly needed sanity check for some of our more outrageous digressions. Similarly, Toni Dzubay (our resident SQL and database expert) gave Part II a meticulous review; her technical and editorial suggestions were invaluable. Others who contributed in a variety of ways include Hoot Thompson, Lisa Sokol, Katharine Murphy, David Ray, Tony Castellano, and Ava Arnone.

Finally, to our families we say a heartfelt: Thanks!

Stephen Morse
David Isaac

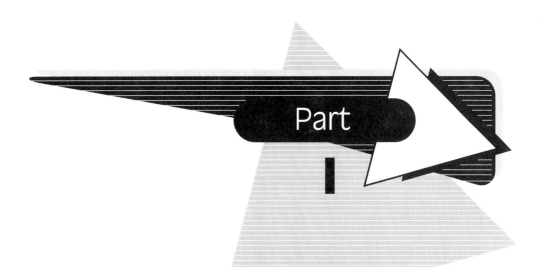

The Hardware
Platform

In Part I we consider three types of parallel hardware architectures on which parallel database software can execute. In Chapter 1 we consider symmetric multiprocessors. This shared memory architecture is by far the most commonly encountered in commercial practice, and illustrates well the difficulties of scalability that must be addressed for large data warehouse implementations. In Chapter 2 we turn to distributed memory architectures. We shall see how the scalability advantages of this architecture make it a strong contender for very large databases. In Chapter 3, distributed shared memory architectures are described. This is an emerging technology that attempts to combine the best features of the other two. Finally, a chapter is provided on I/O and storage issues as they relate specifically to parallel machines executing large

1

data warehouse applications. As we shall see, efficient design and parallelization of the I/O is often determinative for overall delivered performance.

Unlike generic sequential machines, in which much of the hardware detail can be hidden from the programmer, user, and administrator, the major hardware architecture features of parallel machines have a strong impact on how the software is designed and (just as important) on how the storage is partitioned and managed. It is this need to be aware of hardware detail that makes programming and administering these machines challenging and that must be taken into account in considering a parallel implementation of a data warehouse. Hardware issues will arise at several points in Part II, where we discuss the way in which parallel RDBMS software attempts to exploit the underlying hardware. Thus Parts I and II are companions, with Part I providing the necessary hardware concepts and terminology to ground the discussion of software architectures and algorithms introduced in Part II.

Although our primary focus is on the RDBMS as an SQL server for large DSS applications, a related concern is the use of the parallel machine as a platform for the execution of data mining algorithms. These may be custom code, for often data mining algorithms are not easily expressible in SQL. The result is that the software development environment of the machine can be an issue, and readers will find occasional digressions along these lines.

Chapter

1

Symmetric Multiprocessors

In this chapter we consider the most widely used parallel architecture, the *symmetric multiprocessor* (SMP). In Section 1.1 we present the basic ideas by discussing a generic top-level diagram for SMPs. The issues surrounding system-wide cache coherence are then discussed in some depth in Section 1.2. Issues that arise in optimizing the operating system for SMPs are presented in Section 1.3. Finally, in Section 1.4 we consider areas of strength and weakness, focusing particularly on lack of scalability. As throughout the book, the discussion focuses specifically on issues that are of concern for large data warehouse implementations.

1.1 BASIC CONCEPTS

The ideas behind symmetric multiprocessors (SMPs) have been around for a long time (see Figure 1–1). The *central processing unit* (CPU) is an expensive component, and in early

3

architectures the CPU would be forced to assist in input/output (I/O) operations. While I/O was going on, the CPU could not be involved in other, more useful work. This is illustrated graphically in the generic computer section of Figure 1–1. Data can move between memory and the I/O interface only by passing through the CPU.

Figure 1–1 Evolution of Symmetric Multiprocessors

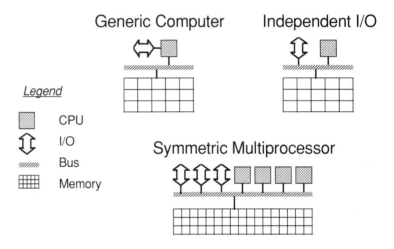

The next stage was to offload the I/O processing onto a relatively less expensive component which we might call an *I/O interface*. This device can access memory directly, without the assistance of the CPU [this capability is sometimes referred to as *direct memory access* (DMA)]. A protocol (that is, a prearranged sequence of signals) enables the CPU to notify the I/O interface where in memory the data should be put (for input) or where to go in memory to fetch the data (for output). Once the DMA data transfer is under way, the CPU can get back to its more important tasks. This is illustrated in the independent I/O section of Figure 1–1.

During periods when the CPU and the I/O controller are active simultaneously (the CPU processing a task using one portion of memory, and the I/O controller accessing a different portion of memory), a simple form of *parallel processing* is taking place. Different, independent operations are occurring *concurrently* (that is, *in parallel*). Further, as should be clear from the picture, both components (the CPU and the I/O controller) are accessing the same memory, although different portions of it. In standard parlance, the *memory* is being *shared* between the two components. Or, more to the point, a simple *shared memory architecture* has been constructed.

Once it became possible for more than one device to access the same shared memory space simultaneously and concurrently, the shared memory architecture was born. A simple illustration of a symmetric multiprocessor is shown in Figure 1–1. What you see is a number of independent CPUs and a number of independent I/O interfaces, all sharing access to a single, large memory space. In a typical configuration, each CPU can be executing its own job (or program) completely independent of the other CPUs. Similarly, each I/O controller can, simultaneously and independently, perform input/output operations at the request of various CPUs.

By assigning separate portions of the memory to the various components, the operating system (in this book, the Unix operating system is of most interest) enforces a strict separation between the ongoing operations. Even though the memory is physically shared, the operating system ensures logical separation; one CPU cannot "step on" the memory that has been allocated to another CPU (or I/O interface).

The most common way in which SMP architectures are used is to assign a separate job to each CPU. While one is executing (say) an accounting package, another might be supporting data analysis, while yet another is servicing an external file transfer request. All these operations can be going on independently, within the same machine, because (as we mentioned) the operating system keeps the processes separate from each other. To any one process, the system looks just like the simpler architecture shown on the top right of Figure 1–1. An important consequence of this approach is that applications intended for execution on a single-CPU sequential machine can execute just fine on an SMP—the program cannot tell the difference because by enforcing the logical barriers in memory, the operating system tricks the program into thinking that it has the entire machine to itself.

This way of running the machine, called *multitasking*, is a simple first step away from the earlier sequential architectures. A more challenging approach, however, involves letting several (or all) of the CPUs cooperate on a single program or application. The reason one might choose to do this is to make the application execute faster. The hope is that by putting (say) five CPUs to work on the problem, the problem gets done (say) five times as fast (or, alternatively, that a problem five times as large can be completed in a reasonable time). It is this second, more challenging way of using an SMP that truly deserves the name *parallel processing*. Simply to execute several different, independent programs on the same machine is useful, but it does not fully utilize the power of the architecture. In this book, whenever we speak of *parallel databases*, we mean a single, unified database application that uses multiple CPUs, concurrently, to get the job done faster (or to permit *larger* jobs to execute in the *same* amount of time).

These ideas are illustrated in Figure 1–2. On the left, a five-CPU SMP is executing five different jobs, labeled A through E. You can see the portions of memory assigned to each job (blank areas of memory have not yet been assigned and are available for use). This illustrates the *multitasking* use of the machine. On the right, the same set of CPUs are executing two jobs, marked F and G. Notice that four of the CPUs are cooperating on job G, and share all the portions of memory labeled G. By *sharing*, we mean that *any* of the four CPUs running job G can access *any* of the blocks of memory labeled

G; the operating system has taken down the logical barriers that separated the jobs in the multitasking scenario and permits the various CPUs to truly share access to commonly held areas of memory. Also note that as far as jobs F and G are concerned, the logical barriers imposed by the operating system still exist; job F cannot get to G's memory, and G cannot get to F's memory. So we see that in this example, multitasking (two tasks, F and G) and parallel processing (four CPUs working together on G) are actually both going on at the same time.

Figure 1–2   How SMPs Are Used

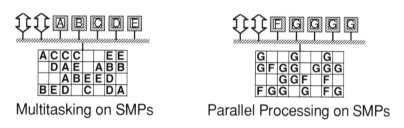

Multitasking on SMPs   Parallel Processing on SMPs

The success of SMPs in the marketplace is due almost entirely to the ability to execute in the multitasking mode. The machine is seen as a server that executes, on demand, any of a number of possible jobs on behalf of any from a large population of users. It is not necessary to buy a separate machine for each job; and when compared to *time sharing* (in which several jobs may share the resources of a single CPU), jobs execute faster because an entire CPU can be dedicated to each user. However, in the heart and soul of parallel programmers and machine architects, there continues to burn the hope and desire for true parallel processing—putting many CPUs to work, concurrently and in coordination, to greatly accelerate execution time on large, demanding problems—like data warehouses.

1.2 Cache Coherence in Symmetric Multiprocessors

The Need for Cache

What is cache, and why is it important? The answer, in a nutshell, is the growing mismatch between processing speeds of microprocessors, on the one hand, and retrieval rates of commodity DRAM memory parts, on the other. To understand this better, we need to take a short digression on the topic of DRAM.

The acronym *DRAM* stands for *dynamic random access memory*. DRAM is only one of many ways to implement memory using silicon chips, but it has three very (*VERY!*) useful properties. *First*, it is cheap: the cost per bit for DRAM is very low, which makes it ideal whenever price is a driving requirement (and realistically, who *isn't* worried about price?). DRAM is a commodity item, available from many sources, and subject to enormous market pressures to keep the price down, and falling. *Second*, DRAM does not take much power. In any application that needs to run outside a raised-floor computer room (and also in many that do need that environment), the low power consumption of DRAM translates into lower total power consumed, less heat dissipated, and hence longer mean-time-to-failure (*MTBF*, industry argot for the standard measurement of reliability and availability). The *third* property is *density*—that is, the number of memory bits that can be stuffed into a given amount of chip or board real estate. The current practice (mid 1996) is 64 million bits on a single chip. By the year 2000, this is expected to quadruple to 256 million bits of memory per chip. For large applications needing large amounts of cheap memory in a relatively small space (such as databases generally, and data warehouses especially), DRAM is the technology "dream come true."

However, DRAM has one significant problem: Even as the *density* of the technology has increased, the *time to access* a given amount of memory has stayed relatively constant. While processing rates of the microprocessors that access the memory have increased dramatically (the current generation of microprocessor can perform about 150 million operations per second, with this expected to approach 1 billion per second by the year 2000), the speed at which the DRAM memory can supply data to, and accept data from, the microprocessor remains flat. (*Note*: Some new DRAM technologies, such as SDRAMs, EDRAMs, and CDRAMs, are emerging in response to this bandwidth problem.) The result is a speed and performance mismatch. A good metaphor for the situation is a production facility manufacturing, say, diesel engines. It does not help to have ultramodern robotics able to turn out 200 engines a day if the supply lines feeding the factory are geared up to supply only enough raw materials and parts for 20 engines per day. The high-performance microprocessor is the modern factory, and the slow DRAM is the inadequate chain of supply. Another metaphor that is sometimes used to describe this situation is "feeding a linebacker with a soda straw." The soda straw, which can only pass along a small amount of Gatorade per second, corresponds to the low-speed DRAM; and the thirsty linebacker is the high-performance microprocessor. Just as the linebacker wants to drink *a lot* of Gatorade (not just sip it), the microprocessor wants to consume *a lot* of data to live up to its performance potential.

The solution that has been proposed to remedy this situation is *cache*. The main property of cache memory is that it is *fast*. Often, it is implemented on the same chip as the microprocessor—about as fast access to data as you can get. In addition, there is almost always another pool of cache memory implemented in SRAM (*static random access memory*). SRAM lacks all the good features of DRAM—it is expensive, a power hog, and not very dense—but it has the one good feature that

DRAM lacks: It is very fast, and hence is well matched to the speed of the microprocessor.

In a typical design, the cache is implemented using a small amount of fast SRAM. The cache sits between the microprocessor and the large DRAM memory. When the microprocessor makes a memory request, the *hope* is that the data being requested will *already* reside in the cache (this is called a *cache hit*). If it does, the memory access can complete very rapidly, without the microprocessor having to wait for the slow DRAM to complete. Of course, if the data does *not* reside in the cache (called a *cache miss*), the DRAM must be accessed, and no performance gain (for that access) occurs. Thus it will be seen at once that a high cache hit rate (that is, the fraction of accesses that can be completed without needing to go to the DRAM memory) will be a major factor in overall performance. High cache hit rates imply high performance, and vice versa.

What are typical cache hit rates for today's microprocessors and applications? The answer strongly depends on the problem being solved, the compiler used to generate the machine instructions, the size of the cache, and the skill of the programmer. Obviously, the desire is to move the data into the cache *before* it is needed by the CPU. A compiler, for example, can look ahead in the program and detect opportunities for "prefetching" the data.

The most important example of this technique is *locality of reference*. Statistically, it is known that if a program needs a word of data, the chances are strong (and can be made even stronger by a good compiler) that nearby words in memory will also be needed. Thus, when a memory reference is made, several nearby words of memory (called a *cache line*) are moved from DRAM to cache along with the specific word being asked for. The programmer can also help by arranging data layout to take advantage of locality of reference and by reusing data as much as possible. With care, it may be possible in this way for a *single* fetch of data to satisfy *many* subsequent CPU references. Large caches also increase the possibility for reuse, since the data can remain in the cache longer before it is "flushed" by some other data element taking its place. Finally, the nature of the problem being solved will often determine, to a great extent, how many opportunities there will be for such optimizations. Nevertheless, keeping all these caveats in mind, it is fair to say that cache hit rates in the range 95 to 99% are not uncommon for many database applications on SMPs. This is good news, since it means that the extraordinary processing power available in today's high-performance microprocessors is not being wasted due to inadequate memory bandwidth.

Caches in Symmetric Multiprocessors

The key ideas are illustrated in Figure 1-3. On the left we see the top-level block diagram. The high-speed cache sits between the CPU and the bus. Only if the data requested by the CPU does not reside in the cache will a bus-to-DRAM memory transaction be required. It is also seen immediately how caching extends naturally to SMPs. Each CPU in the SMP can have its own local cache. High cache hit rates both allow the CPU to execute faster *and* reduce the traffic across the bus and to the memory. This is illustrated on the right in Figure 1–3.

Figure 1–3   Use of Caches in SMPs

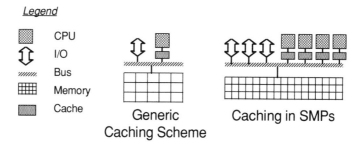

Legend

CPU
I/O
Bus
Memory
Cache

Generic
Caching Scheme

Caching in SMPs

This second benefit—reduced bus and memory traffic— in practice is as significant as the first. The bus and memory are (as the name SMP implies) *shared* resources. This means that only one CPU can have possession of the bus or memory at a time. While the bus and memory are fast, and transactions complete rapidly, there is still a finite not-to-exceed rate on both these components: the ability of the bus to transfer data (called its *bandwidth*, measured in millions of bytes transferred per second), and the ability of the memory to supply and accept data (also called *bandwidth*, with the same unit of measure). Both the bus and memory bandwidth are finite resources, and the CPUs in the SMP contend with each other for use of these resources. By reducing each CPU's need for bus and memory bandwidth, caching in SMPs reduces the likelihood of contention for resources, improves overall system performance, and permits a larger number of CPUs to share the bus and memory.

We can now take up the issue of *cache coherence*. The problem arises in the following way. Caches work by making a *copy* of data and placing the copy in the cache. The underlying "real" data still is held in the slower DRAM, but a copy of it resides in the higher-speed SRAM cache at each CPU. As we saw earlier, in a true parallel implementation, several CPUs in the SMP can cooperate on a single problem, in large part because they each are granted common access to shared areas of memory (recall Figure 1-2). In a caching SMP we see that it is possible for each of several CPUs to have its own private, cached copy of the single underlying true data value held in DRAM. And that's the problem—several local copies of the one single "true" value. Of course, no problem arises as long as none of the CPUs try to change (that is, write to) the value. But what if one of the CPUs changes the value of the copy it holds in its local cache? The other CPUs, with their own local cached copies of the data, had better be told; otherwise, they will continue to use the "old" or "dirty" data, and the result produced will be in error.

Cache coherence (or, more generally, *memory coherence*, or *coherent memory*) is the means by which the multiple locally cached versions of the one underlying true variable are kept logically consistent. The biggest job, as mentioned, arises when one of the CPUs wants to modify the value of the data. How are the other CPUs notified that they should no longer use their local (cached) versions of the data but, instead, should return to main memory to obtain an updated version?

In a bus-based SMP (such as we have been examining), cache coherence can be implemented rather simply by using the bus itself as the means of notification. That is, the bus is used not just to move data between the CPUs and memory but also to permit one CPU to alert the others that a locally cached value has been changed. There are several versions of rule schemes (protocols) for maintaining coherence, but they all have one common feature: They require each CPU to "listen in" or "snoop" on the bus constantly to see whether a "dirty data" message is being sent from some other CPU. These types of bus-based coherence schemes are sometimes called *snoopy protocols*, or *bus sniffing*. They all require the *bus* to be used as the means for one CPU to alert the others that a data modification has occurred. As we shall see, this need for the bus to maintain cache coherence via bus sniffing protocols becomes a major hindrance to scalability as architects try to build systems with large numbers of CPUs.

1.3 OPERATING SYSTEM ISSUES

The operating system (which for the purposes of this book, we assume to be some form of Unix) for SMPs has a number of functions and responsibilities that do not arise in a sequential, uniprocessor environment. We postpone a discussion of I/O, file systems, and external storage until Chapter 4. For the moment there are three items that can strongly affect RDBMS performance on these systems unless they are handled with some care: (1) tasks versus threads, (2) processor affinity, and (3) hot spots. We'll look at each in turn.

Tasks and Threads in SMP Systems

In the early days of Unix SMPs, parallelism was handled by creating multiple Unix processes. These would coordinate with each other by means of standard Unix messaging facilities (*pipes* or *queues*). At any given time, many of these processes might be "active" in the sense of schedulable, but only some would actually be executing on a processor. The rest would be "swapped out" in the time-sharing sense, waiting for their next slice of time on one of the processors.

There are a number of inefficiencies with such a scheme, and other versions of Unix evolved to address these concerns. Perhaps the most serious concern is the overhead involved in setting up and swapping a Unix process. The operating system maintains a considerable amount of information on each process. This information, called the *state* of the process, includes information on memory locations in use, data files that are open (and file pointers), where in the instruction sequence the process is, and so on. All of this information must be created each time a process is created, and must be saved and restored each time a process is swapped out or swapped in. This overhead is costly in parallel applications that only want to parallelize for a fairly short period. That is, the programmer might wish to put several CPUs to work on a particular part of the total problem and then release them again for use elsewhere once that phase is complete.

The reason behind such a programming approach is that not all parts of a problem are equally parallelizable. One part of a problem may be able to make efficient use of many CPUs, while the next may only be able to make use of one. In the technical argot of the community, there are *parallel regions* and *sequential regions* in the code. During a sequential region, a single CPU is at work; during a parallel region, however, many CPUs can be applied.

These ideas are shown in Figure 1–4. The processing time on the parallel regions can be shortened by assigning many CPUs to work on them. The sequential regions, on the other hand, cannot be effectively parallelized, and only a single CPU is assigned. This style of programming—alternating back and forth between sequential and parallel regions in the code—is characteristic of parallel applications on SMPs and, more important, does not fit neatly into the multiprocess, old-style Unix view of the world. What is wanted is a way to make multiple *threads of control* appear and vanish rapidly, as needed, without a lot of system overhead. A single governing thread of control, called a *task* in this way of speaking, corresponds roughly to an old-style Unix process. That task has all of the heavyweight state, but in addition has the ability both to create and terminate as many threads as it may need at any given time.

Figure 1–4 Parallel Code Regions in SMPs

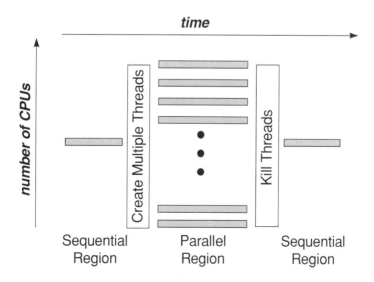

Figure 1–4, then, represents a single task (or program, or process). During sequential regions, it has only a single thread active. During parallel regions, it has many threads—typically, as many as there are CPUs available. When the parallel region ends, all but one of the threads is killed, and it continues with the next (sequential) region of processing. In considering RDBMSs on SMP platforms, the buyer should be cognizant of whether or not the code is *multithreaded* (in this more efficient manner just described).

Even if the code is multithreaded, however, it is good to know what fraction or percentage of the code resides in sequential versus parallel regions. The more of the code that is parallelizable, the faster the application will execute (since, clearly, more CPUs can be applied efficiently to parallel code regions). In perfectly parallel applications (sometimes referred to as *embarrassingly parallel*), there will be only one region, and it will be parallelizable. Most applications cannot do that well, but RDBMSs can typically get parallelism well above 95 to 98%, especially if the query being processed touches a large amount of data.

It is interesting in this regard that the fraction of parallelizable code typically *depends on the size of the problem being solved!* The larger the problem, the greater the fraction of execution time that can be spent in parallel regions, and hence the more efficiently the code can utilize the hardware. These issues, which have great practical significance, fall under the general heading of *Amdahl's law.* A good discussion can be found in Chapter 2 of *Practical Parallel Computing* (H. S. Morse, Academic Press Professional, Chestnut Hill, Mass., 1994). Briefly, Amdahl's law observes that the sequential part of the code (since, by definition, it cannot be parallelized) is a kind of roof or upper bound on how much performance improvement can be achieved *just be adding more processors*: Since you cannot speed up the sequential part by parallelization, you can never make an application execute any faster than it takes for the sequential part, no matter how many

CPUs are available. As we noted above, however, the size (that is, the fraction of execution time) spent on the sequential part depends much more on problem *size* than on the problem type. If the problem is large enough, very many (up to hundreds of) CPUs can be applied efficiently. This is certainly true of all the important database primitives (scans, selects, sorts, merges, and joins).

Processor Affinity

One of the major goals underlying an SMP is that from the user's point of view, it should make no difference which CPU is selected to execute the job. If the job executes on CPU 2 today and on CPU 6 tomorrow, the user should see no difference. In a caching environment, however, this "goal" for SMPs is no longer entirely achievable. The reason is that the contents of a CPU's cache, at any moment, is a reflection of the recent history of the program that has been executing. As the program executes and makes memory requests, the cache of the CPU on which it is running will fill, over time, with data needed by that particular program. Because the cache now contains data (and instructions) associated with the process, it does make a difference which CPU the program runs on. Once the cache has been primed in this way, the program (or, speaking less anthropomorphically, the user on whose behalf the prograram is running) really does prefer the CPU on which it resided most recently. If it were to be moved to a different CPU, the cache local to that CPU would have to be reprimed (that is, data would have to be moved from the slower DRAM memory to the faster cache). During that period, the program would then execute more slowly than if it had remained on its original CPU.

What sorts of events could cause a program to require such a migration? Or, put another way, how often will the situation described above (moving to a different CPU, and hence requiring a cache renewal) happen? The answer will depend, to a large extent, on the operational environment. What contention is there for the resources? How many other programs are waiting in the background to "bump" an ongoing process (as in time sharing)? And once a time slice opens up again for the program, is there any mechanism to ensure that it is reassigned to the CPU from which it was bumped (so that it can recover as much as possible of its prior cache state)?

These are the general issues revolving around *affinity* between processes (or threads) and CPUs. One way or another, we would like the operating system to be aware, when necessary, of the fact that an executing thread may have a lot invested in the cache state of a particular CPU and to make an effort to reassign the thread to the CPU on which it was executing previously. Operating systems on SMPs may or may not offer such facilities. And even if these capabilities are provided, programs and applications may or may not make efficient use of them.

How much performance impact does cache affinity have? Clearly, this will vary both from problem to problem and from machine to machine. The more CPUs are active, the more potentially serious the problem is. If all the threads are trying to prime their local caches simultaneously (not an unlikely situation after a context switch if there is no thread-to-CPU affinity), both the memory bandwidth and the bus bandwidth will be saturated, and the system will execute, in effect, as if DRAM were slower (since it is being shared) and as if no cache were available (since the local cache must be refilled). For large numbers of CPUs, this can result in a considerable slowdown every time a process swap occurs—several times per second is not an unreasonable estimate if the system has several jobs in the queue. Even if only one job is executing, however, the operating system itself has periodic (several times per second) tasks to perform (memory management, checking interrupts, etc.), and each of these events, although short in duration, could cause performance degradation if affinity is not provided.

The moral is that just as with multithreading, a smart buyer of RDBMS software for an SMP platform will inquire both about thread-to-CPU affinity (in the operating system) and about the extent to which the application software uses these facilities. As we indicated, this is likely to be more of an issue as the number of CPUs in the system increases. As a rule of thumb, we suggest that six or eight CPUs is the point at which this may become a performance issue.

Hot Spots

A third area of potential concern from an operating system standpoint is hot spots. They arise naturally in a shared memory system when several CPUs are trying to write to the same memory location. An example will illustrate this problem.

> Example: During the processing of a database query, it may be required to count the number of records that satisfy a certain condition. In a merchandizing application, the query may ask to count the number of items that required special restocking in district A during 3Q95. There are two components to satisfying this query. First, of course, the condition imposed (district A, 3Q95, restock) must be imposed. Second, a count of the records selected by the condition must be made.

> A typical way to parallelize this operation on an SMP is to distribute all the records across all the CPUs and then to have each CPU, in effect, execute the query against its own local subset of the records. At the end of this process, each CPU has a count taken from the (small) set of records it handled; what is now required is to add up all these local counts to get the aggregate count. This is usually handled, in an SMP, by using a shared variable guarded by a lock. Each CPU will read in the current value from the shared memory location, add to it its own local value, and then return (write) the new sum back to the shared location.

> The lock that guards this variable is to ensure that the CPUs access the shared value one at a time; without the

lock, two CPUs might read and modify the same value; whichever wrote back latest in time would "win the race" in the sense that its value would have been added in, but the value from the other CPU (the one that "lost the race") would have been lost. By ensuring that only one CPU at a time has access to the shared variable, the lock guarantees that the correct sum is generated. <>

Using this example, we are now prepared to discuss hot spots. The lock guarding the shared variable is, potentially at least, a hot spot. All the CPUs are contending, each wanting to add its own local value to the global sum. To get access to the shared variable, however, each must first obtain access to the lock—itself a shared variable taking the two possible values OPEN and CLOSED. Each CPU will read the lock repeatedly, hoping to find it OPEN. If it is OPEN, the CPU will immediately change the value of the lock to CLOSED (notice that other CPUs with their own cached values of the lock variable will be notified of the modification via the cache coherence mechanism). It can then read and modify the shared variable holding the sum. When that is completed, the CPU resets the lock to OPEN (again, cache coherence notifies the remaining CPUs of the change), and the next CPU (whichever is lucky enough to get the lock next) can have its turn. This continues until all CPUs participating in the global sum have contributed their values.

The situation is exactly the same as waiting in line to use the rest room after the movie is over on a transcontinental flight. As each passenger, in turn, uses the facility, he or she slides the lock lever, which marks it as "in use." Sliding the lock lever back resets the signal to "available," and the next passenger can take his or her turn. You can see that if there is a long line (lots of CPUs), the wait time can be lengthy. Again, it is the lock which assures that passengers get access one at a time.

What makes the lock a hot spot is that many CPUs are trying to modify it simultaneously. Each repeatedly (in a loop,

called a *spin wait*—each CPU is "spinning on a lock") tests the
status of the lock—is it OPEN or CLOSED—until the OPEN
status occurs (it has become OPEN because the most recent
CPU, whichever it was, has finished). But all the CPUs are,
independently and concurrently, executing the same loop,
and thus are all trying to read and modify the same variable.
As should be clear, this results in a lot of bus traffic to the
memory. All (or most) of the bus bandwidth is being used by
the CPUs to test the lock; none of them are doing "useful"
work. This use of the bus bandwidth also slows down the
other CPUs (the ones that have completed or that may be
working on another task entirely). The bus bandwidth is a
shared resource, and the system (as a whole) works well only
if its use is evenly distributed. What happens with a hot spot
is that this valuable shared resource (bus and memory bandwidth) is (unfairly?) consumed by the spinning CPUs, each
waiting its turn at the shared variable. The effect, if it is not
handled carefully, can be a serious degradation of overall system performance and is experienced by the user as longer
delays.

The example given above—a shared variable, with a
lock, used to compute a global sum—is only one of many possible uses that can potentially result in hot spots. In an SMP,
shared variables, with locks, are the most common means for
the CPUs to coordinate their work. Every time such a lock-
protected variable is used (and they are used all through most
SMP codes), the potential for a hot spot exists.

One way to handle hot spots is to impose a waiting
period between successive tries to the lock. That is, if a CPU
tests the variable and finds that it is CLOSED, the CPU is
forced to wait some length of time before it is allowed to try
again. During that period of time, it is not contending for bus
and memory bandwidth, so it is not consuming the valuable
shared resource. In this connection, then, it is important (1) to
have operating system mechanisms that provide such a delay,
and (2) to have code that utilizes these mechanisms. Another

device to address hot spots is to provide a set of *flags*, separate from the main memory, solely for the purpose of implementing locks. In such a scheme, any flag is accessible over a separate bus in one clock tick from any CPU, and a "test and set" instruction is provided that (again in a single clock) sets the lock if it is OPEN and notifies the calling CPU that it is now allowed its turn at the global variable. Such hardware mechanisms can dramatically improve overall system performance on SMPs by ensuring that bus and memory bandwidth are not excessively consumed by hot spots.

1.4 STRENGTHS AND WEAKNESSES

In this section we consider the strengths and weaknesses of the SMP architecture for use in data warehouse applications. As we noted in Section 1.1, the commercial success of SMPs is due to their ability to execute existing (that is, legacy) sequential applications with little or no modification. They accomplish this by not parallelizing the application; the application itself executes sequentially on a single CPU (just at it would have in an ordinary single-CPU machine). At the same time, one application is executing on one of the CPUs, another application can be executing (concurrently) on a different CPU, and so on. The machine becomes a "throughput engine," executing many applications simultaneously (each as a sequential application) on behalf of many users.

A database application can execute on an SMP in just this way. The separate "jobs" correspond to multiple independent queries submitted by different users perhaps executing entirely different applications. This way of using the machine is sometimes called *interquery parallelism*: many independent queries all executing simultaneously. There is, however, another way of using the machine. In this approach, many of the CPUs cooperate to speed up the execution of a single query. This is called *intraquery parallelism* and is what we shall ordinarily mean by the term *parallel database*. In a parallel database, many (or all) of the CPUs cooperate to respond to a single database query or update. In an SMP environment, we would expect this cooperation to take place as multiple *threads* within a single larger *task* (that is, the RDBMS should be *multi-threaded*, as described in Section 1.3). Even in this restricted sense, however, an organization may find it useful that the SMP is capable of executing other applications besides the RDBMS. For example, we might imagine an operational concept in which the SMP has (say) 12 CPUs. Of these, perhaps eight are devoted to executing the parallel database; in the meantime, the remaining four are available for other work. In particular, if there are legacy sequential (single-CPU) codes to execute, we would expect the SMP to handle these without the need for code modification. The ability of the SMP to handle a large variety of workloads, some portion of which consists of legacy sequential codes, is what has made this architecture so successful.

The most significant limitation of the SMP architecture is *scalability*, and this is perhaps the right place to introduce the relevant terms. As we noted in Section 1.3, the underlying motivation for adding more processors to a system is either (1) to execute a given job faster (that is, to *speed up* the execution of the job), or (2) to execute a larger job in (roughly) the same amount of time (that is, to *scale up* the size of the job that can be completed). As the hints suggest, these two goals are (respectively) referred to as *speed-up* (hold the job size constant and reduce the execution time) and *scale-up* (hold the execution time constant, and increase the size of the job that can be completed). In either case, the ratio of interest is (job size)/(unit time). In speed-up we are attempting to reduce the denominator (the amount of time); in scale-up we are attempting to increase the numerator (the job size). In either case, the hope is that this ratio will, itself, scale in proportion to the number of processors. Speaking simply, the hope is (for example) that by doubling the number of processors, we will thereby double either the speed-up or, respectively, the scale-up of the machine.

These ideas are illustrated in the two (notional) graphs shown in Figures 1–5 and 1–6. In Figure 1–5, the point to observe is that there are different speed-up curves, depending on problem size; large problems will be able to utilize larger numbers of CPUs more efficiently than will small problems. Figure 1–6 illustrates this same point from a slightly different perspective: The scale-up curve will tend to follow the ideal very closely, with the inefficiency (that is, the gap between the achieved versus the ideal) holding fairly constant and hence decreasing as a percentage of total run time.

Figure 1–5   Speed-up Depends on Problem Size

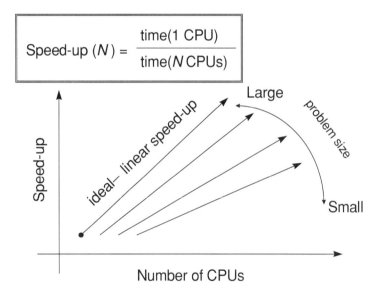

$$\text{Speed-up } (N) = \frac{\text{time(1 CPU)}}{\text{time}(N \text{ CPUs})}$$

Figure 1–6 Large Machines Have Good Scale-up

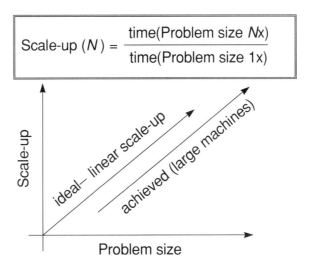

$$\text{Scale-up }(N) = \frac{\text{time(Problem size } Nx)}{\text{time(Problem size } 1x)}$$

The point behind introducing these notions is that the actual shape of these curves, as achieved in practice on a real machine, will depend not only on the type of problem but also on the characteristics of the physical platform on which the job is executing. For standard backplane, bus-based SMPs, there are *architectural* features that prevent large numbers (where *large*, let us say, means more than about 20) of CPUs being used efficiently on a single problem. The most serious issue—the one that most directly limits the ability of the machine to scale to large numbers of CPUs—is memory and bus bandwidth. As we noted earlier, even in a cache-coherent SMP, the physically shared memory is a bottleneck. Once the available bandwidth has been utilized, additional CPUs will not speed up the problem. Why? Because they will be "starved" for memory bandwidth. Once the available memory bandwidth is exhausted, every additional word of memory a new CPU retrieves comes at the expense of a memory reference needed by some other CPU.

An agricultural metaphor will illustrate this notion. Consider the physical shared memory to be a trough and the CPUs to be hogs gathered around the trough. The point here is that once all the spaces around the trough have been taken, additional hogs cannot be fed. There is a natural bound (based on the number of spaces around the trough) beyond which the trough simply cannot support additional hogs. And that is exactly the situation faced by the shared memory system in an SMP machine. Once the available memory and bus bandwidth are exhausted (and in practice, that point is typically reached somewhere between 10 and 20 CPUs), adding additional CPUs will not help—either in speed-up or in scale-up. The machine has reached its physical limits.

To emphasize the point—it is not the *size* of memory that does not scale; it is the *bandwidth* to that memory that does not scale. Inherent in a bus-based SMP architecture is a bottleneck (bus and memory bandwidth) that prevents the number of CPUs from increasing beyond a fairly small number. To summarize: *Bus-based SMP architectures are not scalable to large configurations!*

This fact has not gone unnoticed by SMP vendors, and considerable technical ingenuity has been brought to bear on these issues. In Chapters 10 and 11 we shall see examples of innovative approaches by SMP vendors to construct machines efficient at data warehouse–sized configurations. In each case the traditional bus-based SMP has been supplemented by some additional architectural feature that allows the machine to break through this scalability threshold.

One area of the decision support market where SMPs have been and will continue to be successful is the *data mart*. Naively, we may think of a data mart as a minor-league version of a data warehouse. There is no general consensus on precisely at what size a DSS database stops being a *data mart* and starts to be a *data warehouse*. Our intuition is that the breakpoint comes somewhere around 50 gigabytes. Below that the level of processing needed appears to be within reach of a departmental server, and SMPs have been filling this market niche for some time. Above that level—and particularly if the intention is to grow the database significantly over time—an SMP architecture no longer has a growth path to provide suitable response time for complex DSS-style queries (but again, see Chapters 10 and 11 for innovative approaches from SMP vendors).

The advantages of a shared memory—compatibility with the sequential paradigm and ease of programming—have not come without a price: the inability of the architecture to scale efficiently to very large configurations. Of course, for those applications that do not need more computing power than is provided by an SMP, it remains (and will continue to remain) a very attractive solution. However, as the value of large databases for decision support becomes more widely appreciated, the need for correspondingly large machines to process that data will be increasingly felt. In Chapters 2 and 3 we examine two ways in which computer architects have attempted to solve the problem of scaling.

Distributed Memory Machines

In this chapter we take up the most widely used solution to the problem of scalability: *distributed memory* architecture, sometimes referred to as *massively parallel processors.* As in Chapter 1, we begin with a brief review of the top-level block diagram for the system. In Section 2.2 we discuss the most critical component of these systems: the low-latency, high-bandwidth interconnection network that binds the processor array into a single computing engine. Operating system issues (Section 2.3) and a discussion of strengths and weaknesses (Section 2.4) complete the chapter.

2.1 BASIC CONCEPTS

Let us return briefly to the metaphor of the hogs gathered around the trough. Once all the spaces at the trough are occupied (we argued), the trough cannot support more hogs. Similarly, once all the available memory bandwidth from a physically shared memory is exhausted, it will not help to add additional CPUs. How, we might ask, can this problem be remedied? One answer is—give each hog its own private, nonshared trough (like the over-the-neck feed bags used during horse-and-buggy days). Now the number of hogs is no longer an issue. Each has its own trough, and (at least by the logic of the metaphor) the total can grow without bound. This is exactly the solution used in a *distributed memory* (DM) architecture. Each CPU is given its own private, nonshared memory. As the number of processors increases, both the amount of memory and (more important) the memory bandwidth grows. The memory bandwidth bottleneck no long limits the size of the machine. Or, put another way, the ratio of the total memory bandwidth to the number of CPUs—that is, the memory bandwidth per CPU—is constant, independent of the number of CPUs in the system.

These ideas are illustrated in Figure 2–1, which shows a simple top-level block diagram of a distributed memory architecture. The machine is composed of a number (perhaps a large number) of *nodes*. Each node, in turn, consists of a CPU, local memory, and (usually) some I/O capability. Notice that each node is really a self-contained, stand-alone computer (indeed, some DM manufacturers simply use standard boards from their line of workstations as the physical packaging strategy). What is new in this picture is the component we have called the *network interface*. This allows the node to send data to and receive data from a generic network (the central block in Figure 2–1). In the next section we go into more detail about the network. For the moment, we concentrate on the significant differences between this architecture and the shared memory architecture described in Chapter 1.

Figure 2–1 Generic Distributed Memory Machine

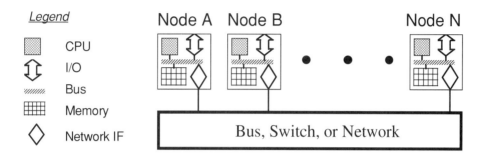

First, notice that the memory is (as the name implies) *distributed* across all the nodes. This is very different from the situation shown in Figure 1–3. There, *all* the memory was accessible from *all* the CPUs. In the DM architecture, however, the only memory available to (that is, addressable by) a CPU is the memory that is local to it. Should a given CPU need data held in some other CPU's memory, a message exchange must take place. That is, the programmer (who, after all, is orchestrating this entire assemblage) must arrange for a message to be sent from the node where the data resides to the node that needs the data. In this simple example, if (say) node A needs data held by (say) node B, node B must formulate a message that contains the data and send the message off to A. Once A has received the message, it has its own private copy that it can use (and modify) as it sees fit. What A *cannot* do is "reach into" B's memory directly and "get" (that is, modify) the data. If it could, B's memory (and memory bandwidth) would be "shared" with A (and with any other node's CPU able to address B's memory directly).

As should be clear from this discussion, the penalty associated with all this scalable memory bandwidth is a programming approach that necessarily contains a lot of messages. Further, the programmer must be concerned about *where the data is*. Look again at Figure 1–2. There, many "blocks" from the physically shared memory are being used, but it is of no concern to the programmer which blocks they are. The operating system takes care of those details, and there is no sense that some blocks are unavailable to some CPUs; *all* blocks are accessible to *all* CPUs. That is a very different scenario from the one presented here.

Suppose, for example, that the task is to scan a large table. In the shared memory approach, *where* the table sits in memory is not important; all the CPUs can get at it. In the DM architecture, however, partitioning the table among the various nodes is central to the task. In a DM architecture, the rows of the table must be physically partitioned and distributed among the memories associated with various nodes. Once that happens, the only way that one node can access the rows residing in another node's memory is via the message-passing mechanism alluded to above. From the programmer's point of view, things are decidedly more complicated. Instead of one large logical table, there are now many small tables (that is, sets of rows), each of which constitutes one portion of the large table of which they are members. Scalability (which was the motivation for the DM architecture) has not come for free.

Before turning to the interconnection network, some additional comments on the generic block diagram are in order. First, although it is not shown, caching usually occurs within the nodes of a DM machine. That is, a high-speed cache sits between the CPU and the local memory. However, there is no notion of "cache coherence" in this architecture. The issue of cache coherence can arise only when a *single logical variable* from the shared memory is *physically replicated* in the caches of many CPUs. However, in a DM architecture, while a copy of data may be replicated, it is the programmer's responsibility to update a changed value (say, by broadcast, using messages) should the program logic require it. It is not the *system's* responsibility to maintain logical coherence; it is the *programmer's* responsibility.

Second, although we have shown each node as having its own I/O capability, that is not always (or even usually) the case. In many DM machines, some (perhaps small) subset of the nodes in the array will have direct I/O capability; the rest will not. When nodes without I/O channels wish to access data, they must apply (using messages) to these "I/O server nodes" for service. The interconnection network is then used as the means to move the data to the requesting node.

Third (and finally), the total number of nodes in such a system can vary considerably—from as few as four to as many as several hundred. DM systems with over 7000 nodes have been built and programmed (but *not* for database applications!). The scalability of memory bandwidth *really does* permit the construction of very large DM systems.

2.2 THE INTERCONNECTION NETWORK

As we noted in Section 2.1, data move around in a DM architecture by means of messages, and the architectural mechanism that supports this capability is the system interconnection network. Logically, all that is needed is a means for any pair of nodes to communicate. Turn back to Figure 2–1. The large box in the center is the focus of our attention for the next few pages.

From an electrical point of view, there are many ways to provide for interprocessor communication. One simple way, for example, would be to use the same kind of technology that is used in local area networks (LANs): say, an underlying Ethernet backbone, with perhaps TCP/IP as the node-to-node communications protocol. In fact, considered from that point of view, Figure 2–1 actually looks similar to a LAN of workstations. In practice, however, such an approach has limitations. The bandwidth (that is, the rate at which data can be transferred between nodes) is small, and the overhead of the TCP/IP protocol (that is, its latency—the time consumed just in setting up the message) is excessively high. To drive home the point—using TCP/IP on Ethernet, we might expect a latency measured in tens of milliseconds and a sustained bandwidth of perhaps 2 million bytes per second. The desired goal for high-performance DM interconnection networks is about three orders of magnitude better: latency measured in microseconds, and total system bandwidth measured in billions of bytes per second.

To achieve such aggressive data transfer rates, the interconnection network must be specially engineered and highly optimized. As much of the message initialization as possible is implemented in hardware, as is all switching and routing along the message path. Along with the choice of microprocessor for the individual nodes, the performance characteristics of the interconnection network is the most important consideration in comparing differences in DM hardware platforms. Similarly, it is the interconnection network that differs most widely among the various vendors, and that they use to differentiate their products.

How important is the interconnection network to overall performance on large parallel RDBMS applications? As we shall see in Part II, *sorts* and fully general *joins* require moving very large amounts of data around the machine. If the pattern of joins can be limited in advance, and if sorting is not required, only modest interconnection performance may be sufficient. For applications such as database mining and for complex DSS-type queries involving fully general joins, the interconnection network is likely to be the system performance bottleneck and is therefore the component most likely to limit the size of the application that can be performed. If the target application is a large database—like a data warehouse—it is best not to skimp on this part of the system.

As the number of nodes in the system increases, the demands on the interconnection network also increase. Thus the ability of the interconnection network to scale smoothly to very large configurations is an important consideration. More nodes mean more data moving around the machine, with correspondingly large stress on the network. As we proceed to discuss the two major approaches to interconnection networks, it will be good to keep in mind two important measures of scalability (both of which have significant practical implications). First, how does the amount of interconnection hardware scale as a function of the number of nodes in the system? Second, how does the performance of the network (measured, say, by sustained point-to-point bandwidth) scale as a function of the number of nodes?

The two most frequently encountered approaches to high-performance interconnection networks are (1) *point-to-point networks*, and (2) *multistage switched networks*. The key ideas for a point-to-point network (PTPN) are illustrated in Figure 2–2. In a PTPN, each node has direct links to some (usually small) number of other nodes, called *nearest neighbors*. A common configuration (shown in the diagram) is a *two-dimensional mesh*: Each node has *four* nearest neighbors (N, S, E, and W). As might be imagined, a technical argot has grown up: The arrangement of nearest neighbors is called the *topology* of the network, and the number of nearest neighbors adjacent to any given node is called the *degree* of the network. Other commonly encountered topologies are *three-dimensional meshes* (degree = 6) and *hypercubes* [degree = $\log_2$(no. of nodes)].

If a message is destined for a node other than a nearest neighbor, a "bucket brigade" is formed, with intervening nodes on the path handing the message along, one by one, until it arrives at the destination. In the example above, the message moves from node A to node B through six intermediate nodes. From the point of view of scalability, the biggest advantage of a PTPN is that the interconnection hardware scales exactly with the number of nodes: that is, (say) doubling the number of nodes will double the number of links—four links per node, no matter how many nodes are in the system. From the point of view of pricing, the interconnection network can be treated as a constant additional factor "per node." The biggest *disadvantage* is that average message latency increases rapidly with the number of nodes (instead of holding constant, or increasing slowly). This is because, on average, the distance (measured by the number of intervening "hops" along the message route) between communicating nodes will tend to increase as the number of nodes increases. On average, it will take longer to deliver a typical message, because the length of the route is greater. (In the argot, the *diameter* of the network—that is, the length of the longest path—increases rapidly for PTPNs.)

Figure 2–2   Generic Two-Dimensional Mesh Point-to-Point Network

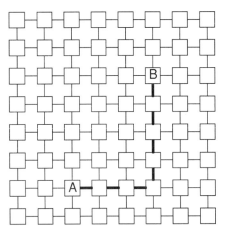

A secondary problem is the potential for *contention*: Two messages, with differing destinations, may, nevertheless, simultaneously require use of the same link. (To convince yourself that this can be a problem, remember that *all* the nodes may be communicating continually, so that hundreds or thousands of messages may be active at any given point in time.) When two messages contend for the same link, one must wait, so that the average behavior (considering all messages in a statistical sense) will suffer.

Depending on the application, clever programming can sometimes alleviate these problems: for example, by arranging the data on the machine in such a way that most messages are exchanged only between nearest neighbors. This means that the distance the message must travel is short (one hop), and there is no contention. However, this requires the programmer to be aware of the placement of data on the physically underlying hardware—a requirement unknown, for example, in a shared memory environment. The requirement that programmers be aware of the physical layout of the underlying hardware topology is one of the reasons why message passing has the reputation for being a difficult programming paradigm. It also affects portability of programs: A program optimized for one machine's topology (say, a two-dimensional mesh) may not be appropriate for the topology of a different machine (say, a hypercube).

In a multistaged switched network (MSSN), on the other hand, there is no notion of nearest neighbor or of machine topology. Consider Figure 2–3. A message begins by being handed off to the first of a series of intermediate *switches* (or *switch elements*) which are physically distinct from the processing nodes. The sequence of intermediate switches a message will traverse is determined by its source and destination. (In Figure 2–3 we show the path a message takes in moving from node C to node E.) However (and this is the main point), the *number* of switching levels the message will traverse does not depend on the source and destination. This means that there is no sense in which some nodes are closer together than others. The latency (measured as a count of switching levels) for *any pair* of communicating nodes is the *same*.

[*Note*: An unexpected convention in wiring diagrams for MSSNs is that the computing nodes are *shown twice*: once across the top of the figure (as *sources*), and again across the bottom of the diagram (as *destinations*). In picturing the path a message takes, we always move from top (source) to bottom (destination) in the diagram. In the physical system, one can imagine the network being folded along an imaginary horizontal line stretched across its middle, so that the top and bottom nodes are made to coincide.]

Figure 2–3 Generic 2 × 2 Multistage Switched Network

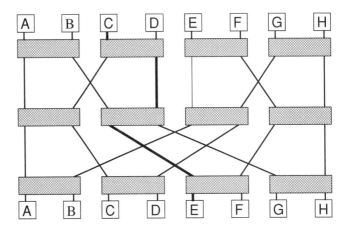

Notice that the switching fabric has two dimensions. One (the horizontal dimension, sometimes called the *width*) varies with the number of nodes. The other (the vertical dimension, sometimes called the *depth* of the switch) determines how many switching levels a message will traverse. In the example shown, the width is 4 and the depth is 3. A message must pass through (depth =) 3 switch elements to get from source to destination.

An important point about MSSNs is that *both* the width *and* the depth of the switch can (and usually will) increase as the number of nodes increases. The *width* is not the problem; doubling the number of nodes *ought* to double the width. However, to provide enough connectivity, doubling the number of nodes will typically also add an additional level of switching to the *depth* of the MSSN. This means that the cost (measured as number of switching elements) will increase *faster* than the number of computing nodes. *Doubling* the number of nodes will *more than double* the number of switching elements (and hence the cost of the system).

An associated potential difficulty is that MSSNs tend to have "magic numbers"—that is, configurations where the addition of just one more node can force the entire network to move up one level. Between these magic numbers, the system scales smoothly (indeed, more processors require no additional switching hardware). At these breakpoints, however, a significant upgrade will be required. In Figure 2–3, for example, we see that adding even one addition node would require an entire additional level of switching: In this architecture, the most nodes that can be supported by a three-stage switch is eight. This unevenness in the scalability of MSSNs can come as a surprise to the uninitiated.

The increased cost for more levels in the switching network is more than just a parts count. Additional cabinetry (footprint, power, cooling) and cabling, above and beyond the cabinets needed to hold the compute nodes, must be purchased to accommodate the additional switching circuitry. The point is: In an MSSN, the physical size (and cost) of the interconnection network scales *superlinearly* [usually, as $N \times \log(N)$] with the number of nodes (= N), and contains "magic number" breakpoints requiring significant upgrades.

There are, however, two advantages for this extra cost ("extra," that is, compared to a PTPN, in which cost scales linearly with the number of nodes). First, the *average latency* for a message in an MSSN grows very slowly. Adding an additional level to the switch increases the latency slightly, but not nearly so fast as the additional message length that will be experienced in a PTPN. Second, because the distance between pairs of nodes in an MSSN is the same for all pairs of nodes (that is, no pair of nodes are nearer, in the switch fabric, than any other pair), the programmer need not be so concerned about data layout as in a PTPN. Optimizing code does not require a detailed knowledge of the network topology; one node is as good as another as far as message latency is concerned.

Figure 2–3 hides many details and should be considered notional. For example, a typical switching element in a real MSSN will have many more than two input and two output ports; eight or sixteen of each is more reflective of today's technology. This means that, ordinarily, there will not be a single path from source to destination, but several alternate paths, through several different combinations of switch ports and elements. This adds an element of redundancy that both improves performance (by reducing the likelihood of contention for a port) and supports fault tolerance (a failed port or switch element does not prevent pairs of nodes from communicating).

2.3 OPERATING SYSTEM AND COMPILER ISSUES

The conceptual model of a distributed memory (DM) machine is very different from that of a shared memory machine. In this section we discuss three of the most important effects: memory management, the message-passing programming model, and the notion of sharing the machine among users. Each of these has a characteristic DM "feel," with consequences for how data warehouses are implemented.

Memory Management

In a shared memory system, the operating system capabilities represent a natural extension to multitasking on a sequential machine. The large shared memory is split up among independent tasks and/or threads, with shared areas (that is, areas that are mapped to the address space of independent tasks or threads) used as the mechanism for communication and coordination. In a DM machine, however, the memory model is very different. In effect, each computing node in the machine has its own *separate, private, nonshared address space*. The addresses available to a given CPU extend only as far as its local memory; the memory accessed by other CPUs (= nodes) in the processor array are, as it were, invisible. This is both good and bad. It means that no other CPU can interfere with "my" data (looked at from a node's-eye point of view), but it also means that data held remotely is not directly accessible; the node must coordinate with that remote node to arrange for data to be sent, using the messaging facilities of the OS.

One consequence of this style is that virtual memory at a node is a dubious concept, at best. For one thing, where will the "disk swap space" for each node be located? There is already a large penalty in process and memory swapping on a high-bandwidth bus-based SMP; if a compute node in a DM system were allowed to take a page fault, one can imagine that the performance penalties would be great. And of course, if all the nodes were regularly to take page faults, the results would be catastrophic.

As a result, the typical programming approach for DM machines has been not to allow (or, at least, to strongly discourage) virtual memory within a given CPU's address space. Programs executing within a node are, for the most part, constrained to operate within the physical memory available at that node. (*Note:* An important exception is when *each* node is provided with a *private disk*, not shared by any other node in the system. In that case, the swap space itself is not shared, so that the possibility of many CPUs contending for shared disk storage is avoided. An example of such a DM system is the IBM SP-2; see Chapter 9.)

What one typically finds at each node of a DM processor array is a Unix-like OS, stripped of its virtual memory (VM) capabilities, and enhanced to support high-performance message passing (see the next section). One consequence is that the amount of physical memory in the system will be, perhaps, a more important consideration than it is when purchasing an SMP. After all, if efficient SQL processing requires that an intermediate table be *in memory*, the amount of memory available becomes a limiting factor in the size and complexity of the queries that can be processed efficiently. Even when a local VM capability is supported, the paging overhead has the potential to degrade performance severely. In our experience, having an adequate amount of physical memory at each processing node is often the difference between success (rapid query response) and failure in large parallel RDBMS applications.

The Message-Passing Programming Environment

In Section 2.2 we talked about the high-performance interconnection network that is at the heart of a good DM architecture. This interconnection scheme is not *just* hardware; it is also necessary that application programs have software access to these facilities with a minimum of overhead. What that means, in practice, is that the message-passing primitives (*send, receive, test, whoami*, etc.) should be implemented by direct traps to low-level kernel routines. It also means that a queue of received messages must be maintained, in system space, at each CPU until the calling process is ready to deal with them. This, in turn, requires adequate local memory at each CPU to implement the queue. In large parallel RDBMSs, both the number of messages and their size can be quite large for typical join and sort operations. Adequate buffer space to store these messages until needed can thus be a substantial issue in properly sizing local CPU memory (see above).

It is also important that the application code be written in such a way that it is independent of the actual number of nodes (= CPUs) in the processor array. For shared memory SMPs this is not an issue, since parallelization is handled at run time based on available resources. For DM machines it means that the number a CPUs must, itself, be a run-time variable. The same code should be able to execute on small or large numbers of CPUs. Typically, the logistics of this are handled using the *whoami* system call. This returns to the application both the total number of CPUs entering into the computation and the index of the particular CPU that made the call. These values can then be used within the application code to control process flow.

A typical approach consistent with these ideas is the *single-program, multiple-data* (SPMD) style of programming. In this paradigm, the same source code executes on every CPU node of the processor array. Instead of having a separate source module for every node, the same source module is replicated. Branching based on processor index is used to handle code segments that only one, or a few, of the nodes are to execute. In this way, a single source code development effort is required for execution on multiple sizes and configurations of the DM processor array.

Often in RDBMS applications, a single host node will be designated to handle the user interface. SQL queries come to this node from the user (or user application) and then fan out (via message broadcast, for example) to the nodes that will process the query. The results then funnel back to the host node to be returned to the user. The number of nodes to participate in a query can be a run-time variable and can change from query to query. It is also typically possible to have multiple queries (possibly from multiple users, and even against different logical databases) active concurrently—within each node, separate Unix processes are spawned, each of which is associated with a separate query. These processes execute in a time-shared fashion under control of the local node OS. This style is typical of parallel RDBMS implementations on large DM machines.

Finally, it is worth observing that compiler technology for DM machines has improved considerably over the past several years. Most important from our point of view is the ability of some compilers to decompose large data structures (for example, arrays of records) *automatically* across the memories of the CPUs in the processor array. This capability permits programmers to treat the large array as a single logical entity instead of as multiple smaller entities, each in the separate address space of a distinct processor. The compiler hides the physical details of the machine behind the abstraction of a single large array. Tying this to similar capabilities in the I/O subsystem (for example, single logical I/O operations from the source code) results in a powerful and friendly programming environment. We can look forward, over the next few years, to similar enhancements in other areas of parallel algorithm development and coding. While these issues are not significant for organizations treating the RDBMS as a black-box server, they are significant if customized data mining applications are required.

Sharing the Hardware

Although some hardware platforms are dedicated to particular database applications, it is also common (for cost reasons) to share a hardware platform among several applications. In the case of DM machines, the idea is to partition the single large processor array into some number of smaller subarrays, each dedicated to a particular job. While it is theoretically possible to time-share multiple jobs within a CPU using the multitasking capabilities of Unix, that is almost never done in practice. Rather, if the machine is to be shared, separate jobs are assigned to physically separate subarrays of CPUs. It is also possible to isolate these partitions and to have them execute separate copies of the OS (or even, different OSs and OS versions).

The issue of allocating CPUs is complicated if the underlying network is a PTPN. The reason is that the proximity of the CPUs in the underlying topology can affect performance.

In a two-dimensional mesh, for example, we would want to allocate subarrays that are, themselves, completely self-contained rectangles consisting of nearest neighbors in the underlying grid. Although it is theoretically possible to have a logical grid consisting of nodes that are physically scattered, that is seldom (never?) done in practice. For MSSNs, however, more flexibility is available, since all CPUs in an MSSN are "equally distant." For example, any subset of CPUs could be allocated in an MSSN without affecting overall performance.

A more thorny issue in a database application is: Which CPUs *own* the data? By "own," we mean "control the disks on which the data is located." If the data needed by the application is resident on disks controlled by CPUs that have not been assigned to the job, those CPUs must be interrupted for I/O support. We go into these issues in more detail in Chapter 4. For the moment it is enough to realize that space sharing on a DM parallel machine must also take into account the way in which data has been spread across the disks and the effect this may have on performance.

Other issues that can have significant practical implications for implementations on DM architectures include privacy, security, and auditing; billing and accounting; failure modes and fault tolerance; managing OS and application software versions and upgrades; heterogeneity (what if not all nodes are identically configured with memory, CPUs, OS versions, etc.); and software licensing costs.

2.4 STRENGTHS AND WEAKNESSES

A major theme of this section has been scalability—the ability of the distributed memory architecture efficiently to scale up to very large configurations. The key to such scalability, which is not possessed by shared memory machines, is nonshared memory bandwidth. Since each CPU possesses a private nonshared memory, adding more processors means that additional memory bandwidth is added as well. The memory bandwidth bottleneck has been circumvented.

If the physical limits of memory bandwidth are no longer an issue, one can still ask whether the applications to be executed on large configurations are able to make efficient use of this bandwidth. Put another way, what are the shapes of the speed-up and scale-up curves for applications executed on DM machines? Part II is devoted to answering this question in more detail, but the basic result can be summarized as follows: *Large* database problems exhibit excellent scale-up curves, even for very large machine configurations. To borrow a metaphor from biology, large DM machines (with high-performance interconnection networks) are almost *Darwinianly* suited for large database applications.

This Darwinian metaphor suggests a pruning process in which less-fitted architectures have been weeded out, with the remaining architectures being those better able to survive in the current environment. That is, in fact, a good picture for what has happened over the past six or seven years. In the early days of parallel processing (where "early" means, say, 1985–1990), vendors relied to a great extent on the federal government (national labs, intelligence agencies, DARPA, etc.) for their major sources of funding. Venture capital, as well, seeded the early efforts. As time went on, however, vendors of parallel equipment were forced to find profitable markets for their machines.

In today's world, profitable means "commercial," and commercial means "database." In fact, only those machines able to show significant performance and cost performance benefits on database applications have survived the harsh realities of the current federal budget climate. The attrition rate in high performance and parallel processing has been high. Losers include BBN (Butterfly, TC2000), Myrias, WaveTracer, Thinking Machines (CM-1, CM-2, CM-5), Multi-Flow (MP-1, MP-2), Intel (iPSC, Paragon), FPS, Kendall

Square, BiiN, CDC, and Ametek. Even supercomputer giant Cray Research recently found its lack of profitability so constraining that they became a takeover target for up-and-coming Silicon Graphics. If we exclude vendors of SMPs (of which there are many), the remaining vendors include Silicon Graphics/Cray Research (Origin, T3-E), IBM (SP-2), Siemanns/Pyramind (Reliant 1000), Hewlett-Packard/Convex (Exemplar), Tandem, Sequent (NUMA-Q), ATT/Teradata, and Unisys (Opus). Of this group, only the T3-E and Exemplar are targeted exclusively at scientific markets. The remainder market aggressively as high-end database engines.

The cost and scalability advantages of a DM architecture make it a very strong platform for data warehouses, especially at the high end. The downside is that few other commercial applications require this kind of horsepower, so that few other software packages have been parallelized for this class of machine. Thus the organization will tend to view a large DM machine as exclusively a database server. There is little opportunity for execution of other applications. Further, in-house development of software for DM machines will be hindered by the complex message-passing paradigm (although this is improving slowly).

At this stage of high-end computer architecture evolution there is a fundamental trade-off between ease of programming (shared memory) and scalability (distributed memory). As a result, SMPs have a rich and varied set of application software but are not able to scale to the largest configurations (however, see Chapters 10 and 11 for innovative SMP approaches to this difficulty). On the other hand, DM machines have only a small application software base but have virtually unlimited scalability. In the next section we take a closer look at an emerging class of computer architecture that attempts to combine the best of both worlds: scalability and programmability.

We close with a brief discussion of an important class of architecture that is quite common in commercial IT shops but that does not fit neatly into the architecture taxonomy we have introduced: *clusters of SMPs*, or simply *clusters*. The idea is to replace each single-CPU node in Figure 2–1 with a modest SMP (with perhaps two to four CPUs per cabinet), and to utilize commodity LAN or channel technology for the interconnection network. The address space for a given CPU extends only as far as the SMP cabinet in which it resides, but within that cabinet the memory is shared. Message passing is then used to exchange data among SMP cabinets. What has happened over the past 18 months or so is that commodity networking has slowly but surely been pushing up toward performance levels previously attainable only with special purpose networks (see Section 2.2). As shown in Chapter 10 (where a specific cluster implementation is discussed in detail), it is now possible to assemble a very formidable and scalable processor array suitable for large data warehouse implementations from off-the-shelf components. To borrow the Darwinian metaphor again, technology advances open up new niches in the architecture ecology which are quickly filled by innovative new designs, competing with and sometimes displacing incumbents. Extinction awaits those who cannot adapt!

Chapter 3

Distributed Shared Memory Machines

In this chapter we consider a relatively recent architecture that has emerged as an attempt to combine the programmability of a SMP with the scalability of a DM machine. The key ideas are introduced in Section 3.1, followed by a detailed discussion (Section 3.2) of how cache coherence is globally maintained without a backplane bus. The difficulties associated with memory management in DSMs are presented in Section 3.3. In the final section, we summarize the strengths, weaknesses, and current "state of play" of this new technology.

3.1 BASIC CONCEPTS

In the first two chapters we stressed the major trade-off between symmetric multiprocessors, on the one hand, and distributed memory MPPs, on the other. SMPs offer a clean software development and porting path, because the memory model supported by SMPs is similar to the memory model supported by traditional sequential machines. The downside, however, is that SMPs based on backplane buses do not scale to large configurations. Memory and bus bandwidth are shared resources that do not scale as the number of CPUs increases. We also saw that this lack of scalability is the chief motivation for distributed memory architectures. As the number of CPUs increases, the memory bandwidth scales upward automatically as well, since each CPU is provided with its own private, nonshared memory subsystem. Unfortunately, however, the ease of program porting and development must be given up. The concept of a single, uniform, shared memory address space does not carry over to DM architectures; processes can share data only by sending messages across the interconnection network—a style of programming unfamiliar to many (most?) application developers.

It has been conventional wisdom in the parallel processing community for some time that fame and fortune awaits whoever is able to reconcile this software-versus-scalability trade-off. One approach that has been adopted by several vendors (and a few research projects) is called *distributed shared memory* (DSM), or *nonuniform memory access* (NUMA). The purpose of this chapter is to explain, at a high level, what the architecture is and its probable ability to support data warehouse applications. Before proceeding, however, a *caveat emptor* is appropriate. The block diagrams that are presented and discussed should be taken as notional. Different vendors have different hardware implementations, and although the concepts extend across many platforms, the implementation details vary from vendor to vendor.

Consider Figure 3–1. What is shown will immediately be recognized as a hybrid of Figures 1–1 and 2–1. In particular, the reader will see that each "node" of this system consists of what appears to be a standard SMP. In this representation I have provided each node with four CPUs, some amount of cache-coherent shared memory, and a single I/O channel.

There is nothing sacred about those choices. Fewer (as few as one) or more (as many as eight) CPUs may appear at each node, and less or greater I/O capacity may be available. The key idea is that each node in this configuration functions just as a stand-alone SMP. In particular, as more nodes are added (just as in a conventional DM machine), more (local) memory and bus bandwidth are added as well. The scalability bottleneck has been broken using the same "replicate the local memory" strategy used by MPPs. Also notice the strong similarity to the *cluster* architecture discussed briefly at the end of Chapter 2.

Figure 3–1 Generic DSM Architecture

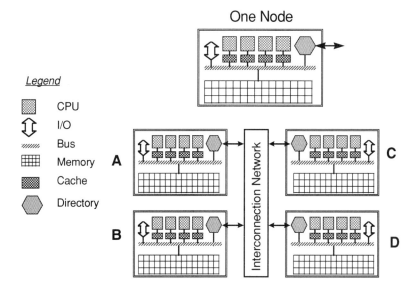

What about cache coherence? The reader will notice a new component, the *directory*, in this block diagram. Its location in the architecture is the same as that of the network interface that appeared in DM machines, but its functionality is considerably more complex. In fact, its purpose is to implement a cache coherence protocol (in concert with its peers at other SMP nodes) that *extends across the entire machine*! A simple example will indicate how the process works.

Suppose that one of the CPUs in node A issues an address (perhaps a *read* instruction) for data that happens to lie in node D's local memory. The following (simplified) sequence of actions must occur. First, the memory management functions in the operating system must detect that the address is not local to node A. This can be accomplished using translation look-aside buffers (TLBs), exactly as is currently done for virtual memory capabilities. Next, the *directory* in node A must be notified that a remote memory access is required. At this point, the two directories—one in node A, and the other in node D—must coordinate the exchange, in a series of four steps. (1) Node A's directory notifies node D's directory that a certain data element (cache line) is desired. (2) The directory at node D retrieves the data from its local memory, makes a notation in its local data structure that A now has a copy of the data, and sends the data along to node A. The directory at node A can then complete the process in one of two ways. (3) It can store the data locally and notify the requesting CPU (in which case the local CPU completes by retrieving the data itself); or (4) it can pass the data directly to the cache of the requesting CPU (with no other local copy made).

The situation becomes somewhat more complicated if a *write* operation is desired. Recall that the major problem that arises in cache-coherent systems is when one CPU wishes to modify the value of a variable for which multiple copies have been issued. The CPUs holding those copies must be notified that the copies are no longer valid (*dirty data*, in the technical argot). SMPs, we saw, use a bus sniffing technique. In DSMs, however, the procedure is more complex. If the CPUs holding multiple copies all reside on the same node, things can proceed as with an SMP. However, if the nodes holding the copies reside on different nodes, an exchange across the network is required. The following is an example of what might take place.

Suppose, for example, that the CPU in node A wishes to modify (write to) the value of the variable it received from node D. The following six steps (or their functional equivalent) must occur. (1) First, using bus sniffing, the directory in node A becomes aware that the locally cached version needs to be modified. It immediately (using the interconnection network) notifies the directory at node D (the original *owner* of the data). (2) The directory at node D has been maintaining records on which other nodes have requested copies of its data (see step 2 in the previous read example). For example, a CPU in node B might also have a local copy. The point is that the directory in node D *knows who to tell*. (3) The directory in node D notifies the directories at all affected nodes (any that have local copies of the affected data) that their copies are no longer valid. Depending on the implementation, it may also (4) wait for a reply from these nodes that the invalidation operation has completed. At this point, (5) the directory at node D can notify the requesting directory at node A that it can proceed. In some implementations, node A has now become the new owner of the data (requests for the data from other nodes will now go to node A instead of to node D). In other implementations, (6) the directory at node A will send back to node D the new value so that it can update its version. In any case, the key functional attribute—notifying CPUs holding a locally cached copy of the data—has been performed.

At this point the reader may be ready to go out and purchase a DSM machine. After all, it appears we have the best of both worlds: the shared, coherent, global address space of an SMP, and the memory bandwidth scalability of an MPP. Well, unfortunately, life isn't quite that simple, as we see in the next section.

3.2 NONUNIFORM MEMORY ACCESS ON DSM MACHINES

To understand the potential difficulty with this architecture, we need to consider the issue of *memory reference latency*. Simply speaking, it is the amount of time that elapses between (1) when the CPU makes the memory request (by issuing the address of the data element it needs) and (2) when the memory request is satisfied (the data element appears in the register of the CPU). Even on simple sequential machines there are several cases to consider (see Figure 3–2). If the data already resides in the register or cache, the memory reference can complete very quickly—often, within only one (or a few) machine cycles. By using latency-hiding techniques such as pipelining and out-of-order execution, the latest generation of microprocessors can often mask even this latency successfully (for example, by overlapping the delays from several concurrent references so that the total latency is highly amortized and the average experienced latency is small).

Figure 3–2   Memory Hierarchy for SMPs and DSMs

SMPs			DSMs		
Size	Type	Latency	Size	Type	Latency
1 KB	Register	10 vsec	1 KB	Register	10 vsec
1 MB	1-L Cache	30 vsec	1 MB	1-L Cache	30 vsec
4 MB	2-L Cache	60 vsec	4 MB	2-L Cache	60 vsec
1 GB	DRAM	150 vsec	1 GB	DRAM	150 vsec
10 GB	Disk	10 msec	4 GB	Remote DRAM	1 μsec
			10 GB	Disk	10 msec

The next big jump in latency comes when the data is not in cache. In that case a reference to the slower (and larger) local DRAM memory must be made. This requires a bus transaction: The memory controller (located at the DRAM) must complete the reference and return the data to the requesting CPU. It is typical that this process takes many times (three to five times is typical) as long as it would have were the data in cache. As we mentioned above, new DRAM technologies may reduce this latency significantly, but still not to cache reference rates.

In standard SMPs, the only other level in the memory hierarchy is disk—that is, virtual memory. Because of swapping, the data may have been moved (by the operating system) from local DRAM out to disk. When such a *page fault* occurs, a disk I/O operation will be needed, and the resulting latency can be on the order of milliseconds. As a result of this very large performance penalty, applications are optimized to ensure that only very rarely will this situation arise (the best optimization, of course, in a very large amount of DRAM!).

In a DSM, however, another level is inserted in the memory hierarchy. This level corresponds to the case when the data *does not* reside in the local DRAM memory at the requesting node but *does* reside in the local DRAM memory of a *different* node. Returning briefly to Figure 3–1, we followed through an example where a processor in node A requests data that happens to have been placed (by the operating system) in memory at node D. We saw that a network transaction, and intervention by the directory at node D, are required. All this adds to the time (latency) needed to complete the transaction.

From the point of view of a CPU executing somewhere in the system, not all memory references are equal. While programmers are used to inequality in latency due to caching and virtual memory, and understand mechanisms (often in the compiler) to minimize these effects, they are not accustomed to this new level in the memory hierarchy. The model in most developers' heads (and the model underlying SMP-style programming) is a *uniform memory access* model: Any location in DRAM is as good as any other, and where the operating system happens to put the data is a matter of indifference as far as delivered performance is concerned. The physical implementation in DSM machines, however, is a *nonuniform memory access* (NUMA) model: Some locations (same-node memory) have significantly better latency performance than others (off-node memory). If the CPU on which a task or thread is executing and its associated data happen to be co-located, performance will be considerably better (because of greatly reduced memory latency) than if they happen to have landed on different nodes.

This is an important point, and a further example may serve to drive home the issues. We saw in Figure 1–2 that on an SMP, the operating system can allow threads executing on separate CPUs to share (that is, have access to) common areas of memory. The task G, for example, was executing on four CPUs, all of which were able to address into (in our example) a total of 15 blocks of memory (all labeled G in the diagram). How will this diagram change on a DSM? Consider the simple DSM shown in Figure 3–3. Here we see two nodes consisting of three CPUs each (about as simple a DSM as one can imagine). The abstract model here is identical to that shown in Figure 1–2: Task F has its own CPU and nonshared memory, and there are four CPUs assigned to task G, with common, shared access to a subset of memory. The abstract programming model is identical, but the actual performance experienced in practice will be very different in the two cases.

In the case of the SMP (Figure 1–2), it really does not matter which set of memory blocks are assigned to task G. Any location in memory is equivalent to any other in terms of experienced memory latency. Clearly that is not the case in Figure 3–3, which illustrates the behavior of DSMs. Suppose, for example, that a thread of task G executing on a CPU from node A tries to access data from a block of memory located on node B. As we have seen, the experienced latency for *that* memory reference will be considerably greater than if the block of memory had been local to node A, because a network exchange (via the directories) is required. The *nonuniform memory access* nature of the architecture will be experienced, in this example, as performance degradation when compared to the same application executing on a true SMP.

Figure 3–3   Parallel Processing on a DSM

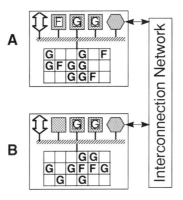

The example given in Figure 3–3 does not do justice to the full complexity of the situation. We showed only two nodes; real DSM/NUMA machines may have dozens, and the memory allocation issue is correspondingly more difficult. Getting the CPU and the memory it accesses "close" can be addressed (theoretically) in a number of ways—moving the memory, reassigning the process to a different CPU, moving both of them, and so on. The algorithms used by the operating system to make these decisions can, at least potentially, be decisive for delivered performance. Similarly, as we noted, the SMP programming model does not provide constructs that capture and allow the programmer to manipulate CPU-to-memory distance. In SMPs the concept is meaningless; in DSMs it is critical. Augmenting current SMP-style language constructs to include this capability is, as of this writing, still very much a research problem. Locality issues will also arise in Chapter 4, since (again) getting the CPU and its working memory close to the needed I/O port can be critical to achieving good performance.

The preceding paragraphs may strike the reader as less than optimistic about DSM/NUMA architectures. In fact, of course, the experienced effect of these concerns will vary largely from application to application and from vendor to vendor. There are ways to address some of these issues, and (as or more important) for some applications and algorithms the issues simply do not arise at all. One of the purposes of this book is to identify the types of relational (that is, SQL) queries that might stress particular aspects of these parallel architectures. Where good solutions exist, we'll identify them. Where problems remain, we'll identify those too. For the moment, the purpose of this section will have been served if the reader understands clearly that nonuniform memory latency is a critical performance issue for DSM architectures that is unknown in the world of SMPs. In the next section we look a bit more deeply at operating system issues that arise in this environment.

Finally, let us return briefly to MPPs. We saw in Chapter 2 that DM machines exchange data using messages. By definition, the "remote access" problem does not appear as a memory latency issue. Because the only memory that a node in a DM architecture can address is its local memory, CPU-to-memory distance does not concern the programmer. What *does* concern the programmer are (1) how to partition large data structures across the memories of the nodes, and (2) minimizing the impact of data exchanges across the network. Both those problems are difficult but are naturally expressible in the message-passing programming style of DM machines. One alternative that is available on DSM machines is to adopt a message-passing approach to programming. Treat local node memory as private, and force processes (and the programmer), when necessary, to move data explicitly around the machine using messages. Put another way, the programmer (rather than the operating system) becomes responsible for data partitioning and management.

Although this is an option in the purely theoretical sense that it can be done, it appears to defeat the original purpose of a DSM machine. Why bother with global memory coherence circuitry if programmers are going to ignore it? One answer might be that different applications require different levels of performance. Maybe the community will consider message passing as a kind of "assembly language" for DSMs, to be used only when highly optimized performance is a top priority. In the context of data warehouses, however, performance and scalability are major concerns. Unless an application has figured out a good way to use the global coherence (for ease of development) and has solved the CPU-to-memory distance problem, it is not clear that it has a significant advantage over a less complex DM architecture. As always, market forces will ultimately decide this issue.

3.3 OPERATING SYSTEM ISSUES

In this section we look more closely at some of the complications that arise when an SMP-style operating system is superimposed on a NUMA architecture. As may be expected, the "distance" (measured in latency) between CPU and data in memory must be taken into account for reasons of performance, and this has far-reaching consequences. Our discussion will touch on three: *placement* (of processes to CPUs, and data to memory), *hot spots* (revisited, but now in a NUMA context), and *data migration and affinity*.

Placement

A basic task of an operating system is to allocate CPUs and memory to processes. That is, the process must be assigned to (that is, placed on) a particular CPU (or CPUs if the task is multithreaded), and portions of main memory must be allocated for use by the process. In a standard SMP architecture, this process is little more than bookkeeping: What CPUs are available, and which blocks of memory are available? There is no performance advantage to be gained by choosing among the available memory blocks—any one will do. In a NUMA architecture, however, some blocks of available memory will be closer to the CPU than others (namely, those that are co-located in the same node). Here, it *does* make a difference which of the blocks of memory are assigned. For efficiency, an algorithm must attempt to optimize both CPU and data placement. Poor choices will result in increased memory latency and (hence) reduced performance.

If a task involves a single thread, so that only a single CPU is needed to execute it, the algorithm is pretty simple: Make sure that the memory and CPU reside in the same node. One way to do that, in turn, is *first* to assign the process to the CPU, and *then* assign the memory. Typically, a process will make memory requests; the memory allocation routine in the OS must have logic that first tries to allocate memory local the requesting CPU's node. By doing the allocation at run time, dependent on the location of the requesting CPU, the CPU-to-memory distance can be minimized.

If the OS can be provided with information about the size of the memory needed by a process before it allocates the process to a CPU, an additional level of optimization is possible. The OS can look for a node where the size of available memory fits well with what has been requested, and place the process there. An interesting side issue (one very relevant to processing large relational tables) is how the OS will react when the memory requested cannot fit within a single node's local memory. The choice of how to spread the large array across the memories of many nodes is a potentially thorny one.

Things become more complicated when the task is multi-threaded—that is, when a single logical task requires many

CPUs to execute a parallel region of code (see Figure 1–4). This is of more than theoretical interest, since multithreaded parallel RDBMSs are the right engine for large DSS/data warehouse applications. To focus our ideas, consider the example shown in Figure 3–4. The logical situation (that is, the situation as viewed by the programmer) is that six threads are needed. For example, we might imagine each thread being assigned one-sixth of a large table; each will process its portion of the table, selecting rows matching the SQL specification, and returning the selected rows to a common area (perhaps as an intermediate table) for further processing.

Figure 3–4   Logical Decomposition of Data and Tasks

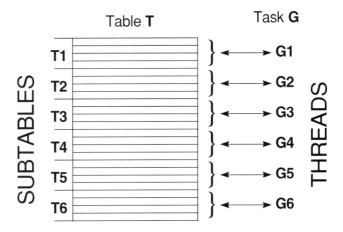

In Figure 3–4, we can imagine each of the threads (and its associated CPU) being assigned its own portion of the table. If the logical task is called (say) G, we will number each of the six threads within G as G1, G2, . . . , G6. Similarly, we might break up the large table, T, into six subtables: T1, T2, . . . , T6. Logically, we want to assign G1 the job of processing T1; G2 will process T2; and so on. Clearly, G1 does not need to access data held in (say) T3. That is, there is a logical independence among separate threads that should be reflected both in the assignment of threads to CPUs and in the decomposition of the table across the physically distinct memories of the nodes.

Figure 3–5 shows one way in which memory allocation might be done—a poor way. Here, the table T is allocated in the sequential region, before the multiple threads have been created. At this point, whatever thread is active (say, G1) will make the request, and the OS will try to place all of T as close to G1 as possible. Subsequently, when the parallel region is entered, the newly created threads G2, G3, …, G6 may or may not be close to the data they need. Because memory allocation occurred *before* the CPUs were assigned, the CPU-to-memory distance could not be optimized. Notice that in a standard SMP, this issue does not arise, since (by definition) once T has been allocated, all CPUs have equally efficient access to any part of it. Our example also indicates the complications that may arise because of prior assignment of other tasks—F and H, in this example.

Figure 3–5 Memory Allocation in a Sequential Region

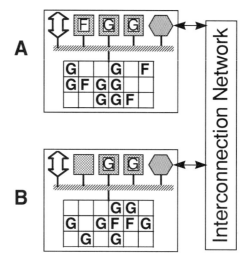

In Figure 3–6 we see a more useful scheme. Here, the allocation of T is done inside the parallel region. First, the threads are assigned; then each thread allocates (local) memory for its part of the table. The logical decomposition of T into pieces matches the physical decomposition of the underlying hardware: T1 resides on the same node as G1; T2 coresides with G2; and so on. The point to notice in this example is that the code designer has to do something different than is needed in the standard SMP. Code ported directly from the SMP environment onto a NUMA machine will almost certainly present opportunities for optimizations of the sort illustrated by this example.

Figure 3–6 Memory Allocation in a Parallel Region

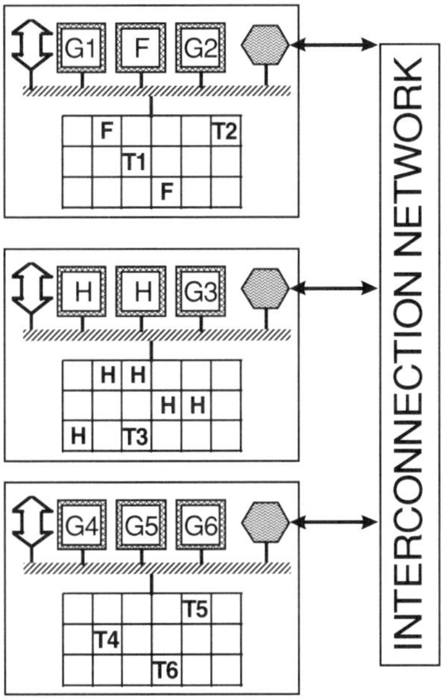

Hot Spots Revisited

In Chapter 1 we considered one of the side effects of a shared memory architecture—namely, the performance impact that arises when many logical processes (threads of control, on

CPUs) are trying simultaneously to access a single shared variable. Often, this variable represents (for example) a lock that guards access to a variable collecting an aggregate (for example, a global sum that will be contributed to by several threads). Sequential access to the shared variable must be enforced—usually, using a lock—and high levels of bus traffic may be generated as all the threads attempt, simultaneously, to seize control of the lock. In an SMP, this is aggravated by the additional overhead of the cache coherence mechanisms, since every process wants to write to the variable, not just read from it. This means that cache line invalidation messages (that is, warnings of dirty data) are also contending for bus bandwidth, and hence clogging the system.

All these problems are aggregated manyfold on a DSM/NUMA architecture. As we have seen in Section 3.1, the latency associated with writes to a shared variable is considerably higher than for reads. The directory at the node owning the data must communicate with directories at all nodes where copies reside, and only then release the requesting process to perform the modification. In the meantime, ownership requests are streaming in from CPUs that have not yet had their turn at the lock. All of this can result in serious performance degradation whenever the global locking mechanism is employed.

In MPPs (that is, DM architectures), the way in which this sort of problem is avoided is through the use of tournament-style global algorithms. Rather than have each node in the system access a single location one at a time, programmers (and libraries that support the programmers) use an algorithm that proceeds by pairing. In the first stage, the nodes pair up and exchange values. One of the nodes then drops out (so only half the nodes are now participating—hence the motivation for the name *tournament-style algorithm*), and the process repeats. With (say) $128 = 2^7$ nodes, after seven rounds the global sum resides in the memory of one node, the tournament winner.

There is no reason why the same sort of algorithm could not be implemented on a large DSM machine. However, on an SMP with a relatively small number of CPUs, the extra coding effort just isn't worth it: The amount of time saved when there are only eight CPUs will never repay the effort to implement the tournament. Further, it is often (usually) not known until runtime exactly how many CPUs will be assigned to the task (that is, the number of threads in the parallel region is typically not known until run time, based on the number of CPUs that are actually available). Hence the tournament code would have to be flexible enough to work for any of a variety of numbers of processes, typically not a power of 2.

In a DSM/NUMA machine, however, the performance hit associated with sequentialized access (and associated hot spots) becomes a significant concern, and (hence) new MPP-like algorithms must be developed. It is not at all clear, however, how this is to be done. The entire purpose of an SMP-style programming approach is to hide the hardware details from the programmer. On the other hand, it is precisely these details that are needed to (for example) construct the tournament in such a way that the pairings occur between CPUs nearby in the memory and network hierarchy. Again, the desire to shield the programmer from the architectural details has had the unintended side effect of hiding just the piece of information needed for good performance.

Data Migration and Affinity

As a final issue, we consider the question of *ownership* of shared portions of the data. In a typical DSM architecture, the primary copy of the data resides in just one node. Other CPUs may request local cached copies, but some node (and its directory) has primary responsibility for the data. (*Note:* An alternative to this approach, called *All-Cache* in some circles, allows multiple copies of the data not just in cache but also in the DRAM memory located at each node. Any node can then be the owner of the data, and ownership migrates from node to node based on write requests.) As we have seen, the principal advantage of being the owner is that CPUs located in that node will have substantially reduced latencies. Thus it makes sense to make the owner of the data the same node as (most of) the CPUs that want to access the data.

One scheme that has been proposed to make this occur is for the operating system to keep run-time statistics on which CPUs are, in fact, accessing the data. The idea is to change ownership if there is an indication that the CPU-to-memory mapping is not efficient. For example, the OS might notice that 95% of the references to a particular block of memory located (say) in node B are actually coming from a CPU located in node A. At that point it seems useful to *move* the block of data from node B to node A. The result of this operation is that node A has now become the owner, and other nodes in the system must come to node A (rather than to node B) to get access to that memory block. Some updating of the TLBs around the system is required, but the benefit is reduced memory access latency and decreased network traffic between the node A and node B directories.

It is also possible, instead of moving the data (and ownership of the data), to move the process. That is, the operating system might choose to migrate the process currently executing on node A (the one that is doing all the memory accesses to B's data) over to an empty CPU located on node B. Assuming that one is available (or can be made available), the desired CPU-to-memory association can be reestablished.

A similar issue arises with thread-to-CPU affinity. In Section 1.3 we noticed that a particular thread might have a considerable investment in the current state of the local cache at the CPU to which it was assigned. After a swap, it might be beneficial for the thread to be assigned to the same CPU. In a DSM, the same issue applies, with the additional proviso that even if the same CPU cannot be used, the CPU that *is* assigned should at least be on the *same node*. The reason should be clear: If a different node is used, the memory references must now travel across the network, and nonlocal latency penalties will be experienced.

3.4 STRENGTHS AND WEAKNESSES

At this point it might be worthwhile reviewing some of the recent history of this architecture. In the parallel processing community, the best known example is the KS-1 machine from Kendall-Square. This machine implemented a global coherent shared memory model through the use of rings. Based on a custom processor, each ring consisted of up to 30 individual processors, plus a directory for the ring. In the model shown in Figure 3–1, a ring of processors corresponds to one SMP-like node. Multiples of these nodes were then linked together by a central ring passing through each directory. Thus, at a hardware level, each SMP bus is replaced by a ring, and the central interconnection network is implemented by yet another, higher-level ring. Cache coherence *within* a node is maintained by passing control and data messages around the ring; and cache coherence across nodes is maintained by a protocol among the directories.

In technical terms the KS-1 was a remarkable success. In market terms it was a failure. It at least proved that the ideas underlying a DSM architecture could be made to work. Unfortunately, the product was not received well by the commercial accounts that Kendall-Square principally targeted. As an outside observer it is hard to know exactly what went wrong, but I strongly suspect that memory latency was a major culprit. It is also true that to some extent, the KS-1 was poorly timed. The business value of data warehousing—the most promising commercial application for very large scaleable systems—was not yet broadly recognized. Whatever the reasons, capitalization for Kendall-Square eventually dried up and the machine joined the list of noble but failed attempts to make a buck off parallel processing.

As of this writing, there are at least three DSM architectures now on the market, two of which see large databases (for example, data warehousing) as major potential markets. In 1994, Convex Computers introduced the Exemplar series. Now a subsidiary of Hewlett-Packard, the Exemplar is exclusively targeted at scientific computing. Sequent (the NUMA-Q) and Silicon Graphics/Cray Research (the Origin) have recently introduced DSM architectures.

The main lesson to be drawn from the KS-1 is that there is a wrong way to do DSM. The Exemplar has focused exclusively on scientific computing, so for our purposes (large-scale commercial DSS systems) it does not offer much help. Can DSM be done well? The difficulties of memory management—that is, minimizing memory latency by optimizing data placement across the machine—are formidable. As DM machines (such as the SP-2 from IBM or the Reliant R-1000 from Pyramid) show, it is possible to do efficient data decomposition across separate address spaces from the application level. Although this alternative is available to DSM machines (that is, program the machine as if it were just a DM architecture), that does not seem to offer much advantage. Only if DSM machines are able to leverage the development work that has been done for SMPs—that is, add scalability without the need for serious reprogramming—do they appear to have a substantial market advantage.

How bad would the performance penalty be if a DSM were to execute unmodified SMP code? To my knowledge, no one knows the answer to that question (although certainly the KS-1 must have tried that approach at some point). If efficient porting to a DSM machine requires a substantial rewrite without significant performance advantages over DM machines, it is hard to see that DSM will have a major market advantage over its DM rivals. Unfortunately, the authors' crystal ball is cloudy.

About the only thing that is clear is that without a broad commercial base in the large-scale DSS arena, DSM architectures will not be able to maintain long-term profitability.

A final point. A marketing strategy that is sometimes used for these architectures is to publish—not the absolute numbers—but the *ratio* between nonlocal and local memory reference latencies. I have seen ratios in marketing literature as low as 2:1 and as high as 4:1. What is not made clear is how those ratios are computed. Notice that having *larger* local memory reference latency actually *helps* the resulting ratio! (That is, using poor numbers for the local reference makes the remote reference look better by comparison.) Thus there is a tendency to choose cases where the local reference is as poor as possible. Similarly, it is not clear how "nonlocal" the nonlocal reference being measured is. For example, if a write operation from a nonowner is involved, a number of network transactions (one to each node with an active local copy) are required. Is that overhead taken into account in the measurement? What about hot spots? Does the published ratio apply to them? The message here is twofold. First, only twice as bad as something that is already pretty bad is no bargain. Second, absolute numbers, with a discussion of the conditions under which they were measured, provide a more solid basis for making comparisons.

During the planning for this book, it had been our intention to include an example in Part III of a DSM/NUMA machine as a data warehouse platform. Our hope was to examine some of the issues raised here firsthand and to illustrate the technical approaches taken by vendors to address them. For various reasons it was not possible to achieve this goal. Nevertheless, we encourage interested readers to pursue this subject directly with the vendors. As noted above, as of this writing the list of DSM/NUMA vendors includes the *Origin* from Silicon Graphics/Cray Research, the *NUMA-Q* from Sequent, and the *Exemplar* from Hewlett-Packard/Convex.

We turn next to parallel I/O architectures. Since many SQL queries are I/O-bound rather than compute-bound, there is a real sense in which Chapter 4 is where "the rubber meets the road."

Chapter

4

I/O in Parallel Systems

In this chapter the important (and difficult) topic of input/output in parallel architectures is discussed. In the initial section we introduce basic concepts and terminology, including especially the notions associated with RAID and striping. In the second section we consider issues of where, within the system, data partitioning is implemented. The strategies for including parallel I/O in each the three main parallel architectures are discussed in the third section, and in the final section we offer an assortment of observations, caveats, and good advice.

This chapter also concludes Part I, which has generally been concerned with issues of hardware architecture. In Part II we take up the question of RDBMS software architectures and algorithms when implemented on parallel hardware.

4.1 BASIC CONCEPTS

Historically, the advent of highly parallel machines is closely tied to the prior and independent development of microprocessors. A famous collection of papers in the field, for example, is entitled: *VLSI and Parallel Computation* (Suaya and Birtwhistle, Morgan Kaufmann, San Francisco, 1990). This might be taken as the motto for parallel machines: The development of the microprocessor made possible (that is, *electrically* and *economically* possible) machines containing significant numbers of CPUs. Prior to the development of the microprocessor, each CPU was an expensive assemblage of a large number (50 or so) of custom components. Both cost and space considerations limited the physical number of these CPUs that could be assembled into a single system, so the path to higher performance lay along lines of increasing clock speed: Parallelism (that is, significantly increasing the number of CPUs) simply wasn't an option. With the development of the microprocessor, however, this view of the world no longer applied. Once a CPU was just another (relatively) inexpensive commodity part, it became possible (that is, *electrically* and *economically* possible) to consider a single machine containing many (hundreds or thousands) of individual CPUs.

The point of bringing up this (by now familiar) bit of recent history is that a very similar process has also occurred in the area of disk storage. Corresponding to the large, monolithic CPU of the mainframe, we have the large, monolithic *DASD [direct access storage device*, sometimes referred to as a *SLED (single large expensive disk)]*. Corresponding to the (relatively) inexpensive commodity microprocessor, we have the commodity disk drive in PC-compatible form factors (5.25 in., 3.5 in.) and interfaces (SCSI, IPI-3). Just as cost per flop for microprocessors gives them a substantial edge over traditional mainframes and minicomputers, the cost per byte of commodity disk drives is very favorable compared to DASDs. Thus, just as with parallel computer architectures, the idea is to construct storage systems for large amounts of data, with very high bandwidth, by assembling many components (individually less expensive, and with less individual performance) in parallel. In a nutshell—what MPP is to traditional mainframes, *RAID* (*redundant arrays of inexpensive disks*) is to traditional DASD.

A complete discussion of the various levels of RAID and their relative performance, cost, and availability characteristics is, fortunately, not needed for the purposes at hand. Our goal is to focus on the data warehouse, and in this context there are a number of working assumptions we can make without exploring all the possibilities or needing to provide extensive justification. The operating characteristics of DSS quickly point toward the "right" implementation.

We begin this brief tutorial, then, with the notion of *striping*. To achieve parallelism, multiple disks must participate in the storage and retrieval of a data set. It might be helpful, for example, to think of the data being stored as a large logical table. Any single disk can provide only a small amount of bandwidth—say, 8 or 10 megabytes per second (MB/sec). For example, if the table is (say) 5 gigabytes (GB), and a single disk can provide 10 MB/sec of bandwidth, we would expect a data read operation to last about 5000/10 = 500 seconds. To improve this situation, the disks can be aggregated; that is, they can be caused to operate on the data set simultaneously and concurrently (that is, in parallel). This can be accomplished by spreading the *single* data set (in some yet-to-be determined manner) across *all* the disks. Then, during a data access, all the disks will participate—each disk, independently, retrieving the piece of the large data file it happens to hold. In our example, if a 5-GB data set is decomposed across (say) 10 disks, each disk will now hold 500 MB. The data retrieval can be accomplished by having all 10 disks each retrieve, at the same time, the smaller amount of data. The retrieval time (subject to some obvious provisos) should be about $500/10 = 50$ seconds; that is, increasing the number of disks by 10 also increased the available bandwidth by a factor of 10 and decreased the access time by a factor of 10.

The idea of parallelism in disks is illustrated in Figure 4–1. There we see the two situations described above. In one instance, the single large data set is assigned to a single disk, and the retrieval time is limited by the retrieval rate of that disk. In the other instance, several (four) disks participate, each retrieving the portion of the large data set that has been assigned to it. The aggregate retrieval time is less because (1) each disk has less to do, and (2) they are all operating concurrently (that is, in parallel).

Figure 4–1 Using Parallelism to Improve Bandwith

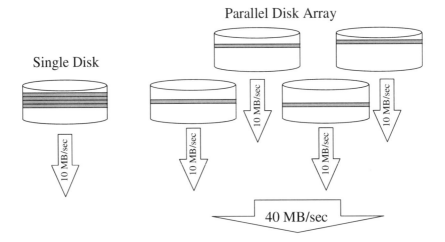

What has increased is not just total storage capacity (obviously, four disks can hold four times as much data as one disk). Just as important for our purposes is that total disk bandwidth—the rate at which the storage system can move data to and from the processor—has also increased. It is this ability of parallel arrays of disks to *scale bandwidth* that makes them so attractive for large data warehouse applications.

The key idea to making this work, however, is to spread the data. Somehow, the single large data set must be decomposed and distributed across multiple disks. Further, these disks must be controlled and synchronized so that they concurrently participate in the data retrieval. The notion of *striping* has to do specifically with the issue of how the data is to be decomposed and distributed across the participating array of disks. In particular, we must imagine the large data set as being (logically) decomposed into a fairly large number (large relative to the number of disks) of small pieces (small relative to the total size of the data set). The size (in bytes) of each piece, called the *striping unit*, is usually a system parameter set in advance and chosen so as to tune performance. For data warehouses, as we shall see, large striping units are appropriate.

Having (conceptually) sliced the data set into a large number of small pieces, we now must assign each piece to its disk. The process that is universally used is *interleaving*. That is, the first piece is assigned to the first disk, the second piece to the second, and so on, in round-robin fashion until each disk has a piece. The process is then repeated, starting again with the first disk, and continued in this way until the entire data set (that is, all the striping units that it comprises) have been assigned.

The process of interleaving is illustrated in Figure 4–2. For purposes of illustration, the large data set T is seen to comprise 20 separate striping units labeled T1, T2, . . . , T20. These striping units have then been interleaved across the four disks: Disk 1 is seen to have striping units T1, T5, T9, T13, and T16; disk 2 is seen to have striping units T2, T6, T10, T14, T18, and so on. When data is retrieved, each of the disks will seek to and return the subset of data it individually holds. The various pieces will subsequently be reassembled into the unified logical data set T. In this way, the goal of achieving high bandwidth through parallelism—that is, striping the data across multiple disks—has been achieved.

Figure 4–2   Interleaving Data across Multiple Disks

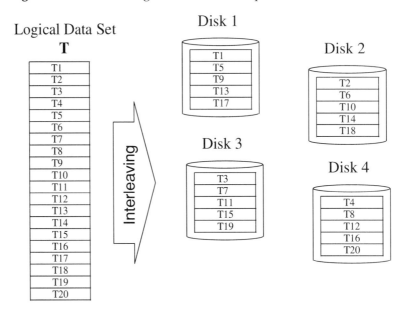

Striping of disks, in the sense described above, has been around for a long time and is not unique to RAID disk arrays. The key letter in the RAID acronym is *R*, which stands for *redundant*. Even though the individual disks used to assemble a disk array have high reliability, the large numbers of disks greatly increases the probability that any one of them may fail. To address this issue of reliability, RAID disk arrays provide extra data, usually in the form of parity, so that the data can be reconstructed automatically even if one of the disks should fail. Using this technique, systems of very high reliability can be constructed. The major differences between the various levels of RAID are (1) the size of the striping unit (from as small as a single bit, in RAID 2, up to fairly large blocks, in RAID 5 and 6), and (2) the way in which the parity/error correcting data is arranged.

Figure 4–3, for example, shows how the parity data is arranged in a typical RAID 5 implementation using five disks. The logical situation is the same as in Figure 4–2: The 20 striping units are still interleaved over the disks. However, for every four striping units, an additional *parity unit* is computed that contains error-correcting data. The additional striping units—those that contain the parity data—are also spread over the disk array. But (as can be seen in the diagram), the disk holding the parity data changes during each pass. On the first pass (corresponding to striping units T1 to T4), disk 5 holds the parity data. On the next pass (corresponding to striping units T5 to T8), disk 4 holds the parity data. After five rounds of this, it is disk 5's turn again to hold the parity data. The disadvantage of this scheme is wasted space: Even though (in this example) five disks are available, only four disks' worth of data can be stored. A 20% storage overhead penalty has been paid. The advantage, however, is high availability: The failure of any single disk will not cause loss or unavailability of the data.

Figure 4–3   Example of RAID 5

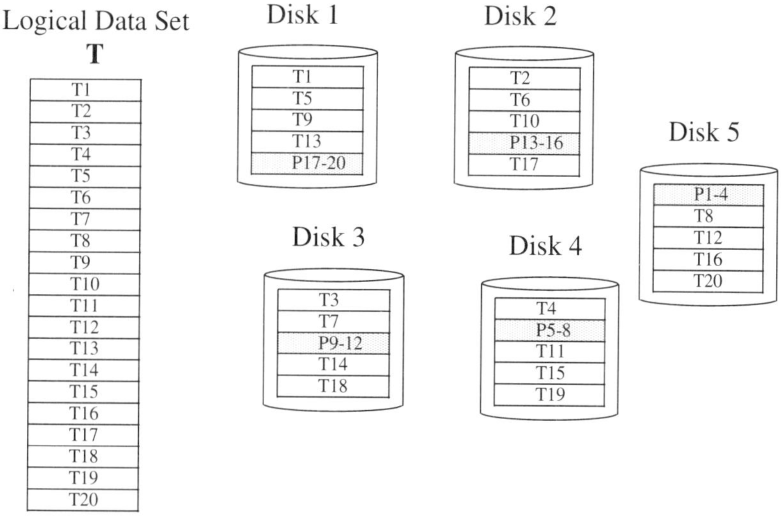

The RAID 5 scheme shown in Figure 4–3 is only one of many possible variations on the general theme. For example, RAID 6 is able to protect against two disk failures, but at the expense of additional storage overhead (and additional latency during a data write). Also, there is nothing special in Figure 4–3 about using five disks: More (or fewer) disks could be used. Using more disks has the advantage of reducing the storage overhead, since only one additional disk's worth of space is needed for the parity data, no matter how many are included in the array. However, it will be seen that once the number of disks in the array reaches a certain point, the aggregate bandwidth they provide will exceed the capacity of the channel into which they are supplying data. For example, it will only take two or three 10-MB/sec SCSI disks to saturate the bandwidth provided by a 20-MB/sec SCSI bus. Putting more disks on that string will not increase bandwidth, since now the SCSI bus has become the bottleneck, not the individual disks. For this reason there is considerable interest in moving to higher-bandwidth buses (ultra-SCSI, Fiber Channel, SSA, SCI, and so on).

4.2 RAID AND STRIPING IMPLEMENTATION OPTIONS

As we saw in Section 4.1, disk striping (and its high-availability relative, RAID) have the twin benefits of (1) increasing total storage, and (2) increasing *bandwidth to a single data set*. The latter point is especially important in the context of a data warehouse and requires further discussion.

It is not especially difficult, and does not require RAID or striping, to provide high bandwidth from multiple disks if the access pattern is to many independent small files, each of which is contained completely on a separate disk. Suppose, for example, that each of three separate, independent disks holds a separate, independent file: file 1 on disk 1, file 2 on disk 2, and file 3 on disk 3. If typical use patterns result in all three files being open and accessed at the same time, the kind of parallelism we have been discussing will not be of much use. The available bandwidth (three disks' worth) is being utilized on three separate simultaneous I/O operations. This type of use pattern, for example, arises in situations where the amount of data required by a typical I/O operation is fairly small, on-line transaction processing (OLTP) being the classic example. Assuming that the requests for data are spread more or less uniformly across the disks and that there are lots of small transactions to deal with, all the disks (three in our example) will be kept quite busy without the need for additional complexity.

It is only when a single operation against a large file is under consideration that the benefits of striping and RAID begin to be felt. If a typical OLTP transaction touches only (say) 20 kilobytes (KB) of data, the response time of a commodity 10-MB/sec disk will be dominated by seek and rotational latency; the data transfer time will be $20/10,000 \sim 2$ milliseconds, plenty fast for any human-in-the-loop system. On the other hand, typical DSS transactions may (and typically will) touch a major portion of the data. At 10 MB/sec, we can access data at only 600 MB/min.

It will typically take today's top-end disks about 15 minutes to read their entire (9 GB) contents. This measure—how long it takes a unit to read or write its total storage—is a good one, since it forms the ratio of *amount of storage* to *bandwidth*. The reciprocal, called the *fill frequency,* may be considered a count of how often the unit can access its contents during a given interval of time. Fill frequency for commodity disks has held pretty steady at about 0.1 per minute over the past several years—that is, bandwidth to the unit has been increasing at about the same rate as storage density.

For DSS transactions, the ability to sustain very high disk bandwidth (using techniques such as striping and RAID) becomes critical to system performance. Let us consider one simple but typical example. We would like system response time to the user to be less than (say) 1 minute, and suppose that a typical DSS transaction touches (say) 10% of the data. On a 3-terabyte (TB) database, this means the ability to read 300 GB of data in less than a minute, or a sustained transfer rate of 300,000 MB/min = 5000 MB/sec = 5 GB/sec = 40 Gb/ sec. Using 10-MB/sec drives, we would need approximately 500 disks *operating simultaneously* to achieve the desired throughput. Note that at 9 GB per disk, we would need about 350 disks just to hold 3 TB of data, so we may say that the data had better be spread over the disks in such a way that *most* of the disks are being used *on every transaction*. In particular, if a single large, central fact table (a common data warehouse schema) must be scanned as part of a typical request, that table in particular had better be striped over a large number of disk units.

There are some strategies to avoid the hard realities contained in the preceding paragraph. For example, it is suggested that the use of such devices as indexes or clever partitioning can substantially reduce the amount of data that is touched by a given DSS query. One strategy for ensuring that "bad" queries are not issued, for example, is to provide the user with a GUI that allows only "good" queries to be constructed and submitted. If such an approach suffices, the full power and scalability of a parallel RDBMS may not be required; such applications fall well within conventional practice. The point of view taken here, however, is that commercially interesting applications do exist where the levels of I/O bandwidth discussed above are appropriate. In those cases, the overriding issue that must be addressed is *sustained bandwidth to single large tables.* As we have seen in our discussion of striping and parallel I/O, the key issue is the decomposition and allocation of data across many (up to hundreds) of separate disks.

It is definitely *not* our suggestion that a single RAID unit should be constructed containing hundreds of disks. In fact, typical RAID implementations are much more modest. Although it is possible to implement RAID features directly in the operating system (for example, the driver software) or in the file system, the current tendency (and one with which we concur) is to implement the RAID features on the disk controller card. The key ideas are shown in Figure 4–4. In one direction the controller card is provided direct memory access (DMA) to main memory. In the other direction, the controller has connectivity to the disks constituting the RAID array. In this configuration the host computer is completely isolated from the internal details of the RAID, which are handled entirely by the RAID controller card. It may even be possible for the controller to handle more than one RAID array (or RAID string, as it is sometimes called) at once. In Figure 4–4, for example, the controller is servicing two separate RAID strings, each containing five disks. Assuming that bus and memory bandwidth is up to the task and that each disk provides 10 MB/sec of bandwidth, each string alone provides about 50 MB/sec of bandwidth, and the two strings together provide 100 MB/sec. To return to our strawman example (300 GB in 60 seconds), about 100 such strings, or 50 such controllers, would be needed to supply the bandwidth desired.

Figure 4–4   Use of RAID Controller to Hide Low-Level Detail

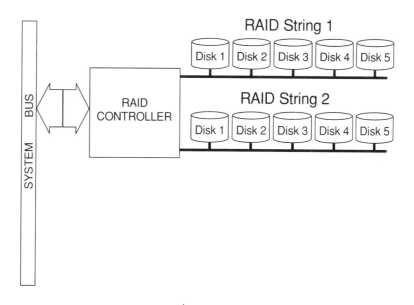

We see that hiding the low-level details of RAID implementation behind a controller has solved only part of the problem. Even if a single RAID string appears as a "device" to the OS (or RDBMS, or file system), there remains the need to spread the data over many such devices. A typical implementation, for example, will *stripe a large table across many RAID strings.* That is, each RAID string is treated as a single logical device (the internal details of the RAID implementation are hidden behind the controller). The application—that is, in our case, the parallel RDBMS—will then itself implement the logic that splits the table and distributes it across the multiple RAID strings. The reader will see, then, that two levels of striping are occurring. At the lowest level, each RAID controller is decomposing the data it gets into striping units, computing parity, and interleaving the data across the disks under its control. At a higher level, the RDBMS is splitting the data according to its own rules and distributing the data across the various RAID controllers.

This situation is illustrated in Figure 4–5. Here the logical table T has been decomposed into six pieces by the RDBMS, one piece for each of the six RAID strings. This splitting is according to rules implemented by the RDBMS, completely independent of the underlying details of the RAID. These six "pieces" are then distributed—two apiece—to each of three RAID controllers. Each controller, in turn, drives a RAID string consisting of five disks. In all, $6 \times 5 = 30$ disks are engaged in I/O, for a total I/O bandwidth of 300 MB/sec (assuming 10-MB/sec disk bandwidth).

In practice, using RAID controllers allows the designer to largely ignore the low-level details of RAID implementation and to consider data partitioning mechanisms at a higher level, one appropriate to the RDBMS application. That does not mean that the choice of RAID level is not important. In fact, the type of data access generated by DSS transactions (long, sequential reads) dictates that RAID 5 is the "right" implementation (see the discussion in Section 4.4). However, at the next level up, the splitting of data across multiple RAID units may be done independently of RAID internals. Often, for example, the RDBMS will wish to decompose a large table at row boundaries, or at column (field) boundaries, or based on key values, or a combination of these. The RAID controller does not need to know about that, and the RDBMS does not need to know about parity. Both types of decomposition are appropriate, and each has been assigned to the level in the system best able to handle it.

Figure 4–5 Decomposing Data across Multiple RAID Units

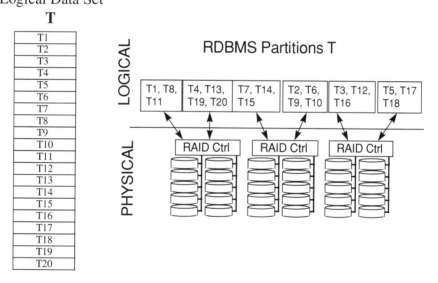

The moral of this section may be summarized briefly: *The aggregate bandwidth to a single table can be no greater than the sum of the bandwidths of the storage devices containing it*. If (as is typical in data warehouses) high bandwidth to single large tables is a requirement, the table *must* be decomposed and distributed across enough devices to achieve the desired bandwidth. It is precisely this issue of how to split and distribute the data that is the *key technical challenge* facing parallel database implementations.

4.3 I/O IN THE THREE PARALLEL ARCHITECTURES

The purpose of this section is to consider I/O approaches in each of the three major architecture classes. We begin with symmetric multiprocessors (SMPs). Based on the discussion from Section 4.2, our focus will be on obtaining high aggregate I/O bandwidth by decomposing and spreading a table across a large number of disks. Within this context we focus on two issues: (1) scalability, and (2) locality of data.

I/O in SMPs

In Figure 1–1 we showed a generic block diagram for an SMP. Let us add a new block symbol representing a RAID controller and its associated disks (as shown, for example, in Figure 4–4). Thus each RAID controller provides the aggregate storage and bandwidth of the disks under its supervision. Figure 4–6 shows two possible configurations. In the top diagram, the controllers have direct, nonshared access to the system bus. The penalty for this is use of a *slot*. The problem arises because the system (backplane) bus for an SMP typically has only a limited number of places along its length to which components (I/O, CPUs, memory, and so on) can attach. Slots used for I/O are unavailable for other purposes (for example, CPUs). In the bottom diagram, we see the RAID controller sharing bus access with a CPU. This permits the I/O bandwidth to scale directly along with the number of CPUs if the customer desires.

The scalability limitations of an SMP are also illustrated in Figure 4–6. The total disk bandwidth is limited by (1) the bandwidth of the system bus, and (2) the bandwidth of main memory. No matter how much bandwidth the RAID controllers can provide, the bandwidth achieved in practice will be no greater than that of the bus and memory. Since (as we saw in Chapter 1) memory and bus bandwidth does *not* scale in SMP architectures, this becomes de facto also a limit on disk bandwidth scalability.

Figure 4–6   Two Approaches to I/O in SMPs

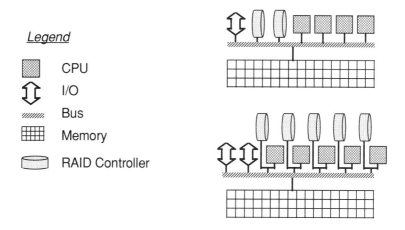

Legend

CPU

I/O

Bus

Memory

RAID Controller

   In fairness, it should be noted that the *amount* of storage attached to an SMP is typically not a problem. Many (hundreds) of disks can be attached to an SMP architecture. The problem is that the bandwidth to those disks does not scale, and hence the strategy of decomposing a large table across many disks to achieve high bandwidth will not work beyond a certain point (that is, beyond the point when system bus and memory bandwidth are exhausted).

I/O in MPPs

Turning next to distributed memory (DM) machines, it is typical to provide each CPU node with the capability of interfacing to an I/O device of some sort. This is well illustrated in Figure 4–7, where some of the nodes have direct access to (or ownership of) disk storage. We should observe at once that it is not necessary for every node to have disk storage. Often, in MPPs, a subset of the nodes are augmented with this capability, and become in this way I/O servers for the rest of the CPUs in the array. On the other hand, in large data warehouse applications, it is often I/O bandwidth that is the driving requirement, and the CPUs are only needed incidentally.

Figure 4–7 Typical I/O Architecture for MPPs

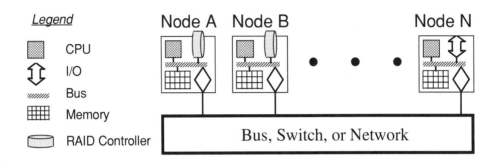

Considering the scalability of I/O bandwidth, the DM architecture has the desirable property that the *ratio* of I/O bandwidth to other system capabilities (especially memory bandwidth and CPU processing capability) *remains constant* as the size of the system grows. That is, I/O bandwidth scales directly as the number of processors. This is (obviously) true, since the *system* ratios are identical to the *node* ratios: The system is just the total of the nodes that make it up.

Just as with the case of memory locality (see Chapter 2), however, the scalability of I/O bandwidth is not without a price. Suppose, for example, that node B in Figure 4–7 wishes to access the data held in the disks attached to node A. Clearly, the high-performance interconnection network will be needed. However, we can imagine two possible implementations. In the first, we imagine the following steps:

1. Node B sends a message to node A notifying it of the data it needs.
2. Node A performs the I/O operation, buffering the data into its local memory.
3. Node A forms a message (or more than one, depending on the size of the data) and sends it off to node B.

In a more efficient implementation, it may be possible for steps 2 and 3 to be circumvented. Assuming that the disk controller is smart enough, there is no reason why the data could not be routed directly to node B's local memory, bypassing the buffering stage completely. It is even possible that step 1 could be avoided, assuming that the disk controller is directly accessible over the network. It that case, the local disk at node A would appear like a "network-attached peripheral" directly accessible from any node in the processor array. The fact that it happens to be local to node A is not relevant.

Even if node "ownership" is not relevant from a logical point of view, it may be very relevant from a performance point of view. The reason is clear to see: Disk accesses to the local disk do not use the interconnection network. This means that they complete more quickly, since the additional overhead of data transfer over the network is avoided. In addition, and just as important, a local disk operation does not utilize any of the (shared) network bandwidth. That means that the total amount of traffic over the network is lower, which (in turn) means reduced contention and more prompt service for other network uses. If all nodes are doing remote disk references, the total amount of network traffic will be very much greater than if all (or most) can be doing local disk references. Thus, just as *locality of data* is the price one pays for scalability of memory bandwidth, *locality of storage* is the price one pays for scalability of disk bandwidth. In decomposing the large table across many disks so as to achieve high I/O bandwidth, it is useful whenever possible to arrange matters so that data on disk is close to the CPU that will be accessing it. This is a major technical challenge facing a parallel RDBMS on a DM architecture: What rules shall be used to partition the large tables across many disks while maintaining proximity between the node where the data is stored and the node that will process the data.

I/O in DSM/NUMA Machines

Turning finally to distributed shared memory (DSM) or NUMA architectures, the issues are identical to those we have just discussed for DM machines. Consider, for example, Figure 4–8. As with DM machines, we see that I/O bandwidth scales with other system parameters: The *system* ratio of bandwidth to processing power is the same as the *node* ratio. But as with DM machines, there is a penalty for nonlocal disk accesses. The NUMA architecture will provide direct disk access from any processor to any disk. However, nonlocal disk references will require transfers across the interconnection network. When many CPUs are making large nonlocal disk requests, this can stress the network and result in contention and (hence) generally degraded network performance. Thus, just as with the DM architecture, the RDBMS will be faced with the need both to partition large tables (so as to provide high aggregate bandwidth) and to position it so that each CPU will be "near" the data it needs to process. The "uniform address space" abstraction of a NUMA architecture can make it difficult for the software designer to express these algorithmic requirements.

Figure 4–8   I/O Architecture for DSM

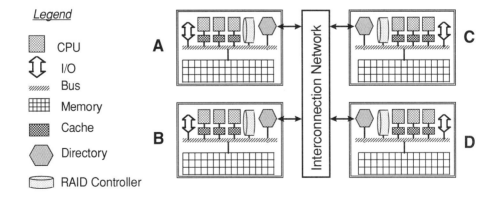

4.4 Observations, Caveats, and Good Advice

A reader already knowledgeable concerning I/O in databases will have noticed a number of points where, for the sake of brevity, complications have been tacitly avoided. It is now time to bring these matters to light.

Channel Bandwidth

We begin with an observation made briefly above but which deserves greater attention. This concerns the fact that at each point where a data transfer takes place, a potential data bandwidth bottleneck exists. Consider, for example, the two diagrams in Figure 4–9. Both are pictures of RAID controllers servicing five disks in a RAID 5 configuration. In the top diagram, the bus servicing the RAID string is (for the sake of argument) a 20-MB/sec bus. This corresponds roughly to current fast/wide SCSI implementations. On the one hand, each of the five disks is capable of sustained transfer rates approaching 10 MB/sec. This means that the bus itself has become a bottleneck: At most, two of the five available disks can fully utilize the bus at any time; only 40% of the *potential* bandwidth is *actually available*, due to the bandwidth limitations of the transfer bus. Here is a case where the system is scalable along one dimension (more disks can be added for more total storage capacity) but is not scalable along another (usable bandwidth does not scale as the number of disks increases).

Now, compare the first diagram to the second. In this case the controller provides a separate, nonshared transfer bus for each disk (up to whatever maximum number the controller can handle; the five disks in our example are for illustration purposes only). This is an example of a scalable approach, since the ratio of bandwidth to storage stays constant as the number of disks increases: more disks means more bandwidth. The key point in these two diagrams is that the bandwidth of the transfer bus itself (this is sometimes called the *channel*) is a key feature to be considered. One of the advantages of a technology such as Fiber Channel is that a larger number of disks can be handled before the channel bandwidth is exhausted. In the first diagram, if the transfer bus bandwidth were (say) 100 MB/sec instead of 20, it should be easy to service all five disks. An advantage of being able to handle more disks on a single RAID string is lower storage overhead for the RAID parity data. If bandwidth limitations force (say) only two data disks per RAID string, plus a third for parity, the storage overhead is $1/_3 = 33\%$. On the other hand, if there is sufficient channel bandwidth to service (say) six disks in the RAID string (+ 1 for parity), the storage overhead for the extra parity disk is $1/_7 = 14\%$, a substantial savings.

Figure 4–9   Two Approaches to RAID Strings

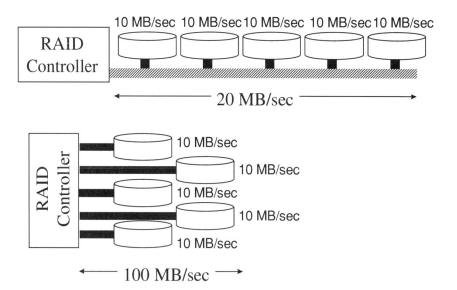

Why RAID 5?

At several points in the preceding discussion we claimed, without further evidence, that the "right" implementation for a data warehouse is RAID level 5 (see Figure 4–3 for a reminder of how parity is handled in this configuration). There are several operational assumptions about the data warehouse that lead to this conclusion; changes to these assumptions might lead to a different result. The first assumption is that high availability is not a critical issue. For the most part, data warehouses are used for analysis, business planning, and data mining. Our assumption is that these operations do not require the kind of 24×7 availability that often characterizes OLTP operations. For high availability, disk mirroring (RAID level 1) and doubled controllers are often required. (Alternatively, RAID 6 can be used to protect against failures from any two disks in the string.)

Another assumption is that reloading of lost data is to be avoided. The point of the data redundancy provided by the RAID controller is not for very high availability but to ease the task of data reconstruction. Data in a data warehouse often reflects a sequence of large data updates over a period of months or years. Losing part of the data means tracking down its source and reloading, a process that may be lengthy and onerous. Having the parity data immediately available means that the reloading process can be avoided.

At current storage capacities (9 GB per disk), a terabyte of data requires about 110 disks. Typical mean time to failure for these disks is on the order or 100,000 hours, about once in 10 years. This, in turn, means that we can expect about one disk failure per month per terabyte of data. The reader can decide whether having the ability to rapidly (on the order of minutes) swap in a new disk and reconfigure the data *without reloading* is worth the additional cost in parity storage overhead and RAID controllers.

Another assumption that is generally true of data warehouses is that lengthy sequential scans of large tables characterize the access pattern. Rather than build indexes to attempt to reduce the amount of data that must be accessed, data warehouse implementations assume that most of the time, a transaction will touch a substantial fraction of the data. In such a situation, the choice of schema will be made to favor fast scans. In such an environment, access patterns take the form of long sequential reads. There is only negligible risk of transferring a block of data only to find that a small part of it is needed. The goal is to open the large spigot and let the data stream.

RAID 5 is ideally suited for such an environment. By choosing a large striping unit (64 KB is not uncommon) and ensuring that the data is read sequentially in the order it was written (sequential scans), very high bandwidths with little seek latency overhead can be obtained. It is worth observing that not all RAID 5 controllers currently on the market are able to achieve these goals. For some vendors, RAID 3 may be the better choice, not because of inherent RAID 3 superiority, but because the vendor has chosen to optimize the RAID 3 controllers for large block transfers. The point to keep in mind is the goal—high sustained bandwidth based on large sequential reads. Although RAID 5 has theoretical advantages, the actual performance of the controller must be taken into account. Under these conditions, RAID 3 may prove to be the better option for some vendors.

Other Types of I/O: Users and Loading

In this chapter we have focused on disk I/O because of its importance in processing complex queries against large tables. Our point of view has been that rapidly scanning large tables end to end is a key capability, and hence we have focused on distribution of the data across a large number of disks. The real world is more complex. I/O involves more than just reading from and writing to disks. User queries must be retrieved and processed and the data must be delivered to the user. Further, periodic loads of large amounts of new data must be absorbed subject to demanding time lines. Both these operations—handling the user interface, and data loading— impose I/O demands that must be sized and often parallelized to meet performance requirements.

Turning first to the user interface, there is considerable variation in both the number and complexity of queries that a DSS might be expected to handle. The focus of this book is on large complex queries. By its very nature, a single such query might require tens of seconds to process even on a large powerful machine, so that implicit in this concept of operations is the notion that not very many such queries are active at the same time. If the goal is to process many (hundreds or thousands) of simple queries concurrently (as is the case, for example, in OLTP systems), the architecture will be quite different from one in which only a few (less than 10) are ever active at once, each of which will require a major fraction of the machine's resources while it is active. We note that vendors who have performed the TPC-D benchmarks at the 300-GB level have all elected *not* to process multiple concurrent query streams, even though this option is permitted.

In this second case, the stress is not on input (it takes only a small message to deliver a very complex SQL query), and there is stress on output only if the query produces a large data set in response. The situation in which such a large output is produced typically occurs when the data is to be input to some other application; only rarely would a user want multiple gigabytes of data. A data mining application, on the other hand, might well use the parallel RDBMS as a sophisticated file server, reducing the data and delivering it in the desired format for subsequent processing. In such a case, a suitable data pipe must be provided, whether the application resides on the same platform as the data warehouse or on a different one.

The historical tendency of an RDBMS (and this tendency is currently enshrined in the SQL standard) is to coalesce the output to a single byte stream. This is clearly counter to this desire for high-bandwidth I/O to the application. If the results of the query are, at some point in the computation, distributed across the memories of the various processors in the array, it may be desirable to leave the data where it is for further application processing, particularly if the application is itself parallelized. One example of such a capability is the use of a parallel file system. This software automatically partitions a single logical file over many devices to achieve high aggregate bandwidth. If the data is already partitioned, it seems a waste to aggregate it and then partition it again. In any case, if the RDBMS forces the data into a single byte stream for output, this could become a bottleneck if large amounts of data are produced.

Whether or not periodic data loads stress the I/O of the system will depend on the amount of data and the time line under which the load must occur. Typically, however, the amount of data to be loaded is small compared to the size of the data warehouse itself (a few gigabytes per day), so that simply reading the data in is not a stressing operation. *Parallelizing* the load operation (that is, spreading it across multiple processors so as to increase throughput), on the other hand, is a technical challenge. Our sense is that conventional I/O capabilities should be adequate to support the data transfers involved.

SUMMARY OF PART I

In these first four chapters we have considered various aspects of processor and I/O hardware architecture relevant to efficient implementation of large parallel databases. We may summarize the four major conclusions as follows:

1. Scalable architectures are those that keep the ratio of the six major system capabilities—processing power, memory, memory bandwidth, interprocessor communications, disk storage capacity, and disk storage bandwidth—constant as the system grows in size. The only way that this balance can be maintained is through simple replication: Provide the desired balance at each node, and replicate.

2. Replication leads inevitably to the issue of locality: Some memory and storage will be close to one processor and distant from another. Efficient implementations must take locality into account by minimizing the distance between the data and the CPU that uses it.

3. Distributed shared memory or NUMA architectures present a system view that masks the underlying hardware locality issues. This mismatch between system view and hardware reality presents a technical challenge.

4. The only way to achieve high aggregate bandwidth to a single table is to spread that table out across many disks and have them all participate in parallel. A major task of a parallel RDBMS, therefore, is to decide how to accomplish this data decomposition and spreading.

In Part II, the issues of data partitioning and locality—among both disks and CPUs—will continue to be major themes.

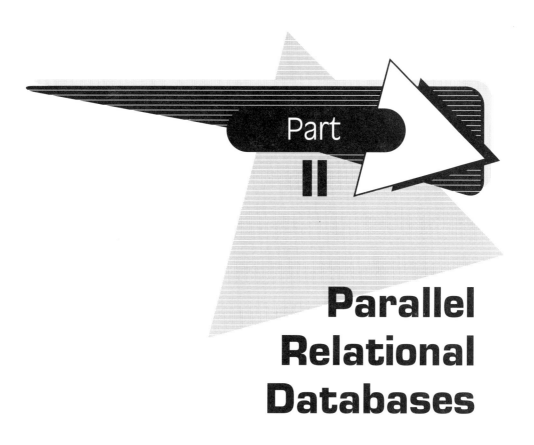

Parallel Relational Databases

In Part II, attention turns to the software that implements the relational database. It is the task of the software to decompose the problem—that is, the SQL query submitted to the database system—in such a way that the hardware is used efficiently. This problem is already difficult on a traditional sequential machine with a large shared memory and uniform access to the entire disk storage system; parallel execution adds to this complexity and introduces issues whose solution may not be immediately intuitive. A major goal of Part II is to sharpen and direct the reader's appreciation for some of these complexities, with particular attention to potential "gotcha's" that await the unwary.

Chapter 5 is a leisurely introduction to parallelism: what it is, the correct conceptual models to bring to the problem, and how these express themselves when the application is a large relational database. In Chapter 6 we present the three standard software architectures for parallel databases: *shared everything*, *shared disk*, and *shared nothing*. The reader will see that these software architectures correspond nicely to the hardware approaches discussed in Part I. The final two chapters in Part II are devoted to detailed discussion of two of the most difficult and important relational operations: joins (Chapter 7) and sorts (Chapter 8). Considerable attention is given to data layout, both in the disk system (to improve I/O performance) and in the machine itself (to minimize interprocessor communications overhead). A database administrator of a parallel RDBMS will find this material of use in planning and utilizing the various options provided by RDBMS vendors for decomposing large tables, developing efficient schema, and allocating storage.

Opportunities for Parallelism in a Relational Database

In this chapter we introduce a number of important concepts regarding parallel software. Although the focus throughout is on database operations (particularly relational databases), there are some notions (load balancing, synchronization, global operations, and so on) that are quite general and that arise whenever a parallel application is developed. In Sections 5.1 and 5.2 we present these more general notions, but using database operations for illustration. In Section 5.3 we take up the relational model, per se, and show the particular form that parallelism takes in this context. In the final section we turn to the general issue of query optimization. This is already a difficult problem for traditional sequential machines, and the addition of parallelism adds an additional layer of complexity. We will see, in particular, how appropriate choice of schema can ease the burden on the query optimizer by eliminating unnecessary complexity and quickly directing the algorithm to the desired behavior.

5.1 BASIC CONCEPTS

Three Types of Parallelism

A good metaphor for parallel processing is a construction project: people building something—say, a large building. In this metaphor, the human workers on the project correspond to the CPUs in the machine; and the structure on which the workers are working corresponds to the problem or application that the computer is executing. To use the workers efficiently, it is typical (and obvious) that we must have them working on different tasks: some erecting the internal structural supports, some pouring concrete, some installing internal plumbing and electrical facilities, and so on. By dividing the single large job (build a building) into many smaller jobs, the work can proceed in parallel—that is, at the same time that one type of job is going on (welding a girder), another type of job can also be going on (attaching an external wall element). That is why so many people can be at work at once: Each is doing an independent task.

These same ideas are at the heart of parallel computation. A single large task is to be decomposed into many smaller tasks, and these small tasks in turn are assigned to separate CPUs. The term *parallel*, in this context, means *simultaneous* or *concurrent execution*: All the individual tasks are executing at the same time. It will be seen at once that the great enemy of parallelism is *sequential dependency*. This is illustrated in Figure 5–1. If the output from task A is required before task B can begin, parallel execution will not improve performance; no matter how many CPUs are available, none of them can get started on task B until task A is complete. The total time for execution will be the sum of the execution times for tasks A and B.

Figure 5–1   Types of Parallelism

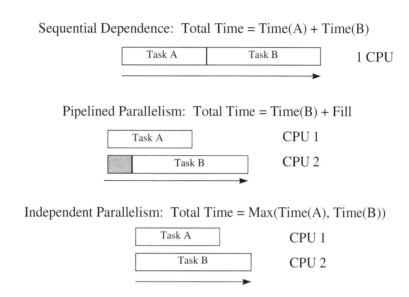

Sequential Dependence: Total Time = Time(A) + Time(B)

Pipelined Parallelism: Total Time = Time(B) + Fill

Independent Parallelism: Total Time = Max(Time(A), Time(B))

A somewhat better situation is shown in the middle diagram in Figure 5–1. Here, even though task B requires task A's output, it does not need all the data before it can proceed. We might think of task A as outputing (say) a long sequence of records. Task B, in turn, examines each of these records in turn and performs some operation on each of them (perhaps adding a value from each record into a running sum). It is clear in this case that task B does not need to wait for all the records from task A to be complete before getting started on the first few. In this case, parallelism (simultaneous execution of task A and task B) is achieved for most of the time. An initial start-up period is needed for task A, after which task B receives input and (concurrently with task A) begins processing. Finally, there will be a short period at the end when task B finishes its final few records, during which task A is idle. The overall execution time has been shortened considerably, because for most of the time both tasks execute concurrently—that is, in parallel.

This type of parallelism, called *pipeline parallelism*, is common in parallel databases. As we will see in Section 5.3, the relational model fits this notion well, since in fact the outputs of relational operators are naturally conceived of as inputs to other operators—that is, the *type* of input and output of the relational operators is the same. At the same time, we will see that the size and types of operations characteristic of large databases (that is, decision support in a data warehouse) makes pipeline parallelism of only limited utility.

The third type of parallelism illustrated in Figure 5–1 is called *independent or natural parallelism*. Applications that exhibit this type of behavior are sometimes called *embarrassingly parallel* because the opportunities for parallelism (that is, simultaneous execution) are close to the surface. In this case, there is no dependency between tasks A and B: Each task can proceed independent of the other (this means that the correctness of the answer does not depend on which one is completed first). Again, we see that the fact that tasks A and B execute concurrently means that the total execution time is reduced. In the sequential case, execution time was the *sum* of the execution times of the two tasks. Now it is the *maximum* of the two times—that is, whichever takes longer. In our example, task B takes a little longer to complete than A, our first example of the effects of balancing the workload. Compared to pipelined parallelism, independent parallelism has the advantage of avoiding the (hopefully small) overheads at the beginning and end of the pipeline, and this is reflected in the formula for execution time.

Although independent parallelism (if it can be accomplished) is best for minimizing execution time, it is the worst of the three types in terms of use of memory. In the first case (sequential dependence), task B never begins until task A is complete. This means that task B can reuse the memory resources that had previously been assigned to task A. That cannot be done, however, in independent parallelism. Tasks A and B are active simultaneously and hence require enough memory for both. In computing required memory, it is as if the two formulas for execution time were reversed: The sequential case only needs enough memory to hold the largest problem (*maximum*), whereas the independent parallel case needs enough for both (*sum*). As before, the pipelined parallelism occupies a middle ground. We assume that the work proceeds "a piece at a time" and hence that only enough memory for the two pieces—one for A, and one for B—is required. Thus the increase in performance has come at a cost: an increase in the total amount of memory required.

Whereas our example shows only two tasks, the general case is more complex. Tens or even hundreds of tasks are not uncommon, but the general principles (and formulas) still apply.

Inter- and Intraquery Parallelism

Turning specifically to databases, the classic example of independent or natural parallelism is OLTP (on-line transaction processing). Here each task is a query to the database generated by a user (or, more properly, the user's application). A common operational condition (often, but not always true) is that the individual transactions are independent; that is, no transaction requires the output of any other transaction to complete. The reason this assumption is made is that the database is assumed to contain a description of the current state, and a transaction is only interested in that state, not a hypothetical state that might have existed if transactions had completed in some other order. In this environment, each transaction can be considered a separate, independent task, a classic case of natural parallelism. Many CPUs (as many as are available) can be kept busy by assigning each task—that is, each query—to a separate CPU.

A metaphor for this scheme is the number queue at a bakery. As each CPU completes its current task, it reports back to a central manager to get the next task in the queue. Similarly, customers (corresponding to the queries to be executed) are assigned number slips as they enter the shop. As they become free after their previous customer, servers (the CPUs) find the next customer to serve by visiting the shop's number dispenser. As long as there is work to do (queries to process, customers to serve), all the CPUs will be kept busy. One advantage of this scheme is that Unix (among other operating systems) provides this "next task" service, often including prioritization and other tuning parameters to help the system adminstrator monitor and control system behavior. This is thus a simple and effective load balancing scheme that requires little or no additional work by the application.

This type of parallelism—many separate, independent queries active at the same time—is called *interquery parallelism*. Its natural setting is OLTP, although there is no reason why decision support could not, at least in theory, make use of the same strategy. One of the operational considerations that makes this strategy work in an OLTP environment is that typically each query is fairly small, small enough that a single CPU can process it in a short enough time to satisfy the user's need for responsiveness. Another operational consideration is the number of queries—typically, a function of the number of users and their rate of submitting transactions. The fraction of available machine cycles that are actually used is driven by the workload, and the system is sized accordingly. One term that is used to describe this environment is *throughput engine*: The workload consists of a stream of independent tasks that are handed off, based on arrival time and priority, to CPUs in the processor array as CPUs become available. It is fair to say that interquery parallelism, and the use of the hardware as a throughput engine, is the most frequent way in which parallel systems are being used today.

An alternative approach, however, is to put many CPUs to work on the same query. The desire here is to speed up execution of a single large, complex query by first decomposing it into smaller problems and then executing these smaller problems concurrently (in parallel) by assigning each subproblem to its own CPU. This type of parallelism, called *intraquery parallelism*, is the chief focus of interest in large decision support systems (DSSs). The reason for this shift of emphasis is twofold. First, unlike OLTP systems, DSS queries tend to be very complex; that is, they tend to touch a much larger fraction of the database than does a typical OLTP transaction. Rather than update or display a single balance line, for example (an operation typical of an OLTP implementation), a DSS query might wish to count the number of occurrences of a certain value across the entire balance table. Here the task of reading in the entire table and computing the required histogram is probably too large to be handed to a single CPU (at least, not if the user wishes to get the result back at something approaching interactive rates). The problem facing the DSS designer is completely different from the OLTP case: Instead of lots of small, independent queries (using the machine as a throughput engine), the desire is to process large complex queries one at a time as quickly as possible (that is, using the machine to speed execution of a large computationally demanding problem).

These ideas are illustrated in Figure 5–2. In the OLTP example we see many small, independent queries waiting in the queue to be processed. The job of the system is to assign these queries, one by one, to CPUs as they become available. In the DSS example characteristic of a data warehouse, on the other hand, we see a single large query to be processed. Here the system must first decompose the large problem into smaller subtasks. These, in turn, are handed off to the various

CPUs for execution. At the end, there may be a final task to assemble the individual results into a package for delivery back to the user.

Figure 5–2 Inter- versus Intraquery Parallelism

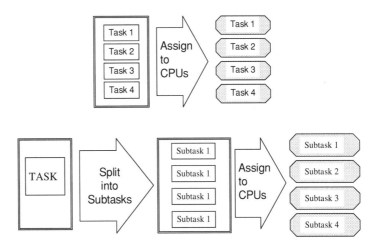

In summary, an OLTP environment consists of many small, independent queries to process. Here, the system is typically used as a throughput engine and implements interquery parallelism. In a DSS environment typical of a data warehouse, the system uses intraquery parallelism to speed execution of single large, complex queries. Because of our focus on data warehouses, it is this second use of a parallel RDBMS that will be of most interest to us.

5.2 TWO IMPORTANT TECHNIQUES

In this section we consider two important techniques in constructing efficient parallel implementations: (1) load balancing, and (2) minimizing global operations. Both of these can have a significant impact on achieved performance. We deal with each in turn.

Load Balancing

Turn back briefly to Figure 5–1, and consider the third diagram. As we remarked in passing, the time to execute task B is longer than the time to execute task A. The effect of this is that during the interval of time after task A completes but while task B is still active, the CPU that has been assigned to task A is "waiting." Machine cycles that might have been used for productive work are wasted. The greater the imbalance between the execution times for tasks A and B, the more severe the problem. Further, the problem becomes more severe as the number of parallel tasks increases. This is because (in the scenario under consideration) *every* task must wait until the *final* one completes. Every task except the longest one will experience some amount of overhead due to the load imbalance—that is, the uneven distribution of workload across the processor array.

To see how severe this effect can be (see Figure 5–3), let us suppose that the usual (expected) execution time is about 5 seconds but that actual execution times vary between 4 and 6 seconds (for the technically minded, the distribution is uniform on [4.0, 6.0], with a standard deviation of 0.6, or 12%). That is, we expect the actual execution time for a task to lie somewhere between a minimum of 4 seconds and a maximum of 6 seconds, with about equal likelihood of any particular time of execution in that range. The expected amount of time that any given processor spends waiting is, then, the difference between the expected maximum (close to 6 seconds) and its expected completion time (about 5 seconds). We see that the average waiting time per CPU is about 1 second, or about 1 sec(wait)/6 sec(total) = 17% of the total available CPU cycles. If we could have spread the load more evenly, so that (for example) the distribution of execution times lay in the range 4.8 to 5.2 (σ = 2.3%), the overhead due to load imbalance would be reduced to 0.2/5.2 ~ 4%.

Figure 5–3 Reducing Overhead by Load Balancing

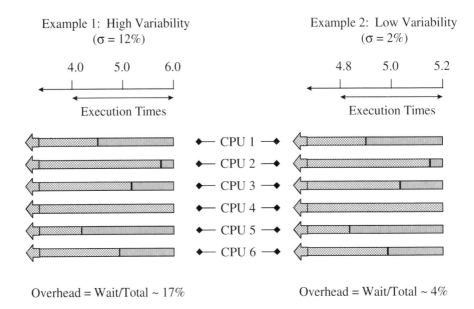

Overhead = Wait/Total ~ 17%   Overhead = Wait/Total ~ 4%

Because of factors like this, designers of efficient parallel algorithms spend considerable effort finding ways to spread the processing load evenly over the available CPUs. Notice that this problem did not arise in our discussion of interquery parallelization. The "pick the next available task" strategy automatically fills in (packs) the available time with work to do, provided that the work is available (that is, provided that there is something waiting in the job queue). In intraquery parallelization, however, the issue is real, and potentially serious. The reason is that in this case, when a processor gets done with its portion of the work (its subtask, as shown in Figure 5–2), there is nothing left to do until the entire task completes. Unlike the OLTP case, there is no work queue holding useful tasks waiting to be done. The CPU is (typically) bound to its query until that query completes, so that the "wait until done" model applies.

As we will see at greater length in Chapters 7 and 8, one of the standard ways of partitioning the workload in a parallel database application is by partitioning the data—that is, assigning each CPU a subset of the data on which to work. Often in these situations, the expected execution time for each CPU will be closely related to the size of the data it has been given—that is, we expect (say) a sort routine to execute in roughly equal times on equal sizes of data. To balance the load in this case means, simply, to ensure that each processor has about the same amount of data to work on. Thus techniques for evenly partitioning the data (and several may be applicable) are motivated by the prior desire to balance the work load evenly.

One important use of *sorting* is related to this issue. We may be tempted to divide the data by considering the values of keys. Naively, we may attempt to divide the key space into equal intervals and to assign each row to a bin based on the interval to which it belongs. Such an approach will fail, however, if the distribution of key values is uneven (think, for example, about text, where some initial letters occur much more frequently than others). Sorting the data, however, gets us out of this bind. In the sorted data we can discover exactly where the breakpoints are to partition the data evenly. This is our first example, among many, of the utility of sorting in large database operations.

Global Operations

A second area that attracts the close attention of parallel algorithm designers is the use of global operations. By this we mean operations that require the close cooperation of all the processors in the array. Examples include:

1. *Global sum.* Find the sum of values held by different CPUs.

2. *Synchronization.* Bring all CPUs to a common point in the processing flow before allowing any to continue.
3. *Locks.* Enforce sequential access to a single entity, often followed by synchronization.

The reason that these operations are of concern is that they inevitably increase overhead. Any global operation will require the exchange of control information among the various CPUs. In an SMP, this will require access to shared data structures, with attendant bus and cache penalties. In an MPP, this will require the exchange of messages across the interconnection network. In either case, the coordination of the operation among multiple CPUs is additional work not required in a sequential process, and hence works against the goal of optimal speed-up and scale-up.

One way of thinking about these issues is to compare the situation against that of interquery parallelism. There, locks are needed to ensure that a modification of data is complete before that data is read and used by some subsequent transaction. However, most of the time, no other currently active transaction will need to access the data. In an OLTP setting it is exceptional that two transactions would simultaneously need "modify" access to the same row. Although the locking mechanism is necessary for data integrity, it tends not to affect overall performance since it is needed only infrequently.

The opposite is true in decision support environments. There, the need for locks is not related primarily to database integrity, since for the most part "modify" operations only occur during regularly scheduled and infrequent load operations. Rather, in a DSS application, locks are used to enforce orderly access to global working variables. In Chapter 1, for example, we discussed "hot spots" in a shared memory machine, but the same issues arise in MPPs and NUMA architectures as well. In such a situation it is *typical* that *all* the CPUs will be involved in accessing and updating the global variable.

The associated overhead, then, has the potential to degrade performance if there is excessive use of this mechanism.

In raising this subject we are not suggesting that the reader will be coding the internals of a commercial RDBMS. Rather, we are pointing toward an analysis technique that needs to be available conceptually during performance tuning and optimization. Sorts and joins, for example, can be implemented in a variety of ways, requiring greater or less use of these types of global operations. Sorts that work just fine up to a certain table size may become excessively and unexpectedly long-running beyond that point. In diagnosing and alleviating the problem, it is good to be aware that inefficient use of global operations, particularly locks, may be the culprit, and that the time has come to shift to an algorithmic approach that is more judicious in its use of these techniques.

5.3 PARALLELIZING THE RELATIONAL MODEL

Relational databases—that is, databases using the *relational model*, and accessed using the *structured query language* (SQL)—have become de facto industry standards. It is not our purpose here to provide a tutorial introduction to the relational model or to SQL. Good references are available (see, for example, C. J. Date and H. Darwen, *A Guide to the SQL Standard, 3rd ed.*, Addison-Wesley, Reading, Mass., 1994), and some familiarity with SQL will help in understanding our examples.

For our purposes it will be sufficient to consider a database as consisting of some number of tables. Each table, in turn, may be thought of as a two-dimensional matrix: that is, as an $N \times M$ array, where M is the number of (named) *columns* in the table and N is the (possibly empty) collection of *rows*. Each row, in turn, contains a single (possibly NULL) value for each column, the value agreeing with the associated data type (including any range constraints). Conceptually, the columns represent attributes, and each row represents one instance, defined (completely) by the values assigned to the attributes.

The relational model achieves generality by insisting that all operations accept one or more tables as inputs and return a single table as output. Simple operations take a single table as input and create a single new table as output. Creating a new output table from a (single) input table by deleting some of the columns is called *projection*. Creating a new output table from a (single) input table by deleting some of the rows (for example, deleting all those rows whose values do not meet some desired condition) is called *selection*. The two operations together—select and project—are referred to informally as a *scan*. It is also possible to create a new output table by *grouping* some of the rows together; each row of the resultant table, for example, might contain the sum (or maximum, or average, or count, and so on) of a defined group of rows from the input table. New columns can be created by performing simple arithmetic operations on values held in existing columns.

The principal way in which two or more tables (as input) can produce a *single* new table (as output) is via the various types of *join* operations (including NATURAL joins, INNER and OUTER joins, UNION and INTERSECTION joins, and so on). As a conceptual aid, consider Figure 5–4, which illustrates how the relational model, and SQL queries against it, behave. *Base tables* (that is, tables that are permanent and endure from session to session) are denoted by boldface letters. Three such tables—**A**, **D**, and **E**—are taken as input to a join operation, and a single intermediate output table, *IT1*, is produced as a result. The table is intermediate because it need never exist (in the sense of having disk storage allocated, and so on) at all. It is a conceptual convenience, not a command for the database system to do anything. This intermediate table is then subjected to a scan (select/project) operation, and another intermediate table, *IT2*, is produced as the result. We see that conceptually, the only function of *IT1* is to serve as input to a scan function that in turn produces *IT2*. The user really does not care about *IT1* at all; SQL allows (indeed, encourages) the user to define and operate on such intermediate tables as a conceptual aid. In a similar manner, the base table **F** is scanned to produce *IT3*. The two intermediate tables (*IT2* and *IT3*), together with the base table **A** (its second use), are then joined (producing *IT4*) and scanned (producing *IT5* as the final output).

Figure 5–4 Simple Flow Diagram for an SQL Query

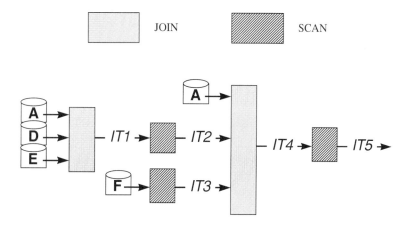

SQL is thought of most appropriately as a formal way of specifying exactly the kind of graph shown in Figure 5–4. SQL programmers, in turn, have learned how to produce desired outputs by specifying a sequence of intermediate tables using a sequence of scan and join operations. The table dependencies (inputs and outputs), which are shown so clearly Figure 5–4, are captured in SQL syntax by *nesting*. That is, in the FROM clause of a SELECT statement, the input tables may themselves result from more deeply nested SELECT and JOIN statements. It is this nesting of calls that gives SQL the appearance of complexity. In fact, the underlying ideas are fairly straightforward (as Figure 5–4 shows).

We turn now to the issue of parallelizing an SQL query represented by a graph like Figure 5–4. The first key point to observe is that there is clearly *sequential dependency*. The overall computation proceeds left to right across the page, and later (rightmost) computations depend for their input on the results of preceding computations. Although we might imagine the potential for pipeline parallelism—that is, later operations might be able to accept partial outputs from earlier ones—there are many versions of join and scan which must have *all* their input available before the computation can begin. Thus to parallelize a graph such as Figure 5–4, *we must be able to parallelize the separate join and scan operations individually*. If we were able to observe the execution of this query in a commercial parallel RDBMS, we would see each of the join and scan operations performed one after the other in sequence; *within* each operation, however, execution takes place in parallel across the processor array. This is shown in Figure 5–5, which illustrates how a parallel RDBMS might execute this query. There are five stages—three joins and two scans—corresponding to the five operations shown in Figure 5–4. Each operation is performed in sequence, to completion, before the next operation is begun. Within each operation, however, all the CPUs are active (that is, operating in parallel). *The total query completes more rapidly because each of its component operations is performed in parallel.*

Looking at Figure 5–5, the reader may wonder where the parallelism is—it sure looks sequential! And at the topmost level, it is: The operations are performed one after the other in temporal sequence. Within each operation, however, it is quite another matter. *Within* the operation, many CPUs operate concurrently—in parallel—to accelerate the computation. Indeed, if we consider Figure 5–5, we can begin to see the types of internal capabilities that must be provided. For one thing, we would certainly like the input to a given stage of the computation to be parallelized. At the far left side of the figure (or, more strictly, whenever a base table is involved), this means parallel I/O from the disks where the base tables reside. In the intervening stages, however, it means that the "handoff" from one stage to the next must be coordinated and parallelized.

Figure 5–5　Parallelizing an SQL Query

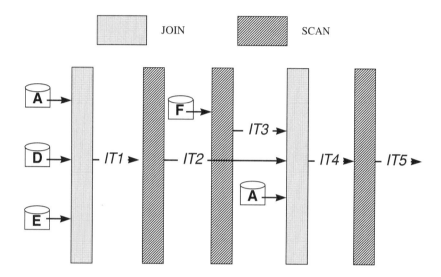

Take, for example, intermediate table *IT2*. It is an output of the second scan stage (the result of a previous join operation using tables **A**, **D**, and **E**). It is also the input to the second join operation, where it will be considered together with the base table **A**. To parallel this (second) join operation, both table **A** and intermediate table *IT2* must be spread (partitioned) among the various CPUs in the parallel array. Just as the data on disk must be assigned to the "right" processor in the array, so also must the data in intermediate table *IT2*. This means that it would be helpful for the scan process that produces *IT2* to know something about the destination for its resulting data. Not only must the scan operation perform the correct select/project, it must also organize (or reorganize) the data in a manner appropriate to the next computational stage.

This "rearrangement" or "splitting" of the data, and the communication of it to its destination processor in the array, is characteristic of parallel RDBMS systems. We might call it a *shuffle* operation (*permutation* is the technical term), and it can occur at various points in the overall flow: at the end of a stage (preparatory to handing the data off to the next stage); within a single stage (as explained at greater length in Chapters 7 and 8); at the beginning of a stage (if the preceding stage has not already prepared the data, and especially when reading off disk); and as the final stage (gathering and sequentializing the data and adding a cursor, for output to the end user). Figure 5–6 shows a notional depiction of some shuffle operations as they might be scattered across the computation.

Figure 5–6 Data Rearrangement Using Shuffle

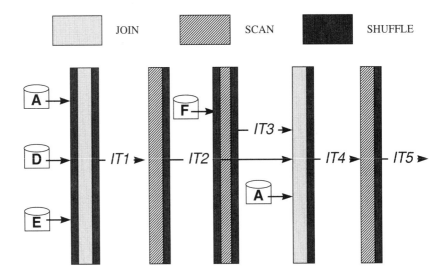

As we proceed, various aspects of the key ideas in Figure 5–6 will be examined in greater detail. How is the shuffle (data rearrangement) to be accomplished on each of the various types of hardware architecture? How can the key database algorithms—scan, join, and sort—make use of the full power of the processor array? How can clever arrangement of base tables improve I/O bandwidth and hence overall performance? These are the topics that will engage us over the next few chapters. Beneath all this, however, lie the central concepts of Figure 5–6, which captures the essential elements for parallelizing the relational model.

5.4 QUERY OPTIMIZATION AND DATABASE DESIGN

An important feature of SQL, which we mentioned briefly in Section 5.3, is that the query is concerned primarily with specifying the *form* of the *final output table*. That is, the intermediate tables that appear in the statement of the query are, as we said, conveniences to the user in conceptualizing and specifying the desired result. In particular, if we consider, for example, Figure 5–4, the user does not really care whether or not the intermediate tables (*IT1*, *IT2*, etc.) actually exist as physical data structures in the memory of the machine. They may or may not—the user does not care. What the user wants is for the final output table, *IT5*, to have exactly the form that has been specified.

This property of SQL—that it is, in effect, a specification of a certain output rather than a specification of the specific steps to be taken to reach that output—is captured by saying that SQL is *nonprocedural*. The SQL language specifies the output and (in the process) verifies that there is *some* way (at least one) to derive the desired table (as output) from the persistent base tables (as input). However, while the specific sequence of joins and scans specified by a query shows one way to produce the table, there may be (and usually are) other ways as well. So far as a relational DBMS is concerned, once the user has specified the desired output table using SQL, the RDBMS is free to use whatever techniques it chooses in order to produce that result. It is *not* required to implement the specific sequence of joins and scans as specified in the query. If some other sequence will produce the same result, the RDBMS is free to use that other method.

Commercial RDBMSs (and parallel versions are no exception) typically have a component called a *query optimizer*. The job of this component is to select a specific sequence of inputs, joins, and scans to produce the desired output table, and to do so in a way that best achieves an approved set of goals and priorities. Starting with the initial SQL query (which always, by definition, provides at least one sequence of operations to produce the desired output table), the query optimizer can apply a number of transformation rules to the query. The effect of these rules is to produce other forms of the query (that is, other scan–join sequences) that produce the same output table. We might call the collection of these alternative versions of the query the *equivalent query set*: that is, the set of queries any of which, if executed, will produce the output table desired.

Corresponding to each query in the equivalent query set there will be a flow diagram such as that shown in Figure 5–6. Using this information, the query optimizer can estimate such quantities as expected time to complete, amount of memory required, interprocessor communication overhead, and so on. Among the results (a separate result for each such query), it can select the query that best meets a predefined set of "goodness" measures. For example, it might be desired to minimize execution time irrespective of the need for intermediate storage. Or it might be desired to minimize use of main memory. Whatever the policy goal, the query optimizer analyzes a large set of possible query execution plans, estimating the resource utilization for each such plan, and selecting the one that best achieves the desired goals.

In estimating resource utilization the query optimizer has a number of facts at its disposal. For one thing, it knows the size and structure of each of the existing base tables (this is part of the *metadata* collected by the RDBMS during table creation and updated as changes to the database occur). It also knows how the data has been partitioned across the disks, how many CPUs are available to process the query, how much physical memory and working disk storage is available, the CPU cycle time, typical cache hit ratios for most standard types of operations, and so on. Further, it has available a stable of possible algorithmic approaches. For example, many SQL operations (for example, GROUP BY, and certain kinds of JOINs) may proceed more rapidly if preceded by sorting the data. Also, some of the tables may have been indexed, making available to the query optimizer a collection of algorithms that would not be appropriate without an index. The point here is that not only the sequence of joins and scans, but also the algorithmic implementations of those operations, can be selected based on estimates of resource utilization.

In its full generality, the problem facing a query optimizer is daunting. Research has shown that even in the sequential case the ability to get the best answer under all circumstances is computationally intractable (for the cognoscenti, query optimization has been shown to be *NP Complete*). Fortunately, however, the practical goal is not to get the *very best possible* answer in every case, but rather, to get a solution that is *good enough* for the problem at hand. For example, both common sense and actual experience suggest that for large databases (such as data warehouses) the input of the data will tend to be a very large fraction of the total execution time for many types of queries. With this in mind one can construct and partition base tables in such a way as to optimize data I/O rates. These design decisions will be known to the query optimizer via its metadata, and its performance models will be constructed so as to select query sequences naturally and quickly, as well as implementation algorithms that emphasize and take full advantage of these features.

The point here is that *if* good design decisions have been made, *then* the query optimizer will be smart enough to know how best to organize the query execution plan. If the design decisions have been poorly made, however, the query optimizer can only do its best with a poor situation. In the world of OLTP, for example, considerable emphasis has been placed on (1) normalization of tables, and (2) use of indexes. By normalizing the tables, the database designer ensures that as few tables as possible will be affected by update operations (normalization ensures that the data is not unnecessarily replicated, so that changes to a value need occur only in a single table rather than in many tables). This, in turn, improves overall throughput, since locks affect much smaller portions of the data, allowing other queries to proceed without interruption. Similarly, in an OLTP setting, the working assumption is that most queries will have very high selectivity (that is, the amount of data required to generate the output table is very small, perhaps only a single record). In such a situation, indexes that point the RDBMS rapidly to the desired row of a table (using logarithmic searches on sorted data rather than sequential searches on unsorted data) can provide a substantial performance gain. The database design, then, reflects the types of queries that will be made (the typical workload), and the query optimizer has available to it a collection of implementation options that will perform well under this workload.

What about a data warehouse? In particular, what about a data warehouse implemented on a parallel computing platform? What kinds of database design decisions can result in superior performance? What is the likely workload, and how can the data be structured so that, most of the time, the query optimizer has available a good set of implementation options from which to select? With this set of questions, we come to the heart of the issue. Indeed, one possible title for this book might have been: *Database Design for Efficient Decision Support Applications on Large Parallel Relational Database Systems*. It is this set of questions that has largely motivated the selection and organization of the material in this book.

It is both naive and misleading to suggest that there is a "one size fits all" answer to this set of questions. However, at the risk of overgeneralization, we mention two general design decisions that may well be appropriate for decision support in large data warehouses: (1) avoid indexes, and (2) don't normalize. Both of these design issues go against the grain of OLTP designs, and will appear counterintuitive to many readers. The motivation behind this advice is, in fact, quite simple. Many (most?) decision support queries will have low selectivity—that is, they will require examination of a substantial fraction of the tables. In such a case, the main goal of the query optimizer must be to achieve very high rates of table I/O. Indexes will just get in the way. The data must *stream* off the disks, and data blocks must be placed sequentially so as to minimize disk head seek and positioning times. When large sequential blocks of data are to be read, the performance advantage of indexes no longer applies. Similarly, the advantage of normalizing the data applies primarily to updates—that is, locking the data when a change is needed. In decision support, however, the database (at least its main central tables) are, in effect, read-only. In a data warehouse operational environment, changes to the database usually occur infrequently (perhaps once a day or once a week), with input data having been extracted from operational (OLTP) systems for loading into the data warehouse. In such a situation, the benefits of normalization (lock management, and data consistency and integrity) are less than in an OLTP environment where updates are frequent.

Further, highly normalized data will tend to increase the number of required JOIN operations substantially. Using denormalized data, on the other hand, a *single* large table can be used where *several* would be required if the data is normalized. JOIN operations work against the goal of fast scans. Even if the resulting denormalized table is larger than the sum of its normalized equivalent (and this is usually the case), the fact that it can be sequentially scanned without the need for JOINs can accelerate performance. This technique, which also goes under the name *precomputed JOINs*, is a staple of data warehouse design approaches.

These design decisions for data warehouse schemas are well known, so are not discussed at length here. The key idea is use of a large *central fact table* surrounded by a small number of *dimension* or *attribute tables* (see Figure 5–7). Join keys and conditions run between the central table and its dimensions. In our opinion the major advantage of this form of schema organization is that it supports the goal of very high sustained rates of data I/O. The corresponding conclusion to be drawn, in a parallel system, is that the partitioning and layout of the data across the disks must be consistent with this design goal. If these decisions have been made well—that is, if the data has been partitioned across the disks in such a way that high sustained I/O bandwidths to single tables can be achieved—the query optimizer will have been given the necessary ingredients to utilize the parallel array efficiently. *Both* the design of the schema *and* the data partitioning must be done correctly if the opportunities for parallelism are to be realized in practice.

Figure 5–7   Typical Schema Design for Data Warehouse

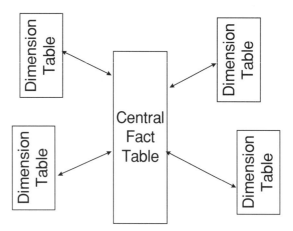

Chapter

6

Software Architectures for Parallel Database Systems

In Chapter 5 we introduced the basic problems and associated strategies that must be addressed by any attempt to parallelize a relational database system. In this chapter we look in greater detail at the three principal approaches that have been taken by commercial RDBMS vendors: (1) *shared-everything systems*, (2) *shared-disk systems*, and (3) *shared-nothing systems*. Separate sections are devoted to each approach, with a brief summary at the end.

It is important at the outset to observe that the meaning of the block diagrams we present is different, in a subtle but important way, from the block diagrams we presented in Part I. There a block in the diagram corresponded directly to a piece of hardware: a CPU, a bank of DRAM memory, a bus, a routing switch in an interconnection network, and so on. In this chapter the block corresponds to a function, or a related group of functions, implemented in software. The distinction is important, because *any* of the three major software architectures can be implemented on *any* of the three major hardware architecture classes presented in Part I. Granted, the match between hardware and software will be closer in some cases than in others. The amount of work needed (for example) to impose a shared memory software abstraction on a physically distributed memory machine is considerable, and the associated overheads are high. Nevertheless, these issues should be thought of as engineering trade-offs, not as hard-and-fast edicts imposed by the hardware platform.

One of our purposes will be to consider the strengths and weaknesses of each possible SW/HW combination. The $3 \times 3 = 9$ possibilities are shown in Figure 6–1. Readers are reminded of the meanings of the various acronyms: SMP, symmetric multiprocessor (Chapter 1); DM, distributed memory (Chapter 2); DSM, distributed shared memory (Chapter 3); SE, shared everything (Section 6.1 below); SD, shared disk (Section 6.2 below); and SN, shared nothing (Section 6.3 below).

Figure 6–1 Hardware/Software Architecture Taxonomy

HARDWARE

		SMP	DM	DSM/NUMA
SOFTWARE	SE	?	?	?
	SD	?	?	?
	SN	?	?	?

As we proceed, we consider the ability of each hardware architecture discussed in Part I to support the software architecture under discussion. In this way, a comprehensive view of the available options will be obtained. In Part III we will see how this abstract evaluation compares with current commercial practice.

6.1 SHARED-EVERYTHING ARCHITECTURES

The taxonomy presented in this chapter identifies two types of sharing: *Memory* can be shared, and *disks* can be shared. Before going further, let us say what it means to "share" memory and disks from a software point of view.

From a software standpoint, sharing memory means that separate threads of control have common access to an address space. In such an environment, a single logical variable (pointing, usually but not necessarily, to a single storage location) can be read and/or written by multiple processes. In Chapter 1 we discussed briefly the programming model usually encountered in a shared memory hardware system, and that model is (naturally enough) what we mean when we talk about a shared memory software paradigm.

Software that uses a shared memory view of the world will permit the various threads of control to coordinate their activities using data structures accessible (that is, addressable) in common by all the processes. For example, such a structure might be a "work to do" list. The process includes code that accesses this global table looking for the next job in the queue. Having found it, the process then branches to (or spawns) the appropriate executable module corresponding to the work to be done. The "work to do" list is a typical and representative example of the "style" that characterizes a shared memory programming model. Other examples include a *lock manager* (that is, a table, accessible to all active processes, of which tables and/or rows in the database are currently being updated by other processes); *global variables* (for example, variables that will hold the sum or maximum of an array of values and that are accessed by various processes responsible for examining different subsets of the array); *global counting arrays* (that is, integer arrays intended to hold counts of occurrences resulting from GROUP BY clauses, which are updated by multiple independent processes scanning different subsets of the table in question); and *buffers* (that is, data currently in memory as the result of an input operation from disk). The programming style marks these variables in the source code as shared, and from that point on the variables behave semantically in exactly that way: Any active process for which the variable has been declared can reference it (read, or write) exactly as any other variable in its address space.

The other type of sharing that occurs in the taxonomy is *shared disk*. By that we mean that any active process can perform I/O operations to any data located on any disk in the system. It does not indicate how the data has been allocated across the disks or what mechanism has been used to divide up the workload among the various processors. Rather, it means that *any* base table can be referenced in the FROM clause of *any* active process, regardless of where, physically, that process is instantiated in the machine.

In subsequent sections we look in more detail at what it means for memory and/or disks *not* to be shared. For the moment we concentrate on the first of the three major classes: shared-everything (SE) architectures. As the name implies, an RDBMS adopting this strategy supports both sharing of memory (that is, common variables and address spaces) and sharing of disks (all tables available as input to all active processes). Figure 6–2 shows the standard way of representing the shared-everything architecture. To achieve higher bandwidth, the tables are distributed across the available disks. Uniquely in an SE architecture, the shared memory is used to coordinate disk access among the various CPUs, as described in the following paragraphs.

Figure 6–2   Generic Shared-Everything Architecture

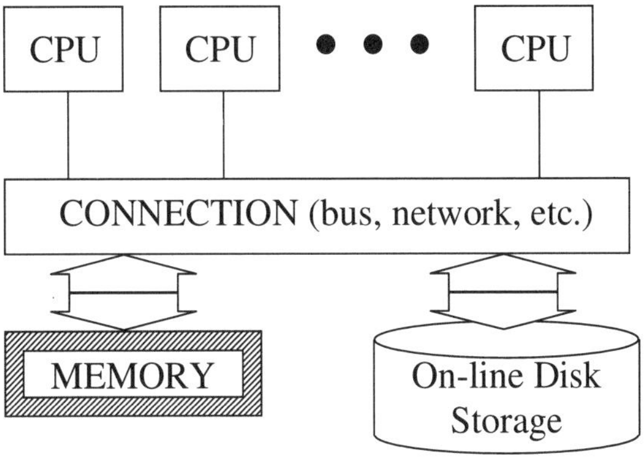

Logically in the relational model, queries access tables. Physically, the tables are partitioned across the various disks in the system. Since a given disk controller can service only one disk request at a time, and since in a parallel system multiple queries can be active at once, a mechanism is needed both to arbitrate which query gets use of the resource (the disk controller) and to maintain consistency. The issue of consistency is identical to that of cache coherence, discussed at some length in Part I. In a database context it goes by the name of *buffer consistency*. Basically, during a disk request, a copy of the data is moved from the disk to a buffer in main memory. The CPU then operates on this local copy. In a parallel system, multiple copies can be outstanding, and a change to one of them must be communicated to others. The lock manager is the formal mechanism for implementing this capability, and a number of protocols and algorithms have been proposed and implemented. In a shared memory machine, the lock manager is implemented using globally accessible data structures. As we shall see in the next sections, the lock management function is handled differently for shared disk and shared-nothing architectures. As with cache coherence, the problem of lock management arises because of the possibility of multiple physical copies (buffers) of a single logical entity (the underlying table stored on disk).

In Chapter 7, where join strategies are discussed in some detail, we look at various approaches for partitioning the data (that is, the table) across multiple disks to achieve high I/O bandwidth. In a shared-everything architecture, there is considerable flexibility, and the "right" choice of data partitioning depends greatly on the workload (that is, the pattern, complexity, and frequency of various types of queries). As we have already seen in Chapter 5, data warehouses will be characterized by very large tables spread uniformly across all available disks so as to achieve maximal intraquery parallel performance.

To illustrate the issues, we trace through the pattern of execution for a single simple query: returning the count of rows in the central fact table (call it T1) meeting some row-based condition (call it <condition>), The SQL might be

```
SELECT COUNT(*) AS NUM
FROM T1
WHERE <condition>
```

How might a shared-everything architecture attempt to parallelize this simple query?

The reader will see at once that much depends on the precise nature of the <condition>. For example, if the <condition> can benefit from the existence of an index (for example, if it involves only values or ranges of values from a primary key), the query might be able to complete with very little I/O. In that case the query optimizer might simply create a single process, assigned to a single CPU, to perform all the necessary I/O and complete the task.

Suppose, however, that evaluation of the <condition> requires a more complex computation involving multiple fields, some of which do not have indexes. In that case there is nothing to be done but to plow through the entire table, evaluating the condition for each record (row) while maintaining a running count of the number of "hits." This is clearly a job at which many processors can help. Each process can be assigned a subset of the data, and a count within that subset can be obtained. The sum of the counts for each of the pieces, then, will be the total count for the entire table. Notice that in this example, there is no implied order; any means of partitioning the data into pieces is about as good as any other, provided only that no process is given an inordinantly large piece (for obvious reasons of load balancing). Given these observations, we can imagine two possible parallelization strategies.

1. Assign to each process (= CPU) an equal portion of the large table. Each CPU then, independently, reads its set of rows and forms the partial count. The final count is assembled after all processes have completed.
2. Form an outer loop, each iteration of which streams in a large block of data from the table. Processing of the block is then parallelized by logically subdividing the block and having each available CPU process its assigned subset. Running totals are summed at the end to obtain the final result.

The advantage of the second approach is the potential for very high sustained I/O bandwidth. If we suppose (as we should in a data warehouse) that the layout of data across the disks has been done so as to maximize the sustainable bandwidth for sequential reads of large, uninterrupted blocks of data, strategy 2 should be a clear winner. The problem with the first strategy is that many processes are, independently, reading many disks. The potential for contention, and frequent access to the lock manager, means that the sustained bandwidth is likely to be much lower that what is achievable if the contention is avoided.

What we are suggesting, in effect, is a special mode of I/O operations—we might call it large sequential block I/O, or nonlock-arbitrated I/O, or some other suggestive name—that is designed specifically to maximize the I/O bandwidth from the full shared disk array into the shared memory. Indeed, the I/O task can be separated from the processing task, so that the participation of a given CPU in the "read" portion of the processing may be different from, and unrelated to, the data it ends up processing once the query is implemented. These ideas are illustrated in Figure 6–3. Instead of many separate streams (one I/O stream for each process/CPU), we have what is conceptually a single large stream filling a single large buffer of the shared memory. Data partitioning and parallel computation then proceed by logically partitioning the (current) large data block among the available CPUs. Because I/O takes place using the faster I/O method, we expect the total processing time for the second strategy to be less than that of the first.

Figure 6–3 Two Parallelization Strategies for SE Systems

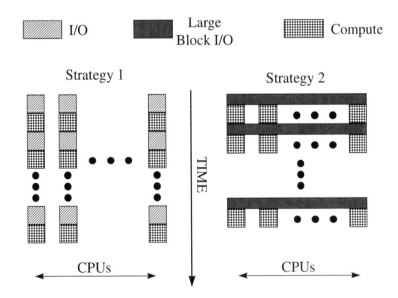

An important practical consideration is the extent to which individual CPUs must be involved in I/O operations. Ideally, we would like the CPU to initiate a data transfer (from disk to memory, or from memory to disk), but we hope that the data need not physically pass through the registers of the CPU on its path. Much will depend on the particular implementation of Unix and other special features provided by individual vendors. Even if the CPU is idle during the data transfer (and it might as well be, since presumably the available bus bandwidth is already consumed with I/O), additional traffic across the bus is required if the CPU must "see and store" each data item. An approach that entails such overhead *first* copies the data into a temporary buffer and *then* copies it into the address space of the process. The additional copy operation is almost always done using the CPU, and we thus have not only the overhead of additional storage (both the buffer and the user's copy) but also additional bus traffic.

Good current implementations avoid this type of overhead. The best approach (see Chapter 16) is to obtain performance numbers reflecting sustained bandwidth on large tables using large block I/O operations. The very high bandwidth requirements of (for example) video-on-demand and high-quality computer graphics are an ideal match for this type of streaming I/O. Further, the fact that the memory is shared makes the data partitioning task easy once the data has been transferred from disk to memory. Here, then, we have the seeds of a general parallelization strategy suitable for data warehouse applications on SE architectures: large block I/Os, followed by subsequent logical decomposition across available CPUs.

We conclude by considering how such a SE approach might be implemented on each of the three hardware architectures we considered in Part I. In doing so, we keep in mind two key features that this parallelization strategy requires: (1)

high sustained bandwidth from the disk to the shared main memory, and (2) high sustained bandwidth from the shared main memory to the individual CPUs.

The SE software model is a natural match to the SMP hardware architecture. During I/O, we may imagine full bus bandwidth being dedicated to disk transfers. Once each large block of data has been brought into the memory, partitioning of the data among CPUs can be done efficiently, since all CPUs have equal (uniform) access to the entire buffer holding the data. The major difficulty is hardware scalability, not software scalability. Memory and backplane bus bandwidth, both for accepting disk I/O and for servicing the CPUs, has been seen to be an architectural limitation for SMPs. Thus, while the SE software approach has no inherent problems on SMPs (that is, this parallelization strategy should work fine on the largest SMP we can build), the hardware architectural limitations of SMPs will prevent an SE/SMP combination from succeeding on very large databases. In contradiction to this general conclusion, however, the reader should examine Chapter 11, in which an SMP-style architecture that does *not* use a backplane bus is able to achieve levels of performance suitable for a data warehouse.

What about an SE strategy on a DM architecture? As far as we are aware, no one has ever attempted to implement the layers of software abstraction required to enable such an approach. For example, in a DM machine, each address space extends only as far as the local memory associated with the CPU. Implementing a software mechanism to trick the RDBMS into believing that it has the ability to address into the memories of other CPUs would entail unacceptably high message-passing overhead. In short, the SE/DM pairing is infeasible based on practical considerations.

We come finally to the SE/NUMA combination. The reader is encourage to turn back to Figure 4–8, which illustrates the NUMA hardware and I/O capabilities. First, we may ask how high sustained parallel I/O can be achieved. We must assume that the table has been partitioned across the disks associated with each node in the system, and that during an I/O operation each disk (or array of disks associated with the node) is accessing the portion of the table assigned to it. Further, we must suppose that the location of the buffer into which the data is placed is local to the node. If not, use of the intercommunication network would be required, simultaneously for all nodes, and the overhead of that exchange would reduce substantially the sustainable I/O bandwidth. Because of these factors, the situation in the DSM/NUMA implementation is very different from that in the SMP. While a single block of data is read into memory, it has been (necessarily) decomposed into several distinct pieces, one such piece for each node. In the NUMA architecture, the single logical block of data from the SMP implementation has been decomposed into multiple smaller blocks; and this decomposition is the direct result of the desire to achieve scalable I/O bandwidth!

The same loss of uniformity occurs when we consider assigning the CPUs to various subsets of the large block that we have read in. In the SMP case, the decomposition does not matter, since all CPUs are equally distant from any portion of the data. In the NUMA architecture, however, it matters a great deal *Clearly*, having already (necessarily) decomposed the data as part of I/O, CPUs must be assigned to access the data that resides in the node's local memory. Such a notion of "locality" is foreign to an SMP view of the world.

The result of this analysis shows that if the local decomposition is used, there is very little traffic across the interconnection network, just whatever is needed to initialize the computation (using a global data structure located somewhere in the machine for that purpose) and to complete the final sum (aggregating the various counts held in each CPU). The implementation should be effective, provided that a level of complexity is introduced (the localized partitioning of the data) not required in the SMP case; or put another way, provided that existing SMP-style implementations are appropriately modified to take into account this aspect of the NUMA architecture. The effect of such modifications will be to make the NUMA machine act more like a DM machine. For the low-level coordination functions (work allocation, lock management, global aggregation), the shared memory model will be just fine. For the heavy-duty block I/O and associated data partitioning, DM-style data locality constructs will be required.

We are now ready to fill in the first line of our SW/HW evaluation matrix:

- SE/SMP: a good fit, but lacks scalability due to SMP memory bandwidth limitations.

- SE/DM: not a good fit; no obvious way to provide a shared memory abstraction on top of separate DM address spaces.

- SE/DSM-NUMA: a good fit, provided that some operations—particularly streaming I/O and data partitioning—use a distributed memory programming model that takes data locality into account.

6.2 SHARED DISK ARCHITECTURES

In our taxonomy, the shared disk (SD) architectures occupy a kind of intermediate, or hybrid, place between the two extremes of shared everything (SE) and shared nothing (SN). Historically, they reflect a stage of development generally known as *clusters*. The hardware configuration underlying this approach might, for example, have been a few (say, three or four) separate machines on a local network attempting to coordinate access to a single collection of disks. In terms of response to customer needs, it was an attempt to increase overall system throughput while making as few modifications as possible to the existing software. Its pedigree thus has much in common with distributed or federated databases. As far as we are aware, no research project (interested purely in formal and architectural issues) has ever been structured around the SD approach, and we conclude from this that there is no *theoretical* justification for the SD architecture. On the other hand, there may be considerable *practical* justification based (for example) on prior investment and risk reduction.

A generic shared disk architecture is shown in Figure 6–4. If we compare with Figure 6–2, the main difference we see is in the (logical) placement of the interconnection network. In the SE architecture, each CPU is provided direct access to all of memory and to all of disk storage. In the SD architecture, each CPU has its own private, nonshared memory, but has connectivity to all available disk storage. In short, disk access is common (shared) across the system, but memory is private (nonshared). There are several implications of this from a software point of view. First, and most important, the coordination of the action among the various CPUs cannot be accomplished using globally shared data structures. Instead, a message-passing protocol is required which uses the inter-

Figure 6–4   Generic Shared Disk Architecture

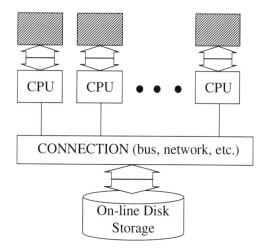

connection network as the mechanism for data exchange. Depending on the performance characteristics of the network (and recall that standard LAN technology was envisioned when this architecture first emerged), the latency could be several orders of magnitude (milliseconds versus microseconds) greater than if a shared memory data structure were available. For this reason, the frequency and detail of coordination among the CPUs in an SD implementation is considerably different than in an SE implementation. For SD, the name of the game is to keep interprocessor communications to a minimum.

The reader will see at once that interquery parallelism is well suited to such a requirement. If the various CPUs in the system are independent, each processing separate and unrelated queries, the amount of interprocessor coordination is minimized. The main job is lock management—that is, making sure that modifications to the data are properly distributed to all the CPUs that may be affected. The good feature about shared disks in such a setting is that the top-level management function—the function that partitions the jobs to the available CPUs—does not need to be concerned about relative placement of CPU and disk. Since every CPU can read every disk, the work manager can assign work on a "next available" basis. As we have seen, this is ideal for load balancing where interquery parallelism characterizes the workload.

What about intraquery parallelism in an SD environment? Let us return to the simple example introduced in Section 6.1. We see at once that sharing the disks is not a particular advantage. Although each CPU may see a single logical view of the large T1 table, the table must be decomposed and transferred into the individual nonshared memories of the CPUs. From a logical point of view, it doesn't much matter if the data is *first* unified (in the shared disk) and *then* decomposed (into the memories of the individual CPUs); or, on the other hand, if the data starts out as decomposed (across nonshared disks) and is then streamed, in parallel, into the local memories. The fact is that decomposition must be done before processing can occur (unlike the SE case, where I/O could occur prior to decomposition). Once data decomposition occurs prior to processing, the major difficulties facing parallelism must have been addressed, and the additional capability of shared disk does not appear to offer much additional benefit. In reality, shared disk architectures are targeted at OLTP implementations, where load balancing over a large number of small queries is the chief performance goal. When SD architectures are used for decision support in large data warehouse implementations, they start to look very much like shared-nothing (SN) approaches. Their SD details tend to reflect both history and the practical advantages of software reuse.

How well can the various hardware architectures discussed in Part I support a shared disk implementation? We begin by looking at SMPs. Consider Figure 6–5. This illustrates a very common architecture in OLTP environments. Each "CPU" from Figure 6–4 has been replaced by a stand-alone SMP. The memories of the various SMPs are distinct and not shared, but within a single SMP the memory is shared. Further, every CPU has uniform access to all of disk storage. This is the well-known "cluster of SMPs" that has been a staple of OLTP implementations since the mid-1980s.

When we consider such an approach for implementing a data warehouse, however, several concerns arise. Most significant, what is the sustainable bandwidth between the shared disk array and the various SMPs? The upper bound on that bandwidth will be set by the interconnection network, and the fact that the network is shared imposes a scalability constraint. To reiterate a point made earlier at some length, as long as each processor is given nonshared bandwidth to a local disk (as in a DM architecture), I/O bandwidth can scale indefinitely. Sharing the bandwidth to the disks, however, results in a bottleneck; such an approach cannot scale to the performance levels appropriate for large data warehouses. To

Figure 6–5   Clustered SMPs in a SD Architecture

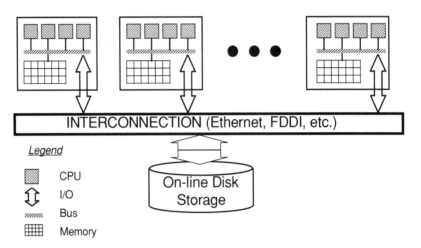

summarize: In considering SMPs as implementations of a shared disk software architecture, we conclude that the approach is a natural one from a software point of view but suffers from the inability to scale to very large configurations.

Turning next to distributed memory hardware implementations, a shared disk approach can be used without much additional overhead. As is clear in Figure 2–1, each disk (or RAID disk array) is still "owned" by a single CPU. The sharing is accomplished by an additional layer of software. When a given CPU wants to access a disk that it does not own, this layer of software performs a message-passing function, requesting the owner of the disk where the data resides to complete the disk access and send the resulting data (using the high-performance interconnection network) to the requesting CPU. This layer of software also performs lock management. Since data can only be accessed by first notifying the local owner, the owner can keep track of CPUs that currently have copies, and can update them, if necessary, when modifications are requested. In an OLTP setting, the additional overhead for this functionality is more than compensated by the load-balancing benefits (a "next available" approach is the right one for interquery parallelism).

In large data warehouses, however, the advantage of this level of software is not nearly so great. The data is already partitioned (it has to be, by definition, in a DM architecture), so it makes sense to make use of that partitioning in constructing intraquery parallelism. By having each CPU only access the data that is in its local disk, very high levels of sustained I/O bandwidth can be achieved. In many cases (as we show at greater length in Chapters 7 and 8), little or no data shuffling may be needed. And when it is needed, the overhead will not be so great as in an SD environment, where *every* CPU is making demands on *every* disk.

In point of fact, SD implementations on DM machines are capable of making these distinctions, so that the SD capability is largely ignored when large table end-to-end scans are required. Locality of CPU to disk—a notion foreign to SD in its pure form—is typically "added in" to the SD implementation, so that the result for decision support applications looks and acts very much like a shared-nothing architecture. Thus the implementation offers a wide range of customers "the best of both worlds": efficient load balancing for OLTP-style applications, and high bandwidth (using shared-nothing ideas) for decision support. We hasten to add, however, that it is still an "either/or" proposition. One cannot have *both* OLTP *and* decision support in the *same* implementation. What one can have is a single software package able to adapt to either one or the other application domain, depending on the customer's requirements.

Turning finally to DSM/NUMA hardware platforms, they appear to be very well suited to a SD style of software implementation. The high-speed interconnection network provides efficient connectivity between CPUs and disks, and the notion of local, nonshared memory matches the physical reality very well. In fact, the shared memory features of the NUMA architecture can be used to implement the message-passing protocols that coordinate activity among the separate processors. From a commercial point of view, it is the ability of NUMA architectures to implement popular commercial SD software efficiently that has been a driving force behind bringing this technology to market. As we noted above, however, the sharing of the disks will not be important for data warehouses. Rather, disk locality, and the ability to stream the data from the local disk into the local memory, will be the dominant factors in performance for large decision support applications.

We are now ready to fill in the second row of our SW/HW evaluation matrix. We begin by noting that no matter what the hardware, *sharing of disks will not help the problem of sustained I/O bandwidth characteristic of large DS applications.* High sustained I/O bandwidth requires partitioned data streaming, in parallel, into local nonshared memories. Disk sharing, on the other hand, is of advantage primarily for OLTP implementations where a "first-available CPU" load-balancing strategy is natural and optimal. With these provisos, we observe:

- SD/SMP: a good fit, particularly when used as clusters. However, lacks I/O scalability for large data warehouse applications.
- SD/DM: a good fit using an intermediate layer of software to handle coordination of CPUs and lock management. SD feature will be ignored in large DS applications.

- SD/DSM-NUMA: an excellent fit, using shared memory features to handle coordination of CPUs and lock management. SD feature will be ignored in large DS applications.

6.3 SHARED-NOTHING ARCHITECTURES

The third major group in our software taxonomy is shared-nothing (SN) architectures. As the name implies, neither the memory local to a particular CPU nor its disk storage is shared by (that is, directly accessible to, or addressable by) other processors in the system. Instead, each CPU (or, more strictly speaking, each process created the system) has only its local memory and, perhaps, some collection of disks—a subset of the total disks—directly accessible to it.

Figure 6–6 has the basic structure, and the reader will observe that it looks a lot like the DM architecture from Chapter 2 (see Figure 2–1). Let us rehearse briefly the software consequences of this approach. First, control structures (lock management, work allocation, global aggregation variables, and so on) cannot be implemented through structures in shared memory. They must be implemented by message passing using the interconnection network. If that network is the low-latency, high-performance network characteristic of top-end MPPs, for example, the performance penalty will be much less than if the network is conventional LAN technology. Second, the disks are not shared. This means that even if a query is assigned to a single CPU (interquery parallelism), other CPUs may need to be involved to extract the necessary portions of the table and route the data to the requesting CPU. Similar complications will arise for temporary working disk space (for example, for out-of-memory joins and sorts).

Figure 6–6 Generic Diagram of a Shared-Nothing Architecture

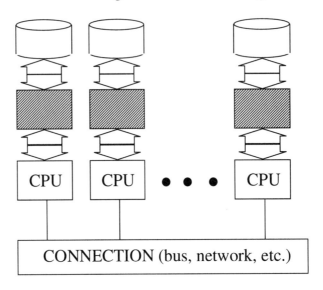

CONNECTION (bus, network, etc.)

Historically, shared-nothing software architectures arose because of the advent of distributed memory MPP-style machines. The scalability and price–performance of those hardware architectures was immediately attractive, and algorithm developments (discussed in more detail in Chapters 7 and 8) showed that even difficult relational operators such as joins could be implemented efficiently. There were, however, two major difficulties. First, in the mid-1980s, when DM machines first appeared, the commercial market was oriented almost exclusively to OLTP. A few specialized database machines (most notably TeraData) exploited massive parallelism for decision support, but that was only a small portion of the total market. In fact, OLTP is not a great match for DM machines (and hence not for SN architectures). The problem is load balancing. As we saw earlier, the natural mechanism for load balancing an OLTP workload is a next-available CPU model in which the tables are highly normalized (because of the frequency of modifications) and queries have very high selectivity (so that indexes are appropriate). DM machines are not very good at any of these things. For example, the next-available CPU model does not take into account data locality—the fact that there is an implied "distance" between each CPU and each disk that must be optimized if good performance is to be sustained. Similarly, the control structures, particularly the lock manager, are much more difficult to implement using messages than using shared memory.

Given these difficulties, what makes DM (and its natural counterpart, SN) so attractive? The answer is simple: *scalable I/O bandwidth*. By partitioning single tables over many independent disks, and by streaming the data into local non-shared memories, it is possible to build machines with virtually unlimited bandwidth. Add to this a high-performance interconnection network to support data rearrangements (sorts and joins), and the capability is in-hand to process queries that are unthinkable in a conventional OLTP setting. The associated penalties, however, must also be noted: (1) the need to partition the data in a single table over many separate "files;" and (2) the need to exploit intraquery parallelism.

Both of the previous architectures we have discussed—SE and SD—employ sharing primarily as an efficient mechanism for interquery parallelism. In the SN architecture, interquery parallelism is largely ignored. What we are most concerned about is processing very large amounts of data—substantial fractions of the total data warehouse—in reasonable amounts of time (seconds or minutes). The assumption is that the standard techniques employed for reducing the amount of I/O required—indexes, bitmapped indexes, high degrees of normalization, and so on—will not work on the types of queries that will be characteristic of a data warehouse. In fact, the only way to process the types of queries under consideration is, in effect, to "brute force" your way through the mountain of data using ultrahigh levels of I/O bandwidth. That, in a nutshell, is the view of the world behind DM/SN data warehouse implementations.

As we saw earlier, whenever an SE or SD architecture implements intraquery parallelism it begins to look a lot more like an SN system. The next-available workload manager is discarded (since there is always only one query to process). The sharing of disks is discarded (since high bandwidth requires paying attention to the locality between disk and CPU). In fact, even on a machine that can support shared memory and shared disk constructs (such as an SMP or a DSM/NUMA), an SN approach may be preferable simply because it forces attention to the major area of concern: data partitioning and techniques for maintaining independence of processing.

Let us consider briefly how the simple query introduced in Section 6.1 (a COUNT of rows satisfying a complex condition) would be implemented in an SN software architecture. First, the large table T1 would have already been partitioned across the array of CPUs and associated disks. Although not required, a common approach is to open separate files local to each CPU and to break the larger table into smaller subtables, each containing a subset of rows. The approaches for how to make that partitioning are discussed at greater length in Chapter 7. For the moment we observe that, in fact, it does not matter for *this* query *how* the division has been accomplished. At a purely logical level, each CPU has its own, independent set of rows to process. Indeed, we might imagine an implementation in which each local CPU is given a separate query, similar to the main query but restricted to the subtable of which it is the owner.

Such an approach—casting the top-level query as a collection of subqueries against independent tables held by the SN participants—is a common way of implementing an SN architecture. In effect, each CPU in the array processes a query just as it would if it were a completely self-contained RDBMS (which, from this point of view, it is). Once the low-level subqueries have been processed by the local CPUs, a merge phase is entered in which the results of the prior stage are redistributed across the processor array, merged with other results, and the process reapplied. In our case the merging is particularly simple: Combine the locally held counts obtained from the subqueries into a single global value.

Although this is (in fact) a fairly simple process, we pause briefly to consider scalability: both the ability to scale to ever-larger tables and the ability to improve performance by adding additional processors to the array. We take as an instructive example the problem of how best to collect intermediate and final results. If we expect the processors to finish at different times, we might arrange to have each of them send its local result to a single processor—the master—for summation (recall that our sample query counts rows). That master processor will receive one short message from every other processor, and (assuming that it is itself participating in the query) it will not be able to perform the final summation until it has finished with its local processing.

Suppose that we were to reason as follows. We expect the CPUs to finish at different times (depending, for example, on internal data dependence of the algorithms employed). Thus we may as well have them send their data along as soon as they have completed processing. In that way, each CPU (except the master) participating in the process can begin work on its next task immediately rather than having to wait for all the others to complete. The problem with this eminently sensible approach is that, over time, the various CPUs will get further and further out of sync with each other. At some point (for example, the beginning of the next query), they must all be at the same point in the processing flow, so the ability to "get started early" is somewhat of an illusion; its real significance is that the CPU will just have longer to wait at the end! Instead of spreading the "wait" periods evenly over the course of the computation in several small chunks, they are coalesced together into a single long wait at the end.

In general, experience has shown that frequent synchronization—forcing all CPUs in the array to a common point in their processing flow—has advantages over a looser approach in which long stretches may elapse during which the CPUs proceed totally independently. While the *user* of a parallel RDBMS need not be concerned with such details, the *administrator* should have a sense of the types of overhead the system may encounter and the options an optimizer might take in establishing the task flow.

If the number of processors in the array is at all large (say, larger than 32), it is likely that the system will perform the global sum required by our sample query using a tournament-style aggregation algorithm. Imagine a tournament in which each CPU is a contestant, with one to emerge as the winner. At each stage the remaining CPUs (those not already "eliminated") pair up, exchange their current values, and form (in our case) the sum of their local values. The loser (determined arbitrarily) drops out, and the winner enters the next round. In an array of (say) $2^8 = 256$ processors, the answer emerges from the top of the tournament (or pyramid) in $\log_2(256) = 8$ steps. The same technique can be used to obtain MIN, MAX, and other global associative operations.

As before, we consider how the SN software approach matches with the three hardware architectures from Part I

- SN/SMP: a poor match. Although SN could be implemented on an SMP, there is no reason to do so.

- SN/DM: a good match. The software and hardware reflect a common philosophy and common assumptions about scalability and independence of operations.

- SN/NUMA: a good match, provided that certain features of the DSM/NUMA machine are ignored. The more the NUMA machine is treated like a DM machine, the better.

Summary

Here, at the end of Chapter 6, we pause briefly to summarize the results of our survey. The matrix introduced in Figure 6–1 now looks as shown in Figure 6–7. Using a crude scoring scheme (P = poor, G = good, E = excellent), we see that the DSM/NUMA architecture has the potential to be a good-to-excellent platform for all categories of SW architecture, *provided* that certain features it provides (especially the ability to disregard the locality of disks and memory) are *avoided intentionally*. Implementations that treat a NUMA machine as if it were just a bigger, faster SMP are apt to be in for an unpleasant surprise. Another important result of our discussion is that the two shared approaches—SE and SD—are most appropriate in an OLTP setting where interquery parallelism characterizes the workload. As soon as intraquery parallelism dominates, as in large decision support applications characteristic of data warehouses, the "shared" aspect fades to the background, and their actual implementations (and this is especially true of SD architectures) strongly resemble SN.

Figure 6–7   Results of SW/HW Applicability Survey

HARDWARE

SOFTWARE		SMP	DM	DSM/NUMA
	SE	G	P	G*
	SD	G	G	E*
	SN	P	E	E*

* Provided that locality of disk and memory are taken into account.

For implementations of data warehouses, the choices are fairly clear. Both SD and SN are feasible, as are both DM and DSM/NUMA hardware platforms. In point of fact, however, even an SD implementation will choose to ignore many of its possible features in favor of SN-style data partitioning and intraquery parallelism. Thus although SD remains an option in theory, in practice we expect SN techniques to predominate. That, in turn, means that the features of a DSM/NUMA machine that could obstruct scalability must be avoided. Just as an SD architecture could serve *if we ignore disk sharing*, so a NUMA architecture could serve *if we insist on locality of memory and disk*. The reader will gather from this discussion that for data warehouses, SN on a DM machine is the target configuration, even if it goes by another name!

Of the four examples discussed in Part III, three fall into the SN/DM category. The fourth (see Chapter 11) represents (remarkably) an SE/SMP approach, a category of which we have been critical. Without wanting to give away too much in advance, the reader will find in Chapter 11 an SMP-style hardware architecture that manages to avoid the difficulties of a backplane bus, enabling it to scale to quite large configurations.

Data Partitioning, Joins, and Utilities

In this chapter attention focuses on methods to partition the data across many disks and the related techniques for combining that data again during query processing. The design decision of how to split up the data across the available disks (Section 7.1) often has significant impact on performance. While the primary motivation for such splitting is to improve overall bandwidth (that is, to have many disks at work reading a single table), the criteria used to do the splitting can have a dramatic impact on the performance of certain types of queries, especially those requiring joins. By considering how joins are implemented algorithmically on a parallel machine (Section 7.2), we will see how performance can be improved by making good data partitioning decisions. Because of their close relationship to data partitioning, two utilities—parallel loading of data and parallel redistribution of data—are of great practical significance, especially in a data warehouse where storage levels are expected to increase over time (Section 7.3).

The general conclusion of Chapter 6 was that even when they go by another name, efficient data warehouse implementations exhibit the major features of an SN architecture executing on a DM machine. In keeping with that observation, our starting point for the discussion in this and the next chapter will be distributed memory machines executing a shared-nothing database architecture. When needed we will observe the differences that might arise for DSM/NUMA machines and/or shared disk software architectures. We also point out from time to time instances where an OLTP style of workload might affect database design decisions and algorithmic implementations. The main thread of the argument, however, continues to be a data warehouse—that is, decision support in very large databases.

7.1 DATA PARTITIONING STRATEGIES

A major theme of the book thus far has been the need for high sustained I/O bandwidth to single tables. As discussed at some length in Chapter 4, the key idea is to spread the table across as many disks as possible. The total available disk bandwidth to a table is then the sum of the bandwidths of the disks accessing the table in parallel. Further, in Chapters 5 and 6 we discussed the top-level software techniques available to support the goal of high sustained bandwidth. For decision support applications in a data warehouse, we saw that certain types of schema designs (see Figure 5–7) made most sense. By decreasing the number of tables (at the price, perhaps, of some loss of normalization), data can stream off the disks at high rates. As opposed to an OLTP-style workload (lots of small queries, frequent updates, interquery parallelization), the focus is on decision support: large queries, read-only, and intraquery parallelization.

There are a number of techniques for data partitioning, and (as we shall see) the choice of how to partition the data can have a far-reaching impact on the performance of several types of queries. When considering the problem of data partitioning, three basic questions must be answered: (1) How many disks should be used to store a table? (2) If the answer to (1) is not "all of them," then which ones should be used? and (3) how should the rows and/or columns of the table be split across the disks selected? Given answers to these three questions, the system should be able to examine an input stream of data, load it according to the partitioning scheme selected, and take account of the partitioning strategy in selecting an optimal query execution strategy.

For large decision support applications, we believe that the right answer to question (1) is almost always "all of them." The reason is straightforward: The more disks involved in retrieving the data, the higher the bandwidth. Of course, if interquery parallelism is employed, it may be possible to keep many disks occupied on several independent queries even if no single query touches more than a small fraction of the data. In such an environment, it might be appropriate to have different subsets of disks service different tables. However, our stated goal is high performance on *intraquery* parallelism on very large tables, and in this context high sustained bandwidth is *the* performance driver. With that observation, question (2) becomes moot. With a more transaction-oriented workload, it could be an important design criterion.

Given that a table is to be partitioned across the disks, what rule or criterion should be used to accomplish the splitting? The most common and important partitioning rules split the data by rows; that is, complete rows are stored together within each partition and the issue becomes how to decide which rows belong together. In effect, we form subtables with the same column structure as the parent table which comprises them.

For completeness, note that it is formally possible to partition the table by columns. Called *vertical positioning*, this technique is used by Sybase in their IQ decision support product. Notice, however, that the schema definition itself could accomplish something of the same effect. By defining multiple tables, each sharing a common key and each containing subsets of the columns of the master table, the database designer can partition a master table by columns using standard SQL constructs. Equijoins (that is, joins on tables that have the same primary key) can then substitute for single table references to the master table.

The difficulty with such an approach is that in a good data warehouse design, the fields of the central master table are typically keys into the associated dimension tables that surround the central fact table (see again Figure 5–7). Queries will include inner joins between the fact table and the dimension tables (that is, the join criteria will include an equality test against the primary key of the dimension table). In such a design we must weigh the possible advantage of reduced I/O (fewer retrieved columns) against the disadvantage of additional joins (one *extra* join for each referenced dimensional column). Such issues cannot be settled in the abstract; we must consider actual data, query workload, and the intended concept of operations. In this connection it is worth noting that the TPC-D benchmark specifications explicitly prohibit the use of "column splitting" techniques during execution of the benchmark.

With this caveat, then, we put aside issues of column splitting (or *vertical partitioning*), and concentrate on row splitting (respectively, *horizontal partitioning*). Suppose that N disks (or, perhaps more accurately, disk controllers or channels) are available. For any given row R of the table for input, we must decide on which of the N disks it is to reside. Three standard approaches are available: *range partitioning*, *round robin*, and *hashing*. We discuss each in turn.

In *range partitioning*, a subset of the fields of the record R is specified to be an ordered key. The standard example is lexicographic ordering on an alphabetic text field, but there are many other (well known) examples. The idea is that each of the N disks is associated with a range of key values. If the key is the alphabet $A, B, C, ..., Z$, we might (for example) assign disk_1 the range $<A - D>$, disk_2 the range $<E - G>$, disk_3 the range $<H - K>$, and so on. During data loading, the input row R would be compared, using its actual key value, against the range criteria corresponding to each disk partition. For example, if the key value associated with row R were (say) F, row R would be stored in disk_2 (because, in the ordering of our example key space, $E <= F <= G$, so that the key value F lies in the range assigned to disk_2). Note that the key selected for range partitioning need not be the primary key of the table.

An advantage of range partitioning is that it acts as a kind of built-in index. For example, if data is retrieved based on the key value (this kind of query is called *associative retrieval*), it is not necessary to scan the entire table; only the disks known to hold the range of values bracketing the key value are of interest. Unfortunately, as we have seen, decision support queries typically do not have this form (which is why indexing techniques are not of much value in a data warehouse). If the typical query will touch a large fraction of the database regardless of key value, range partitioning does not appear to offer much advantage. Further, there is a severe potential disadvantage—data skew. *Data skew* refers to the potential for imbalances in the number of rows assigned to any given disk. We know, for example, that (depending on the application) some letters of the alphabet will occur much more frequently than others. A range partitioning scheme that does not take such skewing into account can result in load imbalances due to unequal distribution of the data (recall the discussion of load balancing in Section 5.2). Even knowing accurately the statistics of data distribution when the database is initialized may not help in the long term, since over time the data warehouse will grow, and data distributions can and will change. For these reasons, use of range partitioning is often avoided for central fact tables, although it may be used in smaller dimension tables where the effects of data skewing are less acute. We take up this issue again near the end of Section 11.3, where we argue that the use of coarse range partitioning may be of value.

Another scheme that addresses the issue of the uneven distribution of data is *round-robin partitioning*, so called because rows are simply assigned to the "next" disk in order regardless of key value. Such an approach assures that rows will be as evenly spread as they can be, and greatly simplifies the loading process. However, a good deal has been given up. It is not just that we can no longer know which disk holds a given record based solely on key value (associative retrieval). Even more significant, we have no way of *co-locating* rows with the *same* key value. Remember that in our approach, *all* tables are to be spread evenly across *all* disks. Suppose that two tables are frequently joined using a shared key. In such a situation it would be of value to have associated rows of the two tables *on the same disk*! In that case, the join could be accomplished entirely by the processor controlling the disk *without* the need to examine the rows held by any other disk or processor in the machine. Using round-robin partitioning, however, such a capability is not possible. The associated rows to be joined will be spread everywhere across the disks of the machine, and any join operation will require movement of data among the CPUs (that is, overhead due to interprocessor communications). This issue is addressed again in Section 7.2.

The third scheme, *hash partitioning*, attempts to have the best of both worlds. Like the round-robin technique, it avoids load imbalance (that is, data skew) by using the hash function on the selected key to, in effect, randomize (and hence evenly distribute) the rows. In this sense, a good hashing function will show little correlation between the distance between values in the key space and the destinations among the disks. However, it has the crucial property that *identical* key values will be hashed to the *same* disk. Thus if the same hashing function and key is used on two different tables, rows from those tables that share key values will be co-located (that is, will end up on the same disk), exactly the state of affairs that had been given up in the round-robin partitioning scheme. Briefly, hashing allows us *both* to avoid data skew *and* to benefit from co-location based on key value.

Before the reader becomes too taken by the cleverness of this approach, however, it should be observed that it will accelerate joins only between tables that share a key value. In a typical data warehouse configuration, there are usually several dimension tables that must be joined to the central fact table. The table, in turn, can only be partitioned for persistent disk storage using the key value of one of these dimensions. For the other dimensions, the data will be as randomly spread as in the round-robin approach. One possible strategy, then, might be the following. Hash partition each of the dimension tables using a separate key appropriate to each. For the central fact table, use a round-robin partitioning scheme (to assure balanced data distribution, and since no dimension deserves priority over the others). Then, when a join is required, the query optimizer can use the key of the dimension table to hash rows *from* the fact table and send them *to* the CPU associated with the corresponding dimension key value. This is the main idea behind the hash join (discussed at greater length in the next section). The point is that in a parallel database, choice of data partitioning strategy plays a role somewhat similar to that of indexes in a sequential database. The query optimizer can use information about how the data has been partitioned in order to choose efficient execution strategies. And *mutatis mutandis*, by devising efficient partitioning strategies in advance through the design, the database designer can lay an effective groundwork for good performance.

An important special case of the data partitioning issue concerns how best to deal with *date* as a retrieval parameter. Writers on data warehouses stress the importance of date as an organizing principle for many types of queries, particularly those that allow comparison and trends analysis of a measure (sales performance, production, costs, and so on). Quarter-over-quarter results for several years running, for example, is an excellent summary result, and many OLAP tools are capable of generating and displaying summary aggregations retrieved from underlying detail data. To process such queries efficiently, it is important that the data be organized such that, for example, a particular week's worth of data can be retrieved without having to retrieve (for the sake of argument) all the data for an entire year.

Although it might appear at first blush that an index is the right strategy, some care must be taken. Our basic goal still has not changed—stream large amounts of data off disk using large block transfers, and if the index points to a lower level than a data block (that is, if it points to individual records within a block), our strategy will fail: We will be reduced to skipping randomly around the spindles looking for one after another of the rows pointed to by the index rather than streaming large blocks of data in parallel. Further, using time for range partitioning among disks is not appropriate. If that were done, then (for example) queries retrieving (say) a week's worth of data would only touch a (presumably small) subset of the disks, thereby greatly restricting I/O bandwidth. What we seek is a means of coarsely eliminating most of the data for time-based queries while retaining high bandwidth access to the portion of the data that is of interest.

One possible strategy for addressing this issue is to use separate named tables for relatively large subsets of data organized by time. For example, we might have a separate named table for (say) each week of data (or day, or month, depending on specific considerations). All the data belonging to the associated time period is placed (at load time) in its associated table. Because different tables have the same column structure, UNION joins should be very efficient, permitting aggregation of data at different periods. And because each table is hashed across all the disks, retrieval rates for any given table should be very good. Finally, when a query is processed that includes restrictions on the range of time involved, only the subtables affected need be retrieved—a big win in terms of reducing the total amount of data that must be processed. Of course, for this strategy to succeed, both the loader and the query optimizer must be made aware of the logical relationship between these time-ordered tables, a capability that may or may not be provided by the database vendor.

An approach like this runs counter to our general advice not to build indexes. An index may be thought of as a way to reduce the amount of data that must be processed to complete a query. The idea is rapid reduction of data volume; less data to process means, in particular, less data to read off disk and hence faster retrieval times. In a data warehouse, we have argued, techniques based on reducing data volume will tend to fail, because queries with low selectivity will require large amounts of I/O, no matter how many indices have been built in advance. Thus the database design should emphasize high I/O bandwidth from the beginning and largely ignore devices that depend for their effectiveness on high selectivity. Although we adhere to this basic viewpoint, the issue of retrievals based on *date* appear to be an important exception. While building of indexes still may not be the best solution, some means of obtaining greater selectivity in time-based queries will usually be appropriate, and the ability of the RDBMS to support this capability is an important evaluation criterion in the procurement process. In particular, this appears to be an instance where careful use of *range partitioning* could be of value.

7.2 IN-MEMORY JOINS

Our point of view in the discussion that follows is that the schema for the data warehouse matches that shown in Figure 5–7. A central fact table is "surrounded" by some number of dimension tables, each containing additional detail. Most columns of the central fact table are simply key values or pointers into the associated dimension tables. Some, however, may contain additional information (date, cost or value, and so on) associated with a specific transaction.

Figure 7–1 shows a classic example of this arrangement. The application is credit card transactions. Each row of the central fact table (Sales) represents one purchase. Associated with the purchase are its date and amount. In addition, there are pointers into two dimension tables: one (Sellers) contains information about retail establishments (address, type of goods, membership in chains, and so on), and a second (Buyers) contains information about customers (address, credit limit, group membership, commercial versus private account, and so on). Operationally, we envision updates to the Sellers and Buyers tables to be relatively infrequent (say, batch updates once per week), and updates to the Sales table to be in the form of append operations: The next batch of transaction data has been downloaded from the on-line operational system.

Figure 7–1 Generic Schema for Examples of Joins

Table 1: Sales

Transaction_Id	Seller	Buyer	Date	Amount

Note: One row per transaction

Table 2: Buyers

Id	Address	Other_stuff

Note: One row per customer

Table 3: Sellers

Id	Address	Other_stuff

Note: One row per retailer

This configuration has many implementation and performance advantages and maps well into the old-style network concept for many-to-one relationships between tables: All the relations between the central fact table and the dimension tables are many-to-one. A given row of the central fact table is associated with *at most one* row of each of the dimension tables (even better, *exactly* one row of the dimension table). Let us suppose that we wish to consider Seller–Buyer pairs for which the total amount of a transaction exceeds some minimum and the geographic distance (between the Seller's business location and the Buyer's billing address) is large; that is, we are looking for large transactions when the buyer is away from home. We suppose that we have a function—built-in or customized—that can take two addresses and return a distance (say, in miles). (For example, the function might be a look-up table based on zip codes.) Our query might look like this:

```
(1) SELECT   Sales.Buyer, Sales.Seller
(2) FROM     Sales, Buyers, Sellers
(3) WHERE    Sales.Seller = Sellers.Id
(4) AND      Sales.Buyer = Buyers.Id
(5  AND      Sales.Amount >= Min_Amount
(6) AND      Distance(Buyers.Address,
             Sellers.Address) > Min_Distance
```

Notice that lines (3) and (4) amount to natural joins between the central fact table, Sales, and each of the two dimension tables, Sellers and Buyers. The link between the Seller's address and the Buyer's address is through the central fact table: We're not interested in all possible pairings of Buyers and Sellers, only those that actually occurred (as represented by transactions in the Sales table).

Let us suppose that all three tables have been partitioned across all the disks using one of the data partitioning schemes discussed in Section 7.1. To perform one instance of the comparison shown in line (6), we must bring together in a single CPU a row from the Buyers table (to get its address field) and a row from the Sellers table (to get its address). Once the rows are co-located in the same CPU, the Distance function can be computed, and the comparison against Min_Distance can be performed. That is, some form of data exchange among the CPUs in the array must take place. At the heart of a join operation, then, is a data-exchange process: bringing initially separated rows of tables together, in the same CPU, so that a test and selection can take place.

Conceptually, it is well to think of each row of each table as having a location at each stage of the computation; that is, at each stage it resides in the memory of a particular CPU somewhere in the array (see Figure 7–2.). As the algorithm progresses, the row migrates around the processor array, moving from one CPU to another as various join operations occur. At each stage, the next destination for the row is identified (perhaps the destination is the CPU where it currently resides, perhaps not). The row is then routed to that destination using the interconnection network, and some local processing occurs: Columns are added or dropped, comparisions against other rows from other tables may be performed, and so on. As a result of this processing, a new set of rows has now been produced, each of which is then ready to be transferred to a new destination for the next stage of processing.

Typically, the destination CPU for a row is computed using the row's current values. This is similar to the data partitioning schemes we saw earlier. There, data values could be used to select the target disk to hold the data. Here, we are doing a similar process: Each row, in effect, computes the location of its next destination using its current values. Note that if two rows, perhaps located in entirely different CPUs, compute the same destination CPU address, then at the next stage they will be at the same CPU: They will have been *brought together*, or *co-located*, or *joined* in the destination CPU's local memory for that stage of the computation.

Figure 7–2 Query Processing Sequence

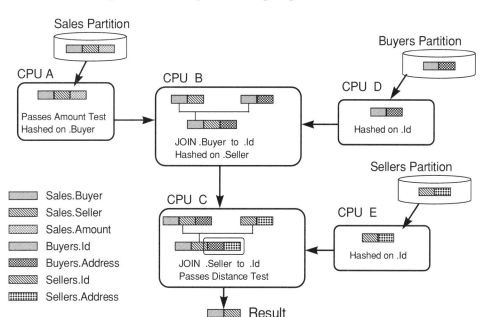

The most common way of computing a destination address for large-scale parallel processing is to use a hashing function based on the field values involved in the join operation. For example, when a row from the Sales table begins its journey from CPU to CPU across the processor array, it resides on the disk of the CPU to which it was initially assigned (as we suggested in Section 7.1, this partitioning decision is often based on its date value). The address of the Buyer and Seller must be found and compared, and the Sales.Buyer and Sales.Seller fields provide the link. In the disk of some CPU of the processor array is the row of the Buyers table whose ID matches Sales.Buyer. However, it is *not* required to know that location. What is required is that both rows—the one from Sales, and the corresponding one from Buyers—must compute the same address for some CPU in the array and be routed there. It doesn't matter *which* CPU is selected; it only matters that both rows, wherever they currently are, both compute *the same* destination address, wherever that may happen to be. Once *both* rows are co-located in the memory of the *same* CPU, the join comparisons can be made.

Hashing of destination node addresses based on row values is the most common way to accomplish this. To join the Sales and Buyers tables based on Buyer.Id [line (3)], every row of the Buyers table computes a destination node by hashing the value in its Buyer.Id field. At the same time, every row in the Sales table hashes the value in its Sales.Buyer field. Rows whose values agree will be routed to the same CPU (irrespective of their present location) because the same hashing function was applied to both. Once co-located in the same CPU, the join comparison operations can proceed in the usual sequential manner.

An important special case of this is when the same hashing function and key is used for joining as was used for initial data partitioning of the base table. In that case, the CPU to which the row was initially assigned (as a result of partitioning) will also be its join destination (since the same hashing function and value were used). The result is that for rows in that table, *no data transfer is required*. When this situation occurs, it can provide significant performance improvement. To see why this is so, picture a CPU that must send a set of rows off to their destinations for the next stage of processing. For each row, a destination must be computed. If the set of rows is very much larger than the number of CPUs (say, 200,000 rows to be redistributed among 100 CPUs), we would expect every CPU to be the destination for many rows. We might think of a satchel, one for each CPU, filled with the rows destined for that CPU. Once the satchels have been filled (by computing destination addresses), each can be sent off to its destination. For 100 CPUs, there will be 99 satchels (since some of the rows will "stay where they are")—that is, the

CPU we have been imagining must send 99 separate messages across the interconnection network. And, of course, that is only *one* of the CPUs; in fact, each of the others is faced with the same task on *its* locally held set of rows. Also, observe that our putative CPU will also be the *recipient* of 99 messages—one message from each of the other CPUs in the array (for, of course, each of them is doing the same operation and will have some rows destined for the CPU we have been considering). One sees from this example that the data-exchange portion of the workload can be a substantial part of the execution time, and that query execution can be improved using strategies that minimize both the number of exchanges and the amount of data per transfer.

Let us follow the route of a row from Sales as it makes its way across the processor array (refer to Figure 7–2). After the row is retrieved from disk, its "owner" CPU (this is CPU A in our example) can perform the "Sales.Amount >= Min_Amount" test. If it fails that test, the row is discarded for the rest of the computation. So suppose that it passes the test. We next hash on the "Sales.Buyer" field to find out where to send the row next, and suppose that the destination is CPU B. A separate retrieval/select/route process also occurs for the Buyers table. In our example, the matching row happened to be located in CPU D. For the row at CPU D whose Id matches the ".Buyer" field of our row, its destination will also be CPU B (since the two fields agree in value and the same hashing function is being applied). Thus CPUs A and D both route their respective rows (based on hashing of the Sales.Buyer and Buyers.Id fields) to CPU B. A local join at CPU B is then performed [as per line (4)], and the corresponding "Buyers.Address" column is appended to our peripatetic row.

The same process is now repeated, except that Sales.Seller and Sellers.Id are used as the hashing key to compute the destination CPU. CPUs B and E both route their respective rows to CPU C based on the hashed value, and a local JOIN is performed within CPU C. At this point, the address fields of the Seller and Buyer are co-located, and the distance test [as per line (6)] can be applied. If the row passes the test, it is ready for output; or if this is a nested SELECT, the result is ready to be routed onward to the next processing stage.

Note that it is possible that CPUs B and D are in fact *the same* CPU. This will occur if the hashing function used to partition the Buyers base table used Buyers.Id as the partitioning key. In that case, rows already at CPU D will stay where they are, saving one data transfer (the transfer from CPU D to CPU B). A similar comment applies to CPUs C and E. If the Sellers base table has already been hash partitioned using Sellers.Id as the key, the transfer of data from CPU E to CPU C can be avoided. As noted above, the performance benefit when this occurs can be substantial.

The query plan adopted here is probably close to what would be used in a real instance. We view the computation as a succession of joins of the central table against any dimension tables that are required. Selection conditions are evaluated as soon as the associated data from the dimension tables has been joined, and the order in which the joins are performed will be based on estimates of how selective each condition is: The more selective, the sooner in the tree of joins it is evaluated. This has the effect of eliminating as many fact table rows as possible as quickly as possible, thus reducing both interprocessor communications and processor load.

It occurs not infrequently that one or more of the dimension or intermediate tables is very small. In that case it may be preferable to move the entire small table rather than to move the rows from the fact table. This involves providing to *every* CPU its own private copy of the table in question, that is, replicating the table over all the CPUs in the array. There are, in fact, very rapid (log time) broadcast algorithms to do this, and the real concern is whether each CPU has enough local memory to hold its copy comfortably. Sometimes called a *broadcast join*, this constitutes an important special case. As an example of how this might be used, here is an alternative join strategy for our example query. Suppose that we join the Buyers and Sellers tables, compute the Distance function on every pair of Buyers and Sellers, eliminate those whose distance is too small, and then form a new table whose two columns are the resulting Buyers Id and Sellers Id. Thus, a particular Buyer–Seller pair is in this table just in case it satisfies the Distance constraint, irrespective of any data contained in the central fact table. *If* the resulting table is small enough, we might then broadcast it to every CPU. Each row of the Sales fact table could then be tested both for the minimum purchase amount [as per line (5)] and to see whether its Sales.Seller and Sales.Buyer pair exists as a row in the precomputed table [line (6)]. Note that *no data transfers of the Sales table rows* are required in this query execution strategy.

An SQL formulation of this approach is as follows:

```
SELECT   Buyer, Seller
FROM     Sales,
         (SELECT      Buyers.Id AS Bid,
                      Sellers.Id AS Sid
                      FROM Buyers, Sellers
         WHERE        Distance(Buyers.Address,
                      Sellers.Address) >
                      Min_Distance) XX
WHERE    Sales.Amount >= Min_Amount
AND      Sales.Buyer = XX.Bid
AND      Sales.Seller = XX.Sid
```

Observe that this formulation yields exactly the same table as the SQL version we considered above. The intermediate table XX, if it is small enough, could be broadcast (that is, replicated) to all the CPUs, and the join condition in the last two lines could then be executed locally against partitions of the Sales base table without the need for transfer of any of its rows.

A major concern that has been left unaddressed is the size of the intermediate tables and data packets (referred to above as satchels). A tacit assumption is that the local memory of the CPUs is large enough to hold the various values in question. A key issue here is how much of the central fact table (Sales, in our example) can be eliminated immediately without the need for further processing (the "amount" test is an example of such an elimination). We expect to have to do I/O on a large portion of the fact table, but we hope that after applying local selection conditions, the number of rows that remain is manageable.

When that assumption is *not* true, we are faced with the possible need for temporary storage of intermediate results. For example, if the size of the rows controlled by a CPU at a given stage of the computation exceeds its available physical memory, the CPU will need to use some of its local disk space temporarily to hold the data. If the operating system at the local node supports virtual memory, the programming may be simple, but the I/O overhead for (first) writing and (later) reading the data for transmission to the next CPU is additional overhead. In Chapter 8 we discuss techniques by which sorting of data can reduce the need for this type of temporary storage for large joins. Experienced database administrators will know that working disk storage is a necessary and often expensive requirement for large complex queries. It is not uncommon for data warehouses to require two or three additional bytes of working storage for every byte of live data.

7.3 UTILITIES AND INTERFACES

In this section we consider a variety of topics related to the operational aspects of a large parallel database: data loading, parallel application interfaces, repartitioning the data as nodes and/or disks are added over time, backup and recovery, and pinning a named intermediate table to memory to support interactive response times. Each topic is discussed in turn.

Loading Parallel Databases

It is well understood within the decision support community that the interface to legacy systems can be, and often is, the most trying and difficult aspect of establishing a large centralized data warehouse. Conversion of data formats, ensuring that the data is internally consistent, reorganization based on schemas appropriate for decision support—these and other considerations make the task of defining and loading a data warehouse difficult, apart from any internal parallelism in the hardware and software. On top of these difficulties, however, parallelism imposes two additional elements of complexity. First, as we noted in Chapter 6, the data must be partitioned across the nodes and disks of the system. This means, in particular, that the loader must be aware of the partitioning strategy for each table and must be able efficiently to route the data to its appropriate location. If indexes are in use, they must be updated appropriately. Second, for reasons of scalability, it is important that this entire process itself be conducted in parallel. This requires that both the input of the data and its processing be distributed across the processor array. Failure to parallelize the load function can result in a crippling I/O bottleneck as the data warehouse grows over time. Like all other system components, the loading utility must be scalable.

Although a detailed discussion of these issues is beyond our present purpose, it is important to note a significant new trend in the industry: the willingness of database vendors to utilize operating system services in support of these functions. What has made this possible is significant improvement, over time, in both Unix implementations and parallel file systems. For example, the management of I/O buffers in Unix has considerably improved, to the point where an RDBMS vendor can consider allowing the operating system to handle this function (as opposed to providing separate code). The recent availability of high-performance parallel file systems points in this same direction. A parallel file system has the ability to stripe a single logical file over many disks and disk controllers. It is able to synchronize input and output operations over this array so as to obtain very high aggregate I/O bandwidths (as discussed in Chapter 4). With such a capability directly available, an RDBMS vendor may choose to utilize it to facilitate external interfaces.

As an example, suppose that the warehouse accepts weekly data downloads from an on-line operational system using tape as the transfer mechanism. A possible loading strategy is first to have the system read the tape into a parallel file. At whatever rate the tape drive(s) supply the data, the parallel file system distributes that data automatically to many separate disks across the processor array. Ideally, this can be done without interruption to ongoing data warehouse operations, since (at this point) the database itself has not been affected. At some future time, the RDBMS can invoke its load utilities *using the parallel file system as the access mechanism to the data*. For this to work, however, the load utilities of the RDBMS must be parallelized—that is, they must be engineered so as to utilize the parallelism provided by the file system. As data is read in, many separate CPUs will receive individual portions of the data. Each processes its own subset of data in parallel with others, coordinating when needed, and using the user-defined data partitioning scheme (for example, hashing) for final redistribution and update.

Historically, parallel loading was not the highest priority of most RDBMS vendors. In an OLTP environment typical of their largest market, updates (two-phased commits, and so on) were of more concern, and those aspects have received correspondingly greater attention. Now that decision support and data warehouses are major RDBMS customers, the need to parallelize the load function has been widely recognized and addressed. Today, a customer can expect some level of parallelization of this function, and the capability is steadily improving. For those considering a parallel implementation of a data warehouse, some attention is advisable to current and planned vendor capabilities in this area. An important question to ask is whether the hardware vendor provides a high-performance parallel file system, and whether (and how) the RDBMS makes use of this capability.

Parallel Application Interfaces

The traditional view of how a database system is used implicitly assumes that the amount of output data generated by a query is fairly small. The reasoning behind that assumption is easy to understand. Typically, the source of the query is a user at a terminal. Even if that terminal is a top-end workstation (and most are not), the total amount of data the workstation could handle would be measured, at most, in megabytes. More often, the response to even a "large" query is measured in a few tens of kilobytes. In such an operational environment, the task of managing the output bandwidth from the query is pretty straightforward. This is reflected, for example, in the programmer's API to SQL: The connection between the application and the RDBMS is a Unix-like byte stream appropriate to (relatively speaking) small amounts of data.

However, the RDBMS in a data warehouse has been used increasingly in quite another way: as a preprocessor and data extraction mechanism for specialized data mining and knowledge extraction algorithms (see Chapter 14 for a more extended discussion). While SQL may be inadequate for the detailed aspects of these algorithms, it can be useful as a means for initial extraction and reduction of data preparatory to further processing. In such a case, the application (say, a data mining algorithm) may extract a table containing many tens of gigabytes, and an efficient data transfer mechanism is required (a Unix byte stream won't do the job!).

Here is another opportunity for the use of a high-performance parallel file system. Rather than sequentialize the output table (that is, have all the processors in the array route their table portions to a single point for output), it is more natural and efficient to have the local CPUs "change hats" and become I/O servers for the parallel file system: that is, output their table portions directly to file in a form accessible from the application code that will be using it. In particular, the internal formatting conventions of the RDBMS can be stripped away in favor of "vanilla" data representations appropriate for custom software developed in-house for specialized applications. Supposing that this software is itself parallelized and able to use the parallel file system, a natural and highly efficient interface between the RDBMS and the eventual application has been achieved.

For data mining custom code, the "I/O bottleneck" has become the "RDBMS bottleneck." If the application interface to SQL is serial, high-performance parallel codes will be severely penalized. A parallel interface to the SQL is required in such a case, and a high-performance parallel file system is, in our opinion, the natural and appropriate mechanism. Already we are seeing vendors providing this capability, and this practice will become more widespread as time goes on. For the moment, however, it is an issue that must be of concern to data warehouse implementations that intend to supplement the RDBMS with custom high-performance data mining applications.

Data Redistribution Utilities

Scalability requires not only the *potential* for hardware processing and bandwidth to grow over time in a predictable manner, it also requires that the potential be *realizable* with a minimum impact to ongoing operations. Consider, for example, what might be required when new processors, and associated disks, are added to an existing hardware platform executing a parallel RDBMS. To make use of the additional I/O and memory bandwidth, the existing tables must be redistributed from the current set of disks to the new (more numerous) set of disks. Further, the space formerly occupied on the existing disks must be released, and then partially reused, to house the newly redistributed tables. Finally, the loader and query optimizer must be made aware of the new configuration to support efficient update and query processing.

Now that we have seen the key ideas behind efficient data partitioning, the reader will see at once how to accomplish the desired rearrangement. However, doing so in a way that (1) minimizes disruption of ongoing operations and (2) continues to support the overriding goal of high aggregate I/O bandwidth remains a nontrivial technical challenge. It is worth exploring with potential vendors their techniques for accomplishing these goals *in parallel* with minimal operational impact.

Backup and Recovery

Decision support applications typically do not have the kind of "7 by 24, 4 nines" availability and reliability requirements that often characterize operational OLTP implementations. While analysis of business data has the potential for very high return on investment, it is usually not time-critical in the same way as operations are. As a result, DSS implementations do not generally require the same level of RAS engineering, and occasional downtime, although annoying, is not crippling. Even so, mechanisms must be in place to recover in the event of a major outage.

First, the use of RAID technology helps substantially. Loss of a single disk in any RAID partition will not halt operations, although it will reduce available bandwidth to that group until the parity blocks have been rebuilt. Since highly parallel algorithms generally proceed at the pace of their slowest component (see the discussion of load balancing in Chapter 5), reduced bandwidth to the disk controller for one CPU can have a disproportionate effect on the entire array. A more realistic operational scenario, in this instance, is to consider RAID not as a way to continue operations (although one can do so), but rather as a very rapid replace-and-repair mechanism. The failed disk is replaced on-line, the parity blocks are rebuilt automatically, and the system is back to its fully functional status very quickly.

Backing up a large data warehouse is a nontrivial task and should be parallelized. Here is another opportunity for use of system utilities and a parallel file system, if they are provided. Just as external I/O can be parallelized with the right set of software, so can tape backups. For the sake of argument, assume the availability of an on-line robotic tape storage system. The bottleneck for data backup will almost certainly be the aggregate bandwidth of the tape drives at the silos; there is no inherent reason why the backup cannot occur in parallel across the processor array. If we assume (current industry practice) that each drive can sustain 20 MB/sec of bandwidth, five such tape drives operating in parallel would take about 3 hours to back up 1 TB of uncompressed data. Alternatively, some installations elect to back up only some of the data partitions each evening, relying on the local log at each partition to bridge the interval between backups.

Pinning Tables to Memory

We conclude by discussing a capability that is only beginning to become generally available, but which has the potential to greatly enhance user response times on complex queries. The basic idea is simple: If the table(s) being queried is already in main memory, the most demanding part of the query processing—the I/O—is eliminated. Further, the query processor is given the advantage of knowing in advance a good deal about the size of the tables involved and their corresponding resource utilization requirements. In short, in-memory processing can proceed much faster than processing that requires disk access.

How might we take advantage of this obvious fact? One proposal is for an interactive session to proceed in two parts.

In the first part, the user "whittles down" the large central tables to a more manageable size by imposing a series of time and other constraints. If the scenario holds true, the table resulting from this initial phase is able to fit completely in main memory. At this point it is treated during the second phase of processing as if it were a base table. That is, it becomes a persistent object (at least until the end of the session, or until the user releases it) against which subsequent very complex queries can be issued.

The reader will perhaps recognize here the idea of a *view*. There are, however, a couple of important differences. First, ordinarily a view is imposed directly onto existing base tables. Here we have a separate realization of the data in main memory. Notice that UPDATEs to this created structure can occur *without affecting the underlying base tables*. This can be a very useful capability; it allows the user to try "what if" scenarios without damaging the integrity of the underlying database. It also (as we observed above) permits very rapid response to queries.

Use of buffers is one way in which databases have attempted to provide similar capability, but a bit of thought about how buffers are used will show that they cannot achieve the same functionality. In the scenario above, we know exactly where the data is, how large it is, and how it is internally structured. We can (if we choose) *sort* the data to achieve even greater efficiencies. None of these options are available using a "look and see if the data happens to be in buffer" approach.

A poor man's version of this capability is sometimes provided in OLAP tools (also see the discussion in Chapter 13). A copy of data from the data warehouse is extracted and transmitted to OLAP software executing at the user's workstation. The OLAP tool can then operate on the data however it wishes (internal to the workstation memory) without affecting the central data warehouse. What we are proposing here is a similar capability, but *using the full power of the parallel processor to support the analysis*.

Summary

In this chapter we have begun to consider at a more detailed level the way in which low-level parallel operators are implemented and the effects that good (or poor) database design can have on the efficient performance of those operators. The underlying technique is partitioning of data, and we have seen how the use of hashing satisfies the simultaneous goals of (1) balancing the load and (2) co-locating identical keys to support joins. These ideas are fundamental to all efficient implementations of intraquery parallelism characteristic of the data warehouse. Finally, we have seen how utilities such as loading, data redistribution, external interfaces, and pinning of tables in memory can have substantial operational impact, and we have encouraged readers considering parallel implementations to take such capabilities into account when considering vendor products.

Chapter

8

Sorting

In this chapter we discuss the importance of, and technical approaches to, sorting very large tables on parallel machines. Sorting (along with graph algorithms) has long been a staple of computer science and lies at the heart of many other algorithms in the general class of knowledge retrieval and data mining. Depending on the circumstances, it can also be used to accelerate the execution of standard relational operators, and it turns out to be a key element in statistical analysis (that is, the construction of histograms and cumulative distributions). If a large parallel machine cannot sort well—both in memory and externally—it will have relinquished a large part of the space for potential applicability in the data warehouse.

Fortunately, it turns out that parallel architectures are in fact nearly perfect sorting engines (in the sense, for example, that a lion is a Darwinianly perfect engine for hunting and killing antelopes). The very things that a large parallel processor needs to do for general-purpose processing—in particular, the capabilities of the high-performance interconnection network that is central to such a machine—are exactly what is

175

needed to perform efficient sorting. Further, if the database design follows the principles identified earlier for obtaining high sustained I/O rates, the machine becomes very efficient at performing external sorts. The message is that the decision to implement the data warehouse on a large parallel machine is completely compatible with the goal of performing sorting operations on very large data sets.

In Section 8.1 we consider sorting in its role of accelerating the execution of SQL queries. As we shall see, there are limitations to this approach that restrict the full use of the capabilities of a high-performance parallel processor. In Section 8.2 we take a broader view of the potential utility of sorting. The RDBMS is thought of as a prefilter to extract data (usually conceived of as very large flat files) for processing by separate (perhaps custom-built) data mining algorithms. We thus begin to break away from a relational view of the world and consider the parallel processor as an engine for executing complex and computationally demanding algorithms. These topics are treated at greater length in Chapter 14. Finally, a capstone section (Section 8.3) summarizes the observations of both this chapter and Part II.

8.1 SORTING IN THE RELATIONAL MODEL

In this section we provide a general introduction to sorting in support of SQL. Separate discussions are provided for implementations of index and ORDER BY, uses of local and global sorting operations, and the standard approach to parallel sorting, the bucket sort.

Use of Sorting to Support SQL

Despite the fact that sorting data is cited routinely as the cornerstone data processing algorithm, it is remarkable how *little* attention is paid to sorting by the relational model. Part of this is intentional. The notion of a table in the relational model states explicitly that "the rows are considered to be unordered." That is, two tables with the same set of rows, but stored in (or accessed in) a different order are, for purposes of the model, equivalent. This is a direct reaction against the *ISAM (indexed sequential access method)* view of the world, in which the sequential nature of the access is "built into" the mechanism. There are definitely important operations— UNION, for example—where ISAM breaks down. The designers of the relational model wanted a set of structures and operations that did not impose this kind of ad hoc limitation; it is exactly this generality that gives the relational model its power and expressivity. Note, for example, that ISAM operations which might be appropriate for base tables can be inappropriate for intermediate tables for which indexes do not exist. A goal of SQL is to avoid precisely this *"Which kind of table is it?"* dependency: All operators must apply equally to all tables.

The only SQL clause that explicitly calls for sorting is ORDER BY, which (in turn) is only associated with the output stream. In keeping with the nonprocedural nature of SQL (recall our discussion in Section 5.3), the ORDER BY clause can only be applied to the outermost SELECT statement (that is, the result table delivered to the application). Thus it is considered to be a matter of *presentation* of data on output rather than an algorithmic intrinsic. In a typical case, the user application is given a CURSOR (essentially, a pointer to rows in the table returned as a result of an SQL query), and SQL allows the sequence in which rows of the table are accessed by the CURSOR to be ordered based on user-defined key values. For our purposes, however, we can see at once that this capability is of very limited utility for (say) data mining operations. A CURSOR is an interactive, sequential abstraction, and inherently sequentializes access to the table. It is perfect for low-bandwidth interactive operations on relatively small tables (for example, scrolling up or down a screen at the user's terminal), but implicit in this model is the notion that the total amount of data to be viewed is rather limited—certainly less than (say) a few megabytes. More data than that would over-whelm an interactive session. Even if the underlying table contains a large number of rows, it is almost certain (based on human factors considerations alone) that the user will want to view only a small number of them.

For this reason, large parallel database implementations will typically not sort an entire large (multi-megabyte) table in response to an ORDER BY request, but will only "skim off" and sort the top few thousand records. Should the user push the CURSOR deeper into the table, the next "chunk" of data (that is, the next set of records deeper into the table) can be extracted, sorted, and returned dynamically in response to CURSOR requests. In this way, the RDBMS saves the effort of having to sort the entire table under the assumption that the user is, in fact, interested in only the top few percent.

If the table generated by the request is small (say, less than 10 MB), an even simpler solution is available: Return the entire table to a single node, which then interacts with the user program exactly like an ordinary sequential RDBMS. Sorting such a table in-core using standard sequential algo-rithms is no longer a challenging problem for the current gen-eration of microprocessors. For most queries using the ORDER BY clause, one or the other of these approaches should be adequate.

Let us look more closely at how this skimming process works in practice. Building on our discussion of parallelizing relational operations in Chapters 5 and 7, we consider the state of the result table produced by the query just prior to output. It will be partitioned across the local memories of many processing nodes, probably as the result of a hash/dis-tribute function beginning the final processing phase. At this point, each processor can sort its data *locally* and is then ready to return (say) the top 2000 rows in response to a CURSOR request. The central controller (the process responding directly to the user's commands) can then locally merge the separate "top 2000" responses, among which will certainly be the top 2000 over the entire processor array. As the CURSOR proceeds down this merged list, subsequent requests to the processor array can return subsequent ordered chunks of data. Thus the scheme of hashing data across the processor array matches well with both styles of CURSOR implementation described above.

Under what circumstances, then, is a true total-table sort operation (referred to as *a global sort* in the discussion below) appropriate for SQL implementations? The most common use in OLTP operations is to generate a *secondary index*. Indexes are of most value when enough is known in advance about the query patterns to know that *a particular key* is very often used to retrieve *a few* records from a certain table. In this case, where query selectivity is high and the key is known in advance, it makes sense to build a direct index into the table storage. Instead of having to search the entire table looking for the row(s) matching the response, the index allows the address of the matching row to be retrieved very rapidly based on its key value. What makes this search process so rapid is that the key values are stored in sorted order in the index, so that a binary "higher–lower" search algorithm can locate the record in logarithmic time, a much faster algorithm than a full table scan.

Use of indexes in sequential RDBMS implementations, particularly OLTP, is now standard practice. The index is typically stored in a *B-tree* structure to facilitate update, delete, and modify operations. In an OLTP setting, where updates are frequent, maintaining consistency of the index is a significant operational requirement. Further, there is significant additional storage required for the index. It is not unusual for the use of indexes to double (or more than double) the required storage for a large table. Building of indexes is by far the most common use of sorting large tables in traditional OLTP implementations.

For data warehouses, however, indexes are not nearly so useful. In a DSS application a typical query may touch a very large fraction of the data, so that the advantages of high selectivity no longer apply. Further, we usually expect DSS queries to be much more ad hoc than in OLTP applications, so that the likelihood of a query matching a retrieval key specified in advance is correspondingly reduced. (*Note: Date* is often an important exception to this general rule, as explained in Section 5.2.)

To summarize: The ORDER BY modifier on an output table is the single explicit SQL command requiring a sorting operation. Because SQL treats the output table as a serial stream, often via the use of a CURSOR, the processing demands on the systems are small, and in this case sorting can be handled without the need for large full-table sorts. Traditional OLTP implementations that make use of indexes can require sorting, but indexes are of less value in large DS environments, where ad hoc queries with small selectivity are common. In the next section we consider how sorting is used internally to parallel RDBMSs in support of standard SQL operations.

Local Sorting in Support of SQL in Parallel RDBMSs

In a parallel implementation of an RDBMS, it is important to distinguish between two different types of sorting operations. In one, called *local sorting*, a given CPU sorts data completely separate from and independent of other CPUs in the processor array. It is as if the CPU is presented with a collection of rows and asked to sort them, without reference to what is taking place in any other CPU in the system. The reader will immediately recognize this as an instance of a standard sequential sort: The CPU will use existing sequential techniques to accomplish the local sorting operation.

The other type of sort, called a *global sort*, is significantly more demanding. In it, a single large table is sorted across the entire processor array. In a typical implementation of such a sort, the first few rows in the key order would be held in (say) CPU 1, the next few in CPU 2, and so on. The *entire table* has been sorted across the local memories of the *entire processor array*. It will be seen at once that interprocessor communications will constitute a large part of this algorithm. Any given row will find itself shipped around the system and compared against other rows at various stages. Eventually, the row will find itself in the local memory of the CPU to which it is assigned in the final sorted order. A parallel sorting algorithm is one that arranges the sequence of comparisons and data exchanges so as to accomplish this task.

We shall look in more detail at an important instance of a parallel sorting algorithm—the bucket sort—shortly. In the meantime, it is an important and somewhat counterintuitive fact that global sorting is generally not of much use in implementing SQL on a parallel system. As it turns out, local sorting suffices for all SQL commands. It is a goal of algorithm designers for parallel RDBMSs to localize sorting as much as possible. When sorting is required, the preferred approach is to begin with an initial one-time data redistribution and then to use a local sort (sometimes called *an intraprocessor sort*) on the locally held data using standard existing sequential techniques. Some examples will illustrate this technique.

Consider, for example, the GROUP BY operator. Here, aggregation operators (such as COUNT, MAX, MIN, and so on) are applied to groups of rows based on shared key value. Sorting is a standard technique for implementing this operator, since after a sort all rows sharing the same GROUP BY key value will be adjacent in the sorted sequence. The point to observe, however, is that in a parallel system we can co-locate rows with the same key value using a hash function. As we have seen earlier in our discussion of JOINs, the first step is to hash each row by key value to identify its destination processor in the array. No matter where two rows with the same key may start out, after the hash-and-send operation, they will end up in the local memory of a single processor—since they have the same key value, the hash function will have sent them to the same destination processor. Once the rows are co-located by the hash-and-send operation, the GROUP BY operation can complete using a local sort exactly as it would in the sequential case. The point to notice is that no global sort is required. Hashing effects the co-location of rows sharing a common key value, at which point a local sort completes the operation.

Exactly the same strategy works for the DISTINCT operator. It is common practice in sequential RDBMSs to implement DISTINCT by sorting. All rows sharing the same key value will end up adjacent to each other in the sorted array, and redundant rows can be dropped out. As before, however, we see that a hash–send–local sort approach will work well here. After the hash-and-send operation, rows with the same key value will be co-located in the memory of a single CPU in the array; a local sort and delete can then complete the operation. As with GROUP BY, the DISTINCT operator can be implemented on a parallel RDBMS without the need to use a global sort function.

Finally, we recall that sorting is a standard way in a sequential machine to implement a JOIN operator. Basically, the two tables to be JOINed are each sorted in the order of the JOIN keys. A merge operation, involving a single pass down both tables, then completes the JOIN. A pointer progresses one by one through each row in (say) table A (the outer loop is over the rows of table A). In the meantime, a second pointer is progressing down (say) table B. Because the two tables are in the same sorted order, each pointer only need move forward through its array; either a match is found, or a higher key value is encountered. In any case, the JOIN on the two sorted tables completes in a single pass through the two tables, a very efficient implementation if the tables are at all large. If an index has been built for either of the tables using the JOIN key, the initial sort itself can be avoided.

As with GROUP BY and DISTINCT, a parallel system can accomplish the JOIN using only local sorts. Again, the rows are distributed across the processor array using a hashing function. Since rows with matching keys will now be co-located as a result of the hash, the JOIN can complete using the standard local sequential sort. In all these examples, the idea is the same: Co-location of matching rows (using hash-and-send), followed by a local sort. Indeed, other than ORDER BY, there is no SQL query that can force an efficient parallel implementation to use a global sort. And (as we say above) since ORDER BY operates on a sequential output stream, other local techniques will almost always suffice.

Counting, Histograms, and the Bucket Sort

Let us briefly review a point made earlier concerning the difference between *range partitioning* and *hash partitioning* (see Section 7.1). The problem with using range partitioning—that is, dividing data among the processors by using intervals in the ordered key space—is the danger of load imbalance. Often data is not evenly distributed over the key space, so that "equal intervals" in the key do not result in "equal numbers" of rows in the partitions defined by the intervals. The classic example of this is the English alphabet, where 26 partitions—one per letter—will result in very greatly differing numbers of rows in each partition. In text, the counts associated with letters like M and S will be greater than counts for letters such as X or Z. Hashing deals with this load imbalance problem through pseudorandomness: The same key values go to the same processor, but different key values, even if they are close together in the key space, will be routed to widely separated processors in the array. It is the desire for *load balancing* that motivates our preference for *hash partitioning*.

When it comes to sorting, however, range partitioning has obvious value. *If* the data has been partitioned by range value, *then* a local sort on the data at each partition *will result in a completely sorted array*! Is there a way to exploit this nice feature of range partitioning to produce an efficient sort? Obviously, the problem is how to overcome the difficulties of load imbalance in range partitioning. Instead of dividing the key space into bins by equal intervals, we want to choose the intervals that define the bins in such a way that (roughly) equal numbers of rows will be assigned to each bin. How can we efficiently accomplish a load-balanced range partitioning function?

One approach is to build a fine-grained histogram of the key distribution. In this approach (which, for example, is at the heart of the radix sorting algorithm), the key space is divided into a very large number of equal-interval bins. Once a count of instances in this finely structured binning has been done (a single pass through the data, incrementing counters in each bin), load-balanced range partitioning is easy. Each partition will be a contiguous run of small bins—enough so that the desired (equal) total number of rows is obtained for each partition.

Figure 8–1 illustrates the approach. Our data set has (say) 100 rows, and we want to use range partitioning to distribute the data evenly over (say) 10 processors. That means we'd like to have about 10 rows per processor. An initial count of the data by equally long key intervals (in our case, 26 bins each one letter long) results in a histogram over the key space. The resulting partitions are then defined as contiguous sets of letters, enough so that each partition results in roughly equal counts. In our example, the resulting partitions are roughly equal: a low count of 7 in the N–O partition, with as many as 12 in the F–G–H and K–L–M partitions. If our initial histogram had been on letter pairs (AA, AB, AC, . . . , ZX, ZY, ZZ), the counts would have been at a finer granularity, so that division points with a more balanced distribution could have been obtained. *More* initial key bins in the key histogram lead to *more even* resulting range partitions.

Figure 8–1 Use of Histograms in Range Partitioning

Initial Histogram

Count	4 7 4 3 2 3 2 7 3 6 1 3 8 5 2 6 2 4 7 6 2 3 7 0 2 1
Key	A B C D E F G H I J K L M N O P Q R S T U V W X Y Z

Results In

Range Partition	Count
A - B	11
C - E	9
F - H	12
I - J	9
K - M	12
N - O	7
P - Q	8
R - S	11
T - V	11
W - Z	10

The preceding discussion is intended to illustrate the very deep relationship between counting and sorting. *If* we can construct the histogram on the key space—a counting operation in which counters at each key bin are incremented as key values in the array to be sorted are encountered—*then* we can (1) evenly range-partition the key space, and hence (2) implement a load-balanced and efficient bucket sort. The converse is also true: *If* the data array is already sorted, *then* the construction of the histogram is trivial.

It is this relationship between counting, on the one hand, and sorting, on the other, that lies at the heart of the use of sorting in data mining operations (and conversely, the use of counting to produce efficient sorts). This relationship might be summarized as follows. If good information about the distribution of the keys is available—either from the exercise of an algorithm, or because running statistics have been kept, or from some other source—then range partitions can be used instead of hashing in data redistribution phases of the parallel relational model. In this case a *local* sort (say, to implement JOIN or DISTINCT) will result in a *globally* sorted array. In a word, bucket sorts based on balanced range partitioning of data provide the added value of globally sorted tables.

It may seem obvious to the reader that counting is always easier than sorting, but that need not be the case. Some reflection on the procedure illustrated in Figure 8–1 will show some of the potential difficulties. For example, we saw that small binning intervals in the key space (to construct the histogram) would result in a more even data distribution. However, it is typically not obvious in advance what the "right" bin size should be. When we think about constructing a histogram over the key space in parallel, we typically think of each CPU constructing its own local version of the histogram (that is, each CPU has its own local counting array, which it uses on the partition of the data assigned to it). The CPUs then exchange and aggregate their local counts in a coordinated fashion (using the interconnection network) to obtain the global counts. However, if the number of histogram bins is too great (that is, if the size of the bin interval is too small), the counting array may not fit in the local memory of a single CPU. In that case the histogram array itself would have to be distributed across the memories of the processor array—a cumbersome approach requiring data exchanges as locally obtained counts are forwarded to the processors holding the associated histogram bins.

In a shared memory system (including a NUMA architecture), a single global histogram counting array can be used. However, sequential access to the cells of this array must be enforced, typically by using one lock per cell. The resulting systemwide contention for locks can seriously degrade performance, and CPUs remote from the location of the histogram array in a NUMA machine will proceed much slower than CPUs local to it. Notice also that sorting avoids the difficulties of defining and updating the histogram bins. Break-points in the sorted data are immediately available based on array position rather than key value. Thus, as suggested, it may in fact be easier in some instances *first* to sort the data and *then* to count it.

One way to avoid having to count all rows in the table is to take a sample. The histogram resulting from the sample is then used as an estimate of the true histogram for the entire table. If this is done well (that is, randomization should be formally incorporated, and the sample size should not be too small), good estimates for balanced range partition points can often be obtained. These, in turn, can then support an efficient bucket sort. It is also possible (although it is not common practice) for the RDBMS to maintain running statistics on various tables and keys of interest. As part of the load and delete process, running counts in associated histogram tables can be updated. This is similar in some ways to the maintenance of indexes, although it is far less costly in terms of storage and processing overhead. These histogram tables might then be used explicitly by the query optimizer in range partitioning and bucket sorts. However, because global sorting is not required by the relational model, commercial parallel RDBMS products do not ordinarily use such data in implementing their internal sorting algorithms. As we show in the next section, however, the need for global sorting to support data mining operations is becoming increasingly apparent. As customers demand this capability, we can expect commercial parallel RDBMS vendors to provide support for balanced range partitioning and global bucket sorts.

8.2 SORTING IN SUPPORT OF DATA MINING AND KNOWLEDGE EXTRACTION

In this section we consider the ways in which physically sorted tables can support computationally demanding algorithms in data mining and knowledge extraction. We will consider two examples of algorithms—cumulative distributions and clustering—that are not easily expressed in SQL but which are fundamental to a number of data mining applications. Assuming that the parallel RDBMS has an interface to application codes executing such algorithms, the ability of the RDBMS to provide the data in sorted order would be a great benefit to such applications. Even better, if the RDBMS provides extensions able to support these types of operations directly, there is the possibility of implementing the algorithm on the underlying data as it exists in the RDBMS without the need for extraction to a flat file.

These notions are shown in Figure 8–2. In the first scenario, SQL is used to extract a large table to a flat file for further processing by application code. If the table can be placed in sorted order, this is an advantage for the algorithm, which must otherwise perform this operation itself. In the second scenario, the algorithm is able to use SQL plus specific extensions without the need for extraction to a flat file. In effect, the parallel RDBMS has already incorporated the necessary operations to support the data mining functionality. Clearly, many

Figure 8–2   Two Approaches to Data Mining

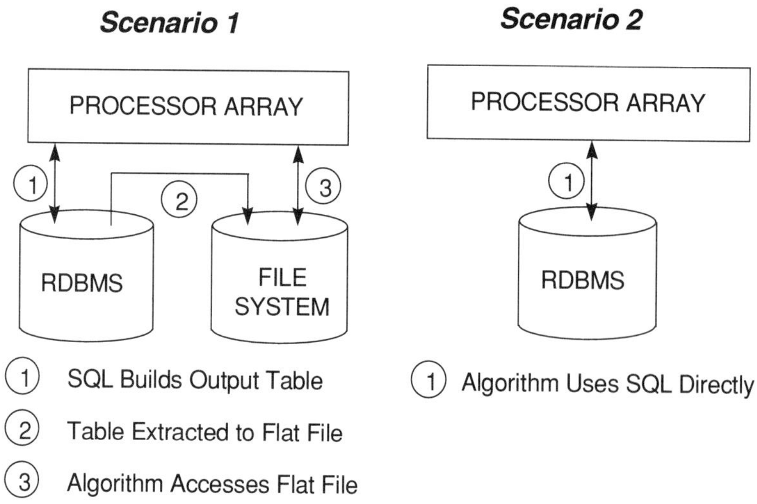

Scenario 1

PROCESSOR ARRAY

① ② ③

RDBMS   FILE SYSTEM

① SQL Builds Output Table
② Table Extracted to Flat File
③ Algorithm Accesses Flat File

Scenario 2

PROCESSOR ARRAY

①

RDBMS

① Algorithm Uses SQL Directly

users would prefer the second concept of operations if it is available (see the related discussions in Chapters 14 and 15).

Histograms versus Cumulative Distributions

It is not difficult using SQL to build histograms. The standard approach is to use the COUNT modifier together with GROUP BY. The effect of the combination of these is that (1) groups of rows with a common key value (as specified by the user) are treated as a single row of the output table, and (2) the COUNT operator counts the number of rows in each group. The idea is to choose a key whose values are discrete (so that the GROUP BY function can test equality) and whose values correspond to the bins desired for the histogram. If the underlying variable is continuous, so that the bins correspond to intervals (*time* is a good example of this situation), the SQL may include a discretizing function. In any case, each bin of the histogram corresponds to a set of rows "lying in" or corresponding to the bin, and the COUNT function returns the number of rows in the set for each bin.

As an example, the following SQL code would return a count of the number of credit card transactions for each customer (that is, a histogram of transactions over the Buyer key space; see Figure 7–1).

```
SELECT      Buyer, COUNT(*) AS Number
FROM        Sales
GROUP BY    Buyer
```

What standard SQL is not able to produce is the associated *cumulative distribution function*. Very often the key space itself has an implied order (while the Buyer key does have a collation sequence, the idea is not particularly meaningful in this example). The idea is illustrated in Figure 8–3. Like the relational model itself, a histogram produced by SQL as above does not have an implied order. Each key value has a count, but there is no implied order within the key space. To take

Figure 8–3   Histogram versus Cumulative Distribution

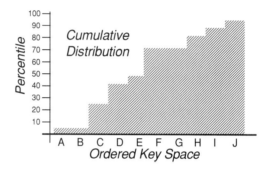

advantage of the order, if any, we ask for the sum of all counts associated with keys up to and including the key of interest. In Figure 8–3 we see how the histogram is used to construct the cumulative distribution function (CDF). For each (ordered) key value in the CDF, we sum the counts of all key values less than or equal to the current key. For example, to obtain the CDF count for key = G, we sum the counts associated with A , B, C, …, G. The resulting total $(1 + 0 + 4 + 3 + 1 + 6 + 0 = 15 \sim 75\%)$ is then associated with the key value G. Notice that the idea of order in the key space is crucial; without the notion of order, we do not know which keys are "less" than G, so we do not know which rows to sum together to obtain the CDF.

An illustrative example is test scores. Suppose that I have a single table "Test" containing the test scores of a number of students. The SQL code

```
SELECT     Score, COUNT(*) As Count
FROM       Test
GROUP BY   Score
```

would tell me how many students got any given score, but it would *not* tell me the percentile: that is, what percentage of the student scores are less than any given score. As we saw in Section 8.1, the GROUP BY operator is naturally accomplished using a local sort on the key value. If the rows are co-located by hashing, a cumulative distribution cannot be obtained easily; the scores will be "randomly" spread across the processor array. However, if the rows are co-located using a balanced range partitioning function, the result will be in globally sorted order, and the cumulative distribution function could be computed easily (although standard SQL does not support it).

The value of the cumulative distribution function is that it enables an algorithm to treat *intervals* of the key space rather than unordered *subsets* of the key space. For many continuous variables (time, cost or value, weight, score, and so on) intervals have a natural heuristic significance that is lost if the data is discretized and noncontiguous bins are grouped together. The cumulative distribution function is a good example of a simple operator that requires global sorting (or, better still, range partitioning) to compute and that has significant value for data mining algorithms.

Cluster Analysis

Our next example concerns a "killer query" that is apt to bring many (most?, all?) RDBMS systems to their knees. The motivation behind this query is the desire to do cluster analysis. The model that is ordinarily used is a weighted graph: that is, vertices connected by edges to which numerical weights have been assigned. A simple but powerful technique on such a structure is to identify subsets of the graph that exhibit a common feature. Sometimes this is as simple as finding connected components; in other cases more sophisticated algorithms must be applied. In any case, the "right" way to represent the graph is to consider pairs of vertices as potential edges and to compute and store the weight associated with the edge as a numerical value. The problem is that the number of edges, E, in the graph can be as large as the square of the number of vertices, V: $E \sim V^2$. If V is already large, E can be unmanageable.

An example of this can be constructed from our Sales table based on credit card transactions (see Figure 7–1). Suppose that we are interested in identifying subgroups of customers based on their buying patterns. One measure of similarity between customers is the extent to which they patronize the same business. That is, two customers are linked if they have a "large" number of purchases from the same set of Sellers. In this case the vertices of our graph will be the Buyers, the edges of the graph represent pairs of Buyers, and the weight of each edge will be the number of different Sellers the two Buyers have in common.

Clearly, the information to construct this graph is available in the Sales table. Since we know every transaction, we know whether or not two Buyers have a Seller in common, adding one more count to the edge between them. Consider the following SQL:

```
(1)SELECT      XX.Buyer AS Buyer1,
               YY.Buyer AS Buyer2,
               COUNT(*) AS Weight
(2)FROM        (SELECT DISTINCT Buyer,
               Seller FROM Sales) XX,
(3)            (SELECT DISTINCT Buyer,
               Seller FROM Sales) YY
(4) WHERE      XX.Buyer > YY.Buyer
(5) AND        XX.Seller = YY.Seller
(6) GROUP BY   XX.Buyer, YY.Buyer
```

The effect of line (4) is to ensure that edges are not counted twice. In line (5) we consider a pair of buyers only if they have a Seller in common. Any redundant pairs (that is, pairs which have more than one Seller in common) are then collapsed in line (6) together with the COUNT(*) operator in line (1). Note that the construction of intermediate tables XX and YY eliminates multiple transactions between the same Buyer–Seller pair. Also, in reality XX and YY are *the same table*. Finally, note that a condition involving an inequality, such as line (4), could potentially benefit from sorting. If the table is sorted, the relative order of two values is implicit in the pointer positions to them without actually having to retrieve their values and perform the comparison. In general, any conditions that involve "<" or ">" operators potentially benefit from sorting.

This simple query, which is not untypical of DS applications, has the potential to "run forever" as they say in the IT business. The computational burden lies in the fact that in lines (2) and (3), a modified version of the large central fact table is being JOINed to itself. To get a better handle on what the computation really involves, consider Figure 8–4. What we want in the table is shown to the far right: For each pair of buyers, we want a count of the number of sellers they have in common. This suggests the following algorithmic strategy. Begin by constructing for each Buyer a list of Sellers from which purchases were made. This *bitmap* (so-named because each cell can be represented by a single bit indicating "yes" or "no") is constructed for each Buyer and saved to temporary storage. Now, to fill in a cell of the Buyer–Buyer table, we can compare the bitmaps of the Buyers in question, counting the Sellers (if any) that they have in common. This operation is illustrated in Figure 8–4. The bitmaps from Buyers M and N are retrieved and compared. A portion of the bitmaps is shown and a match is indicated by "*". The job is to count the number of "*"s and store the count in cell <M, N> of the Buyer–Buyer table.

Figure 8–4 Good Algorithm for Executing Self-Join

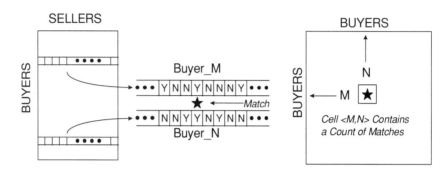

Stage 1: For each Buyer, construct a bitmap of related Sellers

Stage 2: For each pair of Buyers, count the Sellers in common using the bitmap

If we consider this algorithm, there are a number of places where sorting—that is, global sorting—could be of value. Notice that both the DISTINCT and GROUP BY operations can benefit from sorting: one on the Seller key, the other on the Buyer key. By initally sorting the Sales table with Buyer as primary and Seller as secondary, both benefits can be obtained at once (as opposed to two separate data redistributions, one based on Seller, the other on Buyer). Second, we clearly do not literally want to join the Sales table to itself, since the storage requirements would be impossible. By parallelizing a merge join over the sorted Sales table, a reasonably efficient implementation can be achieved. [To translate the preceding sentence into English: Start with the first Buyer in sorted order and compare against all other Buyers, filling in the first row of the final table; repeat for successive Buyers in sorted order, but considering only other Buyers that follow (not precede) in the sorted order. In effect, only the upper-right triangle of the table is computed, per line (7) in the query. Because the number of Buyers to be considered decreases as the algorithm progresses (the triangle gets narrower near the bottom), we may wish to redistribute the remaining portion periodically to achieve load balance.]

A further benefit of sorting can be obtained if the final table can be presented in sorted order *by edge weight*. The benefit of this is as follows. The connectivity of the graph changes if one excludes edges whose weights fall below a threshold. For example, it might be that a good cluster can be obtained if only Buyer pairs with (say) 20 Sellers in common are considered (that is, only edges whose edge weight is at least 20 are considered). Of course, it is not possible to know in advance exactly where the threshold lies. But if the edge table is presented in sorted order by edge weight, we can easily add in additional edges by varying the threshold. The point is that even if the RDBMS cannot perform the actual clustering algorithm, it can substantially accelerate the algorithm by presenting the resulting data in a computationally useful sorted order.

We do not believe that at the current state of the art, parallel RDBMSs are able to achieve the optimal bitmapped form of this algorithm. Of even more concern, however, it is doubtful that many implementations would exploit the advantages of global sorting to accomplish a global parallel nested join. A guess at a possible order of execution might be as follows. <Step 1>: Hash the Sales table on the Seller key, imposing the DISTINCT condition from lines (2) and (3). <Step 2>: At each node, construct for each Seller a list of pairs of Buyers for that Seller. This can be done using a local sort with Seller as primary key and Buyer as secondary key. For each Seller, the cross product of the list of associated buyers with itself is the desired structure. The result is a unique <Buyer, Buyer, Seller> triple—essentially the first table in Figure 8–4, but with a third Buyer dimension added. <Step 3>: Use a GROUP BY on the <Buyer, Buyer> key, plus a count, to complete the operation. This means hashing the table on the <Buyer, Buyer> key followed by a local sort and count.

8.3 CONSIDERATIONS

We have come now both to the end of Chapter 8 (on sorting) and to the end of Part II (on software for large parallel databases). In the next few pages, we wish to bring this material together briefly, summarizing and emphasizing the major points and recommendations. First, it should be clear at this point that data distribution and redistribution is at the heart of parallel implementations of the relational model. Distributing the data across multiple disks allows us to achieve high I/O rates by reading the data in parallel. Distributing the data evenly across multiple CPUs allows us to achieve high performance by operating on the data in parallel. For all this to occur, however, some *method* or *algorithm* for distributing the data must be imposed. The three most obvious and commonly used approaches—round robin, hashing, and range partitioning—each have strengths and weaknesses. Further, the choice of how to partition the data initially across the base tables may be motivated by different considerations than how to partition (or repartition) the data during the course of executing a query. *The most significant single factor to be considered in the implementation of a large parallel database is the effect that data partitioning strategies have, in both loading and query execution.* It has been the goal of Part II to provide the reader with the necessary background and insight to support good procurement and design decisions.

We have also seen that there are unique features of the relational model that support efficient parallel implementations. Since the relational model does not build in order to its tables, parallel database vendors can implement relational operators using the idea of co-location: rows to be joined (for example) need only be brought together (often by hashing), at which point preexisting sequential algorithms can be used to complete the operation. This gives rise to a model of execution in which *local operations* on data alternate with *data exchanges*. The local operations (local sorting, joins, scans, and so on) can use preexisting code, the data exchanges make use of the high-performance interconnection network, and scalability comes "for free" with the proper choice of hardware architecture.

An important distinction that we have stressed throughout this discussion is the difference between *interquery* and *intraquery* parallelism. Because our focus is on decision support in a data warehouse, our emphasis and attention has focused on intraquery parallelism: getting all the available CPUs to cooperate in accelerating performance against single large, complex queries. Under different operational conditions (for example, OLTP), the design decisions and trade-offs would be much different. Historically, RDBMS vendors have focused on OLTP (naturally enough, since this is where the greatest market has been). The development of a market for data warehouses and decision support in the past few years has had a very significant impact on all aspects of the internal design and implementation of an RDBMS. Design rules that worked well for small queries with high selectivity are no longer applicable. Further, applications that have been optimized assuming such design rules may work poorly on database implementations targeted at decision support. When the additional complexity associated with parallelism is thrown into this already volatile mix, it is little wonder that many users approach the data warehouse with trepidation. One of our goals in Part II has been to alert the prospective data warehouse customer to the implications for database design that follow from the parallel decision support operational premise.

The deemphasis of the relational model on sorting is a mixed blessing. On the one hand (as we have seen), it enables a rapid and very clean form of load-balanced parallelism using hashing as the data redistribution mechanism. On the other hand, database mining and knowledge extraction is often one of the main "consumers" of RDBMS cycles in a data warehouse. These application domains *require* sorting for efficient implementation. Indeed, the interface between the parallel RDBMS and the data mining application code (perhaps both executing on the same platform) remains cumbersome due to serialization of the output stream. By moving more explicit global sorting back into the RDBMS, the database system could become a significant participant in data mining rather than a mere file server. Further, explicit global sorting of large tables offers query execution strategies which, although not required for SQL, can nevertheless significantly enhance performance for some computationally demanding queries (that is, self-joins of large fact tables). We have suggested that an increased emphasis on techniques to support *range partitioning* should lie at the heart of such an approach. Although we are aware of the difficulties that data skew poses, we feel that efficient histogramming and sampling techniques should be able to overcome most of these problems. The resulting ability to provide to applications globally sorted tables as the result of local sorts has substantial business value. We expect commercial RDBMS vendors to pursue these lines of development over the next few years.

Data warehouses require hardware and I/O performance that scales to many terabytes of data. Part I showed that such hardware configurations can be and are being built using parallelism. In Part II we have seen that software is now available that can implement the relational model efficiently on such large parallel hardware platforms. The *shared-nothing* software model implemented using a *distributed memory* parallel hardware model appears most scalable, even if a DSM/NUMA hardware platform is the physical basis for the implementation. The reason is that *locality of data* (as we have seen repeatedly in notions of *co-location*) is fundamental to parallelizing the relational model. For intraquery parallelism on large complex queries, the current state of the art is highly partitioned tables ($\Rightarrow$ high I/O), data distribution and localization (hashing or range partitioning), and a shared-nothing software architecture. We can identify nothing in emerging technologies which suggests that this state of affairs will change anytime soon.

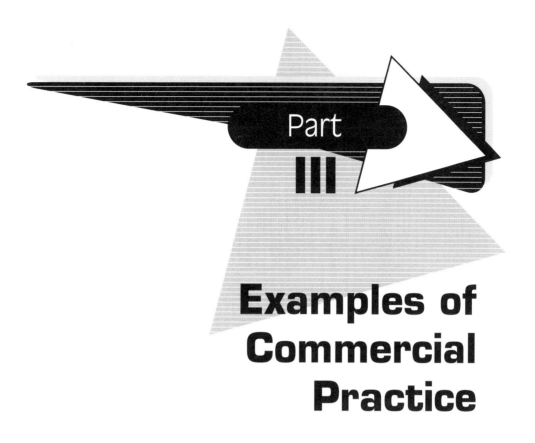

Part
III

Examples of Commercial Practice

The following four chapters canvas a broad spectrum of products typical of data warehouse and decision support in the current marketplace. Four examples have been selected for detailed presentation:

1. IBM DB2-Parallel Edition executing on an IBM SP2 computer (Chapter 9)
2. Informix-Online XPS executing on an HP 9000 EPS cluster (Chapter 10)
3. Oracle 7 executing on a Sun Starfire Ultra Enterprise 10000 (Chapter 11)
4. White Cross Systems database machine (Chapter 12)

An explanation for how this selection was made is in order. The primary purpose of Part III is to illustrate the general principles introduced in earlier chapters using concrete examples. To that end it was important to ensure that major generic hardware and software architectures discussed in Parts I and II were represented. Even within this narrowed scope, however, there are many excellent offerings on the market today, and certainly not all of them appear among the examples we discuss. This list does not indicate specific endorsement of these products, or implied criticism of products that are not presented. Rather, the list should be viewed as representative of best current commercial practice, and hence as indicative of the kinds and levels of service and performance that are broadly available from commercial vendors. Although all the products represented here are worth the attention of prospective data warehouse customers, there are many other fine products not included here that should also be considered.

There is one significant omission that must be addressed. During the planning phase of this book, it was our intention to include an example of the DSM/NUMA architecture as one of the hardware platforms. For various reasons it was not possible to achieve this goal. In Chapter 3 the reader will find references to the current set of DSM/NUMA vendors, and we encourage readers to contact these companies directly.

It is also important to understand that this is not a *Consumer Reports* type of comparison. We are not recommending (or failing to recommend) any specific hardware or software product. We do not discuss such issues as cost, benchmark performance, or competitive advantage. Our sole goal is *to illustrate general principles using concrete examples*. Without such examples, the reader's understanding will remain at an abstract level. By looking closely at real commercial products, the reader will be able to come to grips with the *reality* of large parallel databases rather than merely theory. The fact that these vendors have been willing to have their products presented and examined in this way is an indication of their own confidence in the technical integrity of their work.

Building a parallel database that can scale to very large configurations while meeting customers' expectations for reliability, availability, and features is a very demanding technical challenge. The descriptions presented in the following chapters have been reviewed for accuracy by representatives of the vendor companies. Without their support and participation, this part of the book could not have been written.

As we noted in the preface, the authors have a hidden agenda behind this presentation. It is our belief that with the advent of large parallel databases in data warehouse applications, parallel computing has at last entered the mainstream of commercial data processing. Such a claim, which would have been difficult to support even three years ago, requires substantiating evidence. By considering the examples shown here, we hope the reader will reach the same conclusion: Even organizations adverse to technical risk can now seriously consider the use of parallel hardware and software to implement large decision support infrastructures.

Chapter
9

DB2 Parallel Edition Executing on an SP2

W̲e begin with a look at IBM's entry in the Unix-based parallel database market. This is *not* IBM's only product for data warehouses and decision support. However, this particular combination is interesting from our point of view because it illustrates well both a *distributed memory* machine (the SP2) and a true *shared-nothing* software architecture. A glance back at Figure 6–7 will show that this combination has particular strengths when considering large data warehouse implementations.

The outline of this chapter is typical of all the chapters in this part. We begin with a discussion of the hardware platform (Section 9.1), followed by a discussion of the software architecture (Section 9.2). In the final section (Section 9.3) we gather the material together, address points that may have been bypassed in earlier discussions, and summarize the major issues.

203

The decision by IBM in 1993 to produce and market a parallel machine capable of scaling to hundreds or thousands of processors marked a turning point in the parallel processing industry. Up to that point, parallel processing (for those who considered it at all) was considered a "fringe" technology most properly associated with the national labs and scientific computing. Some commercial applications (seismic processing, molecular modeling for pharmaceuticals) had been developed, but the engine of commercial computing—databases—remained outside the range of suitable applications.

The introduction of the SP2 changed all that. While not turning their backs on the high-performance scientific market, IBM specifically targeted large databases (both OLTP and DSS) as a natural market for the machine. Where other vendors had failed to convince, IBM was able to demonstrate business utility, and for the first time large scalable parallel processing began to be profitable. Further, the decision by IBM to embrace the technology established a level of credibility for parallel processing that has had benefits for the entire industry.

IBM's entry into the parallel processing market also put pressure on marginal vendors to show profitability. Clearly, IBM was making money with a parallel machine, and both venture capital and government funding (for example, DARPA), long tolerant of market failure, now began to expect results from small development efforts that had been drifting along in red ink for years. The resulting shakeout in the industry has been all to the good. The parallel machines now on the market are focused on customer requirements in a way unheard of previously. It is now clear to all the players that a large commercial base is required to sustain profitability, and that in turn means taking large databases and decision support seriously. This sea change in the parallel processing community—*from* "beauty and light" designs unrelated to real customer needs, *to* a situation in which customer requirements come first—is due largely to IBM's presence in the market. That is a contribution that goes far beyond the more narrow issues of the technical characteristics of the machine.

9.1 IBM SCALABLE POWERPARALLEL SP2

Before looking more closely at the hardware internals, some context for the SP2 may be in order. Scalable parallel architectures exploit the dramatic packaging and cost–performance advantages of VLSI memory and microprocessor technologies. In the case of IBM, this means specifically the RS6000 processor, which is at the heart of their business in high-performance Unix workstations. (*Note*: IBM's version of Unix is called AIX.) A fundamental design decision was to exploit the large existing investment in AIX and the RS6000 in building a large scalable parallel machine. Thus when we consider the individual processing nodes of an SP2, it is not far wrong to think of them as RS6000 workstation boards with some hardware and software extensions to support (1) a high-performance interconnection network, (2) a parallel processing software development environment, (3) reliability and availability features, (4) global system management and administration capabilities and (5) services required for parallel processing. Thus the SP2 development was conceived of as *additions to* an existing proven hardware and software base.

The SP2 is a classic example of what we have called a *distributed memory* hardware architecture (see Figure 2–1). Every processing node consists of a full-functioned processor (the RS6000), memory (up to 2 GB of DRAM per node), a private hard disk (typically 2 GB), and an interface to the *high-performance switch* (HPS). Because each processing node is given its own non-shared disk, all the virtual memory features of AIX can be used (for example, swapping to the local disk). This local, private disk space is in addition to and separate from whatever general storage may be required for the database itself. It enables AIX to execute as it would on a workstation. It also enables a single SP2 processing node to execute the full range of AIX application software. Some SP2 customers use the machine in this way: as a server for single-threaded AIX applications. We note that the RS6000 processor is a state-of-the-art RISC processor supported by a rich software development environment and an extensive set of applications. Single-chip microprocessors (the 604 series) are already appearing in the SP2 product line, and this trend will continue.

Although configurations of an SP2 are supported that use LAN technology as the interconnection mechanism, a large data warehouse will need to use the high-performance switch (HPS). Using the terminology introduced in Section 2.2, HPS is a *multistage switch network* (MSSN). That is, rather than individual nodes communicating directly using point-to-point links, the switching fabric provides connectivity between pairs of nodes by routing the message through a sequence of intermediate switching elements. The switch element in the HPS provide eight input and eight output ports. These are "paired" so that they may logically be considered a single set of eight bidirectional "links." Each link may connect to a processor or to the link of another switching element. As an example, a single switch board contains eight switching elements. At eight links per element, this is total of $8 \times 8 = 64$ bidirectional links. Sixteen of these links are used to connect directly to processors, 32 are used to connect the switch elements to themselves on the board, and the remaining 16 are available to connect to higher levels in the switching network. Typically, a group of 16 nodes resides within a single cabinet, and messages among them need not leave the cabinet. Higher numbers of nodes are supported by cabling together switch boards located in different cabinets, or (for large configurations) by adding cabinets dedicated to switching circuitry. As we noted in Chapter 2, MSSN hardware grows superlinearly (that is, faster than the number of nodes), but the available network bandwidth *per processor* grows linearly (unlike point-to-point networks, where per-processor bandwidth tails off for large configurations).

Starting with research begun on the Vulcan switch, IBM has developed a number of enhancements to increase bandwidth, decrease latency, and provide high levels of reliability and availability. Low-level messaging protocols are embedded in the AIX kernel, and a separate microprocessor with DMA capability is provided to offload communications processing from the CPU. Multiple redundant paths are provided both to reduce contention (alternate paths) and to support availability (routing around failed switch components). The HPS—both hardware and software—is the most significant addition to standard RS6000 hardware technology needed to build the SP2.

The SP2 is intended to support a variety of customer requirements, not just databases. The high-performance scientific computing market is also a major focus of the SP2, and many features and capabilities are provided to support the needs of those users. Most significant for our purposes are (1) compilers and libraries, (2) a parallel file system, and (3) a robust software development environment, including interactive debuggers and profilers. As we discussed in Chapter 8 (and return to in Chapter 14), it is often not possible to implement data mining algorithms directly from SQL. In those instances, separate application code must be executed, often after having exported a large table from the RDBMS. The SP2 is an excellent platform for executing those types of algorithms. The features mentioned above form the basis for developing high-performance parallel application code. The fact that this code can execute on the same platform as the underlying RDBMS is a great advantage, since it permits a direct RDBMS-to-file system transfer without the need to traverse an external network. Given the size of tables on which data mining algorithms execute, the network download could become a serious bottleneck. This bottleneck can be avoided if the SP2 can execute both the database and the data mining application code on the same platform.

There are many storage options available from IBM on the SP2; we consider just one of them. The *serial storage architecture* (SSA) is a state-of-the-art approach to providing high availability coupled with high bandwidth for disk storage subsystems. We may think of an SSA loop as consisting of a controller and several disks (see Figures 9–1 and 9–2). Data moves in both directions around the loop. Thus, even if the loop is broken at a point, data can still move between the controller and the disks. Typically, we think of the controller as implementing some level of RAID (for data warehouses, this is probably level 5) among the disks under its control. This is implemented by the controller itself, so that higher-level application software is provided with a simple interface. Enough disks can be placed on each single loop to exhaust its bandwidth. At this point, adding more disks to the loop can increase the amount of storage but will not increase the rate at which the data can be accessed.

Figure 9–1 One Device in an SSA Loop

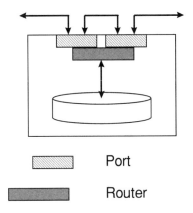

Port

Router

Figure 9–2   Typical Twin-Tailed SSA Loop

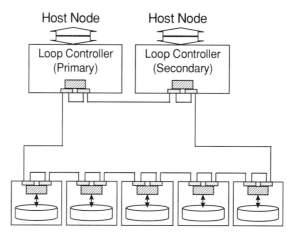

For purposes of reliability and availability, we may choose to place two controllers on the same SSA loop: one primary and the other secondary, in case the first fails. Often, the secondary controller on a given loop is itself the primary controller on some other loop. Should the first controller fail, the second must do double-duty (driving its own disks plus those of the failed controller). Performance has been degraded temporarily but continues without interruption. This combination of RAID and redundant controllers is a flexible and reliable approach for data warehouse implementations.

High levels of storage capacity and I/O bandwidth are obtained by using multiple SSA controllers. A single processing node can physically support many such controllers, but a caveat is in order: The aggregate bandwidth of the controllers attached to a node should not exceed the bus bandwidth to which they are attached. Otherwise, the controllers will not be able to execute at their full rate. Similarly, if the data streaming off the controller is destined for routing across the network, the bandwidth of the network links can become the limiting factor. If sustainable I/O bandwidth is the driving concern (as it often is in large data warehouses), one SSA disk controller per node may turn out to be the optimal design point.

As explained in Chapter 4, we would expect single large tables to be partitioned across multiple SSA controllers; these controllers, in turn, implement RAID and stripe the data internally across the disks on the loop in a way transparent to the application. As a result, a single table read can result in up to thousands of disk spindles, associated with up to hundreds of SSA controllers, all accessing the data simultaneously. As we mentioned earlier, SSA is only one of the storage options available from IBM on the SP2. It illustrates, however, the principles discussed at some length in Chapter 4 and shows how very high aggregate I/O bandwidth can be obtained using today's off-the-shelf commercial technology. Compared to the state of affairs even four or five years ago, this represents an extraordinary acceleration of I/O capability for large decision support applications.

The most "natural" use of the SP2 storage approach is for a given processing node to access the data from the controller local to it. This corresponds to the shared-nothing parallel architecture, and is in fact the approach taken by DB2/PE (see Section 9.2). However, IBM has also provided a level of software that permits efficient implementation of a shared disk architecture. Called *virtual shared disk* (VSD), this allows any processing node in the system to directly drive a controller located elsewhere in the system. Using the interconnection network as the data transfer mechanism, it is as if the processor were accessing a local disk when, in fact, it is accessing data located at some other remote node. VSD is part of the SP2 design philosophy to support both major scalable parallel database architectures. An example of a commercial parallel RDBMS product that utilizes a shared disk approach is Oracle (see Chapter 11). In fact, Oracle executes in parallel on an SP2 using VSD as its shared disk access mechanism.

Up to this point, we have spoken of a processing node as if it were a single CPU. Although that can be the case, the situation is richer than that, due to recent changes in the RS6000 workstation market. We remarked earlier that the SP2 processing nodes are very closely linked to RS6000 workstations executing AIX. For its workstation market, IBM has introduced a line of multiprocessing SMP-style products. Thus standard boards now include multiple cache-coherent CPUs, and these boards can now appear as single processing nodes in an SP2. In effect, an SP2 processing node can consist of multiple CPUs addressing a *locally* shared memory. The memories of distinct nodes are still distributed, and message passing over the HPS is still used to exchange data among nodes. Within a node, however, the memory is shared (in SMP fashion) among the CPUs at that node. This hardware configuration gives rise to a hybrid programming model: multithreaded shared memory *within* a node but distributed memory message passing *between* nodes. We discuss the software implications of this in the sections that follow.

The SP2 also has a number of enhancements to increase reliability and availability. We have already noticed such features in the network (alternate routing) and the disk storage architecture (RAID, dual controllers). It is important to distinguish between services provided directly by the system, on the one hand, and software executing in the application that utilizes these services, on the other. A division of responsibility exists, and the application must direct the action to be taken in response to the detection of error or component failure. The SP2 system services include a heartbeat (nodes periodically send status messages notifying neighbors that they are alive and well) and the ability to designate groups of processors (membership services) that can coordinate restart actions in response to a failure of one of their members. As noted, the application software is responsible for utilizing these services and directing the resultant recovery activity. Specific applications may or may not choose to make use of this infrastructure. Finally, as would be expected, the SP2 supports the full range of networking and connectivity options needed by a large IT installation. A list of hardware and software protocol standards supported includes Ethernet, FDDI, ATM, HiPPI, SNA, TCP/IP, NFS, AFS, DFS, and UDP/IP.

To summarize: The SP2 utilizes state-of-the-art RS6000 processors executing an industry standard version of Unix (AIX) as the individual processing nodes in a classic distributed memory architecture. A local nonshared disk at each node supports full virtual memory capabilities and permits individual nodes to execute standard AIX applications. A high-performance multistage switch network, the HPS, provides high-bandwidth, low-latency connectivity across the processor array. Partitioning tables (or striping files) across multiple RAID controllers enables the architecture to sustain very high aggregate I/O bandwidth to single tables. In addition to a shared-nothing approach natural to a DM machine, the SP2 also provides a virtual shared disk service (VSD) that can efficiently support a shared disk RDBMS software architecture. Because of its investment in software development tools for its HPC customers, the SP2 also provides an excellent environment for developing and executing customized data mining applications. The result is a scalable hardware platform very well suited to large decision support and data warehouse implementations.

9.2 SOFTWARE ARCHITECTURE OF DB2
PARALLEL EDITION

Just as the SP2 is based on and closely linked to the RS6000/AIX workstation, so DB2/PE is closely tied to the IBM DB2 product targeted at the RS6000. And just as the SP2 made extensions and modifications to its RS6000 baseline to facilitate scalable parallel processing, so DB2/PE required modifications and extensions to exploit the computational advantages of massively parallel processing. Before looking more closely at the internals, it should also be said that DB2/PE is capable of good performance on *both* decision support applications and traditional OLTP applications. Our focus here is on decision support and data warehouses, but there are many features and capabilities of DB2/PE that are not especially relevant for data warehouses but that would be relevant in an OLTP setting. The following discussion is not intended to be a comprehensive treatment of all of DB2/PE's strengths and features. Our focus is on decision support on large databases.

Using the taxonomy from Chapter 6, DB2/PE is a classic *shared-nothing* parallel RDBMS. The IBM terminology for this type of architecture is *function shipping*, and it is intended to contrast with a shared disk approach, which IBM refers to as *data shipping*. The idea behind this terminology is to "ship functionality" to where the data is rather than to "ship data" to where the functionality is. Recall, however, that both shared disk and shared-nothing architectures require extensive data movement across the interconnection network (for example, complex joins).

One intention of the DB2/PE approach was to reuse as much code and functionality from the original DB2 as possible. Our discussion in Chapter 6 on parallelizing the relational model shows that such an approach should work well. The computation is viewed as a succession of data exchanges (using data partitioning techniques and the interconnection network) followed by local scan–sort–join operations on co-located data at the individual processing nodes. These local operations are virtually identical to standard operations in a sequential database, so that extensive code reuse should be possible. The largest new items required for parallel execution include (1) data partitioning and redistribution algorithms and services, (2) query optimization, and (3) parallelized utilities. We discuss each in turn.

Data Partitioning and Redistribution

Data partitioning is at the heart of parallelizing a database, and IBM offers an approach with considerable flexibility. Partitioning a table across multiple disks is done by hashing on a user-specified key (which can span several columns). However, rather than hash directly to a disk storage node, the hashing function hashes to an intermediate logical structure containing 4096 "buckets." The buckets are then mapped, in a second stage under user control, to the actual storage nodes where the data will reside. This two-stage approach—first hash to a bucket, then map the bucket to a storage node—has the advantage that redistribution of data does not require rehashing of the data. Once a row has been hashed to its logical bucket, its storage location is subsequently and independently determined by the map assigning the bucket to a disk. If a bucket is assigned subsequently to a different disk (say, to add new disks or to rebalance the load), the underlying logical bucket number for the row has not changed.

To facilitate the bucket-to-disk mapping, DB2/PE has introduced the notion of *node groups*. A node group is a named subset of storage nodes, from as few as one to as many as the entire set of available disks, in any combination desired. When storage for a table is defined, the table is assigned to a named node group. This enables the system to create the map from the hashing buckets to the storage nodes. If at a later time the set of nodes in the node group changes, or if a different named node group is desired for the table, the system can (1) redefine the bucket-to-disk map, and (2) rearrange the data on the new set of disks accordingly. Note that rehashing of the data is *not* required.

In addition, two SQL extensions are available to make use of this two-level mapping capability: NODE and PARTITION. The NODE scalar function returns the node number to which the row has been assigned, and PARTITION returns the logical bucket assigned by the hashing function. This enables rapid queries for counts based on node number, so that data skew can be detected quickly. By redefining the bucket-to-node map, data skewing can be corrected.

As we have said, for large data warehouse applications we will usually want to partition a table over the entire set of available disks so as to obtain the greatest possible I/O bandwidth. Thus our default is a node group consisting of all disks. In other types of applications (for example, OLTP), the ability to form disjoint node groups could be of value. Separate tables could then be accessed independently, a useful capability for interquery parallelism (see the discussion in Chapter 5). In decision support, where intraquery parallelism is the main goal, partitioning of tables across partial subsets of disks does not appear to offer any advantage.

During the course of executing a join, all the join options discussed in Chapter 7 are available. The data can be redistributed using a hash key, followed by a co-located local join (called a *redistribution join*). Alternatively, if one (*directed join*) or both (*co-located join*) of the tables are already partitioned based on the join key, one or both of the data transfers can be avoided (since the data is already appropriately distributed). Finally, it is possible to replicate a copy of a small table at all nodes (called a *broadcast join* in DB2/PE parlance).

To perform the necessary data redistribution functions, a number of internal services have been provided. One of the most interesting is *table queues*. Conceptually, we think of the results of a local scan/join operation completing before the next data redistribution function begins. In fact, part of the table may be available for processing before the entire table has been completed. Thus a table queue can be thought of as an intermediate table whose rows are available for processing as soon as they have been completed. Both "send" and "get" (push or pull) styles of access to the queue are supported, and the HPS is used as the data-exchange mechanism.

The use of table queues supports pipelined parallelism (see the discussion in Chapter 5); subsequent stages in the processing sequence can begin before the prior stages are complete. As we noted at the time, however, this kind of parallelism is more appropriate to interquery parallelism, where the latency of a single small query is of most concern. In the processing of a large query using intraquery parallelism, all processors typically work on a single stage until all have completed, at which point a data exchange occurs (see Figure 5–6). Thus for large decision support applications, table queues are of most interest as the means by which table repartitioning and redistribution is carried out.

Query Optimization

Two significant areas of choice for the query optimizer are (1) the sequence in which joins are performed, and (2) aggregation strategies. We look at each in turn.

Concerning join sequences, it is often the case that queries can be logically restructured to produce the same result but using alternative internal sequences of join–select operations. The job of the query optimizer is to consider these possible sequences and to choose the one that is "best." In our discussion of these issues in Chapter 7, we implicitly assumed that all the nodes would participate in the query. In DB2/PE, however, the introduction of node groups complicates this assumption. A base table may be stored on a *subset* of nodes (the node group), and the associated node groups for different tables need not be the same (they may be identical, or they may overlap, or they may be disjoint). All of this greatly increases the number of possible join options (as opposed to our implied case, which was that all the nodes always participate). To simplify this, DB2/PE does not attempt to try every possible join data redistribution option. Rather, it considers using only the nodes where one or the other table currently resides (especially valuable if the partitioning key matches the current join key on one of the tables), or it considers using all the available nodes (that is, even if the tables are locally grouped entering into the join, the redistribution will result in the table being spread over the entire processor array).

The DB2/PE optimizer is able to optimize either against time or against resource utilization. In the first case, the optimizer chooses the plan resulting in the fastest time to complete the query. In the second case, it chooses the plan that utilizes the least amount of system resources (memory, temporary disk, and so on). The first is more appropriate for large decision support queries; the second is more appropriate for OLTP. In making its estimates, the query optimizer uses full knowledge both of how the data is distributed and of the cost associated with data communications over the HPS. This overhead includes the amount of data to be sent (raw bandwidth) as well as estimates for contention and latency overheads. By adjusting internal parameters, the optimizer can be "tuned" for the specific SP2 configuration and for the specific data partitioning and storage allocation policy. As with the DB2 optimizer on which it is based, a *greedy* heuristic is used to locally optimize execution strategies,

There are a number of global SQL operations (COUNT, GROUP BY, and so on) that require coordination among the various nodes participating in the operation. The fewer the nodes, the less overhead associated with (say) obtaining a global sum by aggregating the local sums held in each node. The query optimizer is able to select the appropriate global aggregation function and to incorporate its costs (time, resources) in its cost estimates. The need to use these global aggregation functions is one source of overhead in parallel computations not faced by serial processes. Deciding when and how to implement these operations is properly part of the optimization task, and the overhead associated with these operations is also taken into account by the optimization algorithm.

Parallelized Utilities

In addition to complex query processing, most data warehouse implementations will require support for heavy-lifting operations (such as bulk loads and deletes). In a parallel system, this means that these operations should be parallelized. For loading, two different strategies are supported by DB2. In the first, a single large flat file is input, and all the storage nodes assigned to the table cooperate in partitioning the input data stream and appending the new data to the end of the existing table. In the second, utilities external to the DB2/PE proper, but provided with the system, can externally partition a large file into many separate files, corresponding to the internal partitioning scheme supported by DB2/PE. These files can then be read and processed independently by the storage nodes. This enables the input itself to be parallelized, and hence greatly increases the achievable bandwidth. In the next section we mention the ability of an interface to the parallel file system to support high-bandwidth external interfaces.

As discussed above, the two-level bucket-to-disk table partitioning scheme supports efficient data reorganization as a result of upgrades to the system configuration. Thus as new disk space is added, the database is able to reorganize the data across the new storage efficiently and in parallel, using the notion of node groups. Similarly, tables can be reorganized to account for data skew (as discussed above) by explicitly modifying the bucket-to-disk map structure, or to achieve specific application objectives. The PARTITION and NODE scalar extensions to SQL are useful for this task.

Backup and Restore operations function on a node-by-node basis. Parallelism is limited only by the number of backup devices available, and multiple nodes can be backed up concurrently. Restoration, in turn, requires that the restored partitions be consistent across the node group(s) holding the restored table(s). This can be accomplished procedurally (always reload the entire database) or by using the database logs to roll forward to a specific point in time. Clearly, when an error occurs at a particular node, it is preferable to restore just that node (using the logs to roll forward to point in time consistency) rather than restoring the entire database. A related operational approach is to back-up only *some* of the nodes each night, on a rotating basis. Adding finer granularity to the backup function accelerates the restore operation, since only the (hopefully small) part of the database that has been affected by the error need be restored. Coming releases will provide additional capability in this area.

Finally, as we discussed in Section 9.1, the SP2 provides an infrastructure based on which high-availability software can be constructed. DB2/PE is able to take advantage of these services. An example of such a service is HACMP (high-availability cluster multiprocessing). Availability can also be achieved by the use of on-line spares. The functionality of failed nodes is taken on by the spare node, which is mapped into the node group and given a copy of the failed node's local tables. Again, the flexibility of the two-level bucket-to-disk mapping scheme is apparent.

To summarize: DB2/PE exhibits a classic shared-nothing software architecture. The various algorithmic techniques discussed in Chapters 5 through 8 apply directly here, including the use of hashing for data partitioning and distribution. Each local node of the system executes software very similar to DB2, and this is then supplemented by message-passing software (called *table queues*) to support the necessary data redistribution stages. A two-level scheme to support data partitions offers considerable flexibility in being able to configure and reconfigure data layout with a minimum of impact to ongoing operations. Finally, a robust collection of fully parallelized utilities provides the necessary support for large data warehouse operations.

9.3 CONSIDERATIONS

The architectural overview of DB2/PE in Section 9.2 does not address many of the features that any database management system should provide to be useful in a commercial IT setting. IBM products are well known for both the range and robustness of these features, and DB2/PE is no exception. For example, client applications and external systems are provided with several connectivity options, including *ODBC (open database connectivity* standard) and *DRDA* (IBM's protocol that permits connectivity between different databases). Many data warehouse operations are now charging usage time back to client departments, and accounting software is available to support that capability. A query governor is available to detect the presence of queries that are especially long-running or that are otherwise utilizing system resources excessively (for example, locks held, rows accessed, CPU time). The priority of the query can be adjusted or other action taken in response. System management tools are available to provide immediate interactive display of and access to the system state. Although these items are not uniquely parallel, they show that parallel implementations such as DB2/PE have the "industrial-strength" features that large IT customers have come to expect.

The product itself is fully supported and subject to an ongoing process of enhancement and extension. As this book goes to press, areas where performance improvements have taken place include support for outer joins, support for CASE expressions, a local bypass feature that allows a query to execute to completion within a single node for high-selectivity queries, optimizations reflecting improved use of the second-level cache, and support for RAID level 5 in the SSA controllers (*not* specific to DB2/PE but of importance to data warehouse implementations). IBM has also announced that *DB2 Common Server* (the workstation version) and DB2/PE products will shortly be coming together into a single product line called *DB2 Universal Database*. This will include support for objects (see Chapter 15), OLAP, web functionality, and JAVA. The release is targeted for 4Q97. Interested readers can find additional information about *DB2 Universal Database* at *www.software.ibm.com/data*.

An area we have not discussed, but which deserves attention in the context of large decision support and data mining applications, is the availability of a parallel file system. Unlike other RDBMSs, DB2 and DB2/PE use the Unix file system (that is, AIX) to retrieve and buffer the data. Thus, instead of managing raw disk partitions, the software utilizes the file capabilities of the operating system. This is possible because, over time, IBM has invested considerable effort in making Unix industrial strength. The AIX file system is fully journaled, supports both mirroring and striping, and operates on both large files (up to 64 GB) and large file systems (up to 1 TB). The 64-bit AIX extensions provide an evolutionary entree to greater levels of performance.

A key software component in this strategy is the development of a fully parallel high-performance file system. Although this is especially useful for the high-performance scientific part of the SP2 market, it is also of interest for large database and data mining implementations. The potential (which at this writing is not yet a supported capability) is to provide a simple interface between the database, on the one hand, and large data mining application codes, on the other. The issue is that SQL does not inherently provide a parallel interface to large tables produced as the result of complex queries. The computational model provided by SQL is one in which the output is sequentialized in client–server fashion and returned to the user's application serially. A parallel file system, on the other hand, is capable of striping large flat files over many (hundreds) of disk controllers so as to enable high bandwidth disk I/O. This capability is critical for large scientific codes and would also be useful for many types of data mining algorithms not easily expressible in SQL. What we envision, then, is a direct interface between the RDBMS and the file system, which, in turn, is used by the data mining applications as its data access mechanism.

Certainly with the introduction of its next-generation parallel file system, the SP2 will have all the pieces in place to make this a reality. Fully parallelized global sorting, for example, could easily be implemented by moving back and forth between the internal database representation and the parallel flat file. This, in turn, would enable load-balanced range partitioning schemes, so that the RDBMS and data mining capabilities are working together in a seamless, coordinated fashion. This vision of the future of data warehouses is technically achievable and offers many commercial possibilities for the next level of capability in data exploration and exploitation.

We have seen that the RS6000 line is already making extensive use of SMP-style multiprocessing at the workstation and department server points of its product line. This, in turn, is now showing up in the SP2, as individual processing nodes are, themselves, fully parallelized SMPs operating on large shared memories within the node. This is architecturally similar to *clusters*, an approach to scalability that is used widely in commercial IT shops. In a cluster, individual SMPs are loosely coupled using LAN interconnection technologies, and with software support to balance the workload, enhance on-line redundancy and availability and provide shared access to storage. Interquery parallelism on clusters has been effective for some time, since extensive communications are not required (that is, the LAN level of interconnection technology is adequate). In replacing the LAN with the HPS, the SP2 is able to extend a cluster-style approach to effective intraquery parallelism. Just as DSM/NUMA architectures attempt to bring scalability to shared memory, the introduction of SMP nodes into the SP2 may be seen as an attempt to bring the benefits of a shared-memory programming style to what is an inherently scalable DM architecture. Thus both camps (DM and SMP) are pushing hard to incorporate into their offerings the benefits of the other. It will be interesting to observe the continuing evolution of the SP2, and in particular to see whether IBM will elect to take the final step toward a true DSM by extending a coherent address space across the entire machine.

The approach taken by DB2/PE to these changes in the underlying hardware architecture has been evolutionary. The first step (current implementation) is to treat each of the processing elements in the SMP node as if it were an independent distributed memory node. This is accomplished by providing each CPU with its own nonshared memory space within the large physically shared memory of the node. The chief enhancement is that when communications are between CPUs on the same SMP node, the interconnection switch is bypassed, and the data is exchanged using the shared memory. This reduces network traffic and has much lower latency than if message passing over the HPS were required. The next step (future) will be to treat each SMP node as a single entity (as opposed to separate entities, one per CPU), and to multithread the software at the SMP node. This step should not be difficult, since it is an easy transition from multiprocessing (which is already supported) to multithreading.

Chapter 10

Informix-OnLine XPS on a Hewlett-Packard 9000 EPS

This chapter provides an excellent example of a widely used architecture, *a cluster of SMPs*, that combines the characteristics of both shared memory (SMP) and distributed memory (DM) architectures. We shall see that Informix-OnLine XPS provides a shared-nothing software architecture that not only complements the DM characteristics of the hardware but also provides a multithreaded implementation that uses the resources of SMP machines efficiently. We shall also see that the HP 9000 EPS exploits both the favorable price–performance characteristics of SMP and the scalability of DM architectures, and integrates these two successfully into a single system. Successive sections cover the hardware architecture (Section 10.1), the software architecture (Section 10.2), and considerations (Section 10.3) on the general approach.

A Brief Architectural Digression

The hardware architecture of this example—a *cluster of SMPs*, or simply a *cluster*—represents a hybrid of the SMP and distributed memory (DM) architectures introduced in Chapters 1 and 2. The basic idea is simple—replace each single node in a DM architecture (recall Figure 2–1) with an SMP. Like a DM architecture, the address spaces of each node are still distinct; and like a DM architecture, message passing over the interconnection network is required to move data between distinct nodes. However, processors co-located within a single node can communicate using the shared memory of the SMP. Further, code executing within a single node can make use of threads and other SMP-style programming techniques. Based on the taxonomy introduced in Part I, we shall (somewhat arbitrarily) choose to regard a cluster of SMPs as an important subvariety of the basic DM architecture.

Using the ideas from Chapter 2, we recall that the performance of the interconnection network, in both latency and bandwidth, is often determinative of overall performance and scalability. Often, clusters of SMPs make use of commodity off-the-shelf LAN network technology as the interconnection mechanism. That is, rather than engineer a scalable high-performance network specifically for the parallel machine, clusters will utilize existing commercial interconnection technology supplemented by operating system and software devices to improve latency and bandwidth. With off-the-shelf networking now approaching 100 MB/sec, this is not nearly as liable to the charges of lack of performance as would have been the case, say, three or four years ago. Thus improvements in commodity networking can now be exploited to provide levels of interconnection bandwidth appropriate to true DM parallel processing.

A cluster represents an amalgam of SMP and DM ideas, and it is useful to compare it with the other major approach to such a merger, the DSM or NUMA architecture described in

Chapter 3. The primary difference between DSM and clusters is that DSM uses hardware (cache coherence directories) to make the existence of distributed memory transparent to the software; clusters do not. As a result, clusters present a unique challenge to the system software, which must contend simultaneously with both an SMP architecture within each node and a DM architecture among nodes. As we noted above, communication between two processors in the same node can utilize shared memory, whereas communications between processors on distinct nodes must rely on message passing. Clearly, clusters were not developed to make life simple for programmers!

What has led to their popularity are the dual forces of cost and scalability. An SMP machine with relatively few processors will typically be lower in cost than an equivalently configured MPP machine. This is because the SMP machine shares hardware components among several processors. However, as discussed in Chapter 1, this sharing of components in general, and the memory bus in particular, limits the scalability of SMP machines. As we noted earlier, however, scalability is the *forte* of DM architectures. Clusters attempt to take advantage of the best qualities of both SMP and DM architectures, but in a more simplistic way than do machines using a DSM architecture. Each SMP node within a cluster can be scaled up with additional processors to the limits of SMP; beyond that, several separate SMP nodes can be connected in an MPP fashion to scale beyond the limits inherent in the SMP architecture. Further cost reductions can be realized from the synergy of the two architectures. Knowing that the DM architecture can be relied upon to provide the needed scalability, the SMP nodes can be configured with relatively few processors, allowing the use of commodity backplane buses for memory access and cache coherence rather than more exotic (and more expensive) hardware.

Although the reasoning behind clusters is sound, many organizations have actually adopted clusters simply by default: They started out with their data warehouse on a low-cost SMP machine, and eventually outgrew it. In this situation, clusters represent an attractive growth alternative to discarding the initial machine in favor of an entirely new MPP machine. With this as background, we are ready to turn to a more detailed look at the hardware platform.

10.1 HARDWARE: HP 9000 ENTERPRISE PARALLEL SERVER

Like other major computer system manufacturers, Hewlett-Packard Company offers systems that range from low-cost machines for the desktop to high-end machines aimed at the most demanding technical and commercial computing applications. Our focus here is on the HP 9000 EPS family, which comprises a range of systems that use SMP machines as building blocks of larger systems. In particular, our focus is on a configuration that uses a midrange departmental server as the SMP building block, which HP calls their K-class machine. Although HP certainly makes more exotic (and more expensive) SMP machines, we will see that using fast, low-cost machines as building blocks and relying on clustering to scale-up performance results in systems suitable for very large data warehousing applications, yet with excellent price–performance characteristics.

Figure 10–1 depicts the HP 9000 EPS architecture. Each node is *functionally* an HP 9000 SMP machine, but *physically* the nodes and the Fibre Channel switch are packaged together in a small number of cabinets to reduce the total cost and footprint. More important, HP has provided support in both hardware and software to allow the multiple nodes to be managed as a single machine. This capability covers system management, system administration, network configuration, and performance monitoring. For example, HP's Multi-Computer System Environment allows systemwide monitoring of I/O activity on a single system console. Utilities to manage the resources within the system, such as job scheduling and load-balancing software, are also provided. HP calls this integrated cluster a "parallel SMP" machine. This integration is important to the success of the system because as we noted above, the mix of both SMP and DM architectures in clusters is visible to the software. If this complexity were, in turn, visible to system administrators, end users, and database applications, these machines would probably not be well received. By hiding most of this complexity under vendor-provided software, the integrated parallel SMP system avoids a major potential drawback of clusters.

Figure 10–1 HP 9000 EPS Architecture

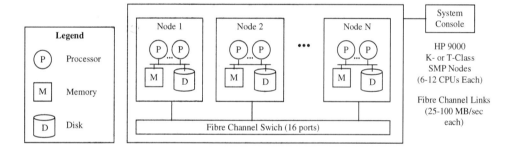

In the HP 9000 EPS, the SMP nodes are interconnected via Fibre Channel through a nonblocking switch. Each K-class node can contain up to six processors (12 processors using T-class machines). With a 16-port Fibre Channel switch, this means that a system configuration can be scaled from only a few processors up to hundreds of processors (12 × 16 = 192), depending on the requirements of the application. Fibre Channel is a standard, generic transport for networking and peripheral connection. Its low latency (10 microseconds) and high throughput (25 to 100 MB/sec per link) qualify it as a feasible MPP node interconnect. Fibre Channel supports several network topologies, including point-to-point, arbitrated loop, and cross-point switched. The HP 9000 EPS uses a cross-point switched topology, which gives each node the full interconnect bandwidth to any other node, without contention for either the network media or the switch. To support more than 16 nodes, a second level of switching is required.

Data transfers using Fibre Channel are memory-to-memory, requiring no CPU resources for the transfer itself. In addition, HP provides lightweight communication protocols that keep the total communications overhead low. For example, by taking advantage of the reliable message delivery provided by Fibre Channel, these protocols do not have to include lengthy code paths to identify and retransmit lost packets as general-purpose protocols must. These are the types of recent advances in commodity network technology that have enabled interconnection performance adequate for large-scale parallel implementations.

Looking inside each node, we see that the K-class machines use a simple, fast bus architecture, depicted in Figure 10–2. The emphasis within a node is not just performance, but *price–performance*. Although this architecture can accommodate relatively few processors (see Chapter 1), it is less expensive than the crossbar-switch architecture used in HP's higher-end machines. The idea is to use proven technologies to keep costs down in each SMP node and to add nodes to scale up to large configurations.

The two caches per processor, one for instructions and one for data, help reduce the demand on the shared memory. The primary caches in this system are 1 MB each, reflecting the belief of the PA-RISC designers that large primary caches are essential for good performance. Rather than squeeze a small amount of primary cache on the CPU chip, the designers elected to place all cache off-chip, where it can be made larger. Single clock cycle access between the CPU and cache is achieved by tightly integrating both of these into a small module that is used, in turn, as a component in building the system. The PA-8000 CPU itself is a state-of-the-art, 64-bit superscalar RISC processor capable of executing four instruc-

Figure 10–2 Block Diagram of an HP 9000 K-Class SMP Node

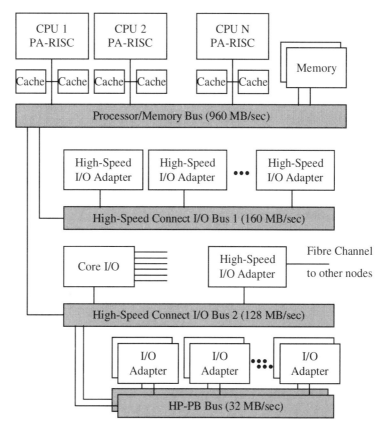

tions simultaneously. Cache coherence between processors is maintained by a snoopy protocol on the backplane bus. Thus each HP 9000 EPS node conforms exactly to the ideas introduced in Chapter 1.

SCSI disks can be connected to the built-in fast/wide/differential SCSI port on the core I/O adapter, and by plugging SCSI adapters into the any of the high-speed I/O (HP-HSC) adapter slots. On the K460 machines, there are five HP-HSC slots; one is needed for the Fibre Channel adapter, leaving four for SCSI adapters. A reasonably configured K460 machine, then, might have five SCSI channels. This is not a large number of channels, but at 20 MB/sec each, this provides 100 MB/sec of I/O throughput per node. Using HP's high-availability disk arrays, which hold 20 disks each, gives us 100 disks for data storage while maintaining a dedicated SCSI channel for each disk array. With today's 4-GB+ disks, one can reasonably put 0.5 TB of disk on each node, for total system storage in the multiterabyte range. Adding multiple arrays per SCSI channel can increase disk storage capacity by another factor of 10.

Note, however, that even with a dedicated SCSI channel per disk array, the available bandwidth from the disks far exceeds the bandwidth supportable by the I/O channel. It seems clear that Fibre Channel attached disks could help each node achieve higher I/O bandwidth, which is critical for data warehousing applications. Currently, HP supports use of the Fibre Channel adapter only for connecting EPS nodes. With this technology in hand, however, it is likely that they will support the use of this adapter in the near future for attaching disks as well. In any case, it is important to note that additional nodes provide additional I/O bandwidth, not just additional processing power. Thus if I/O bandwidth is a driving requirement (as it often is in large DSS environments), the number of nodes may be driven as much by the number of I/O channels needed as by the number of processors needed. As a rule of thumb, we suggest maintaining a ratio of at least 200 MB/sec *sustained* I/O bandwidth per terabyte of disk storage, not just for HP systems but for any large data warehouse. One way to remember this ratio is that the entire disk storage system should be readable in about an hour and a half.

HP began building SMP systems in the late 1980s and has made good use of the experience they have accumulated since then. For example, their Unix operating system, HP/UX, has evolved to be more efficient for SMP through finer granularity of the kernel processes. This finer granularity prevents one processor from holding onto key system resources for too long, which would cause other processors to stall while waiting for the resource. As observed in Chapter 1, there are many aspects of the operating system that can dramatically affect scalability of performance within the SMP node as additional CPUs are added. The HP/UX product incorporates lessons learned over the past decade to achieve smooth speed-up and utilization curves as processors are added to each node.

Two recent announcements show the direction of HP's thinking in the highly competitive parallel server market. First, HP's recent acquisition of Convex has provided HP with technology for high-end SMP systems that is already reflected in HP's technical computing servers. This same technology is finding its way into HP's commercial product line. The high-end Exemplar machines use a true NUMA architecture, so that HP is now well positioned to pursue DSM technology for database servers should it choose to do so. Second, HP and Intel are jointly pursuing development of a common processor architecture (IA-64), which would be used by both companies (Intel will manufacture the processors). The market credibility and cost advantages resulting from this effort should benefit the entire HP computing product line. In particular, high manufacturing volumes are critical to reducing processor costs, and there is no better place to find high volumes than the market for personal computers based on Intel processors. Market analysts have reacted positively to the HP/Intel alliance.

10.2 SOFTWARE: INFORMIX-ONLINE XPS ARCHITECTURE

In 1991, Informix redesigned the architecture of their OnLine DBMS product in anticipation of the need to support parallel hardware architectures. This new "Dynamic Scalable Architecture" made its debut in Version 7 of their OnLine product and gave Informix the stable foundation needed to build parallel implementations that have been at the forefront of the parallel DBMS industry. The first of these, Informix-OnLine

Dynamic Server, targeted decision support (in addition to traditional OLTP) on shared-memory machines. OnLine Dynamic Server put all the resources of an SMP machine to work on a single query and achieved industrywide recognition for the speed of its parallel scans and the completeness of the parallel implementation. The second of these, Informix-OnLine Extended Parallel Server (XPS), targeted distributed memory machines, including both MPP and clustered SMP systems. OnLine XPS provides a true *shared-nothing* database architecture and parallel SQL operations to deliver high performance, scalability, and fault tolerance. Because the shared-nothing architecture of Online XPS maps directly to the distributed memory architecture of MPP and clustered SMP machines, the scalability advantages of the underlying hardware are fully realized. And because OnLine XPS leverages the heritage of OnLine Dynamic Server, it is also able to exploit parallel processing efficiently *within* a single SMP node. It is this dual ability to exploit both shared memory and distributed memory architectures that makes OnLine XPS particularly well suited for use on clusters. In the following paragraphs we dive progressively deeper into the architecture of OnLine XPS to understand how parallelism is supported at the system, node, and processor levels.

Cooperating Co-servers

At the system level, Informix XPS provides a single-system image to end users and applications issuing SQL queries. Thus the complexity of the clustered SMP architecture is completely hidden from view. Hiding these complexities "under the covers" allows applications to remain unchanged in the face of changes to the physical data layout as disks, processors, or whole nodes are added. Within the system, however, remember that each SMP node is essentially an independent machine. Informix retains this independence in the DBMS software. Each node in a cluster executes its own instance of the DBMS services (called a *co-server*) for logging, recovery, lock management, and buffer management. Although it would be possible (indeed, simpler) to centralize these functions on a single node, serializing these control functions would eventually limit scalability, even if queries themselves were handled completely in parallel.

To provide the image of a single large server, one resource, the system catalog, must be logically centralized. This is because the catalog describes how data are distributed across nodes. Note that the catalog will naturally be needed by every node executing a query and thus will have a high access rate. To optimize performance, the catalog is cached across all nodes.

True to the shared-nothing architecture, each co-server "owns" a set of disks and the partitions of the database that reside on these disks, as depicted in Figure 10–3. A co-server will typically have physical access to other disks owned by other co-servers for fail-over purposes, but in normal operation, each co-server will access only those disks that it owns. OnLine XPS provides both partitioning and replication to fully enable parallelism. *Partitioning* (or in Informix's nomenclature, *fragmentation*) allows very large tables to be divided

Figure 10–3   Independent Co-servers in Informix-OnLine XPS Architecture

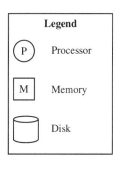
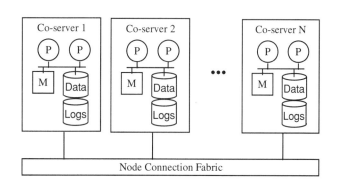

across multiple nodes in a true shared-nothing structure, and (as we discussed in Part II) is the fundamental mechanism for enabling scalable parallel data access. At the other extreme, *replication* can be used to provide local copies of small, frequently used tables (such as a state code-to-state name lookup table) on each node to minimize internode traffic.

Different clients can connect to different co-servers (see Figure 10–4). The co-server to which a client is connected manages execution of the query, including coordinating the activities of other co-servers that own data needed by the query. This coordination is achieved by making intelligent decisions about how to divide a query and where to send the SQL operations to be performed on different nodes. The OnLine XPS services responsible for making such decisions include the request manger, the query optimizer, the metadata manger, and the scheduler. These services are tightly integrated into the core of OnLine XPS.

Figure 10–4 Structure of Services in Informix XPS Architecture

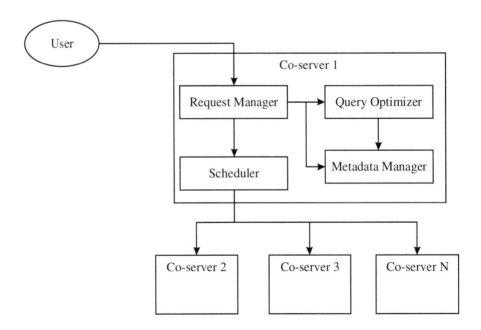

The request manager is responsible for overall management of the query, including coordinating with request managers on other co-servers needed by the query. The query optimizer is responsible for determining the best way to perform a query, such as the order in which tables are read, how they are read (by index or sequentially), and how they are joined with other tables in the query. The query optimizer is "parallel aware" and considers the effects of parallelism in calculating the cost of alternate query plans. The metadata manager stores (among other things) information about how data is distributed across nodes for use by the query optimizer. The scheduler is responsible for activating the query plan such that the proper resources are locally available. Note that as discussed in Chapter 6, the role of the scheduler is particularly important in a parallel system because of the need to balance the processing load.

Iterators, Virtual Processors, and Threads

To fully exploit the underlying parallelism of a clustered system, OnLine XPS employs several complementary mechanisms, including iterators, virtual processors, and threads. *Iterators* are the primary logical mechanism for decomposing a single query into its basic components for parallel execution. Iterators perform functions such as scanning, joining, grouping, sorting, and merging streams of data. As depicted in Figure 10–5, they may be connected together within a dataflow model (see the discussion of parallelism in the relational model in Chapter 5). Connecting iterators together in sequence enables pipeline parallelism, while replicating the iterators enables partitioned parallelism (Informix calls these *vertical parallelism* and *horizontal parallelism*). The dataflow model makes it easy to spawn as many iterators as can usefully be employed in executing a query. The key to horizontal parallelism in this model is a special *exchange* iterator. The exchange iterator is inserted by the query optimizer to reparti-

Figure 10–5 Interserver and Intraserver Parallelism

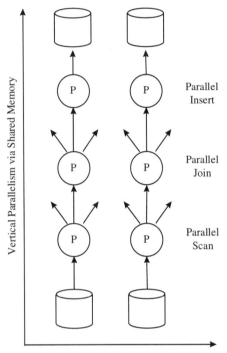

tion data and redistribute it to other iterators (possibly on other nodes) for further processing.

Note that an exchange is another name for the "shuffle" discussed in Chapter 5 (see, for example, Figure 5–6). Because an exchange frequently deals with large volumes of intermediate results, efficiency in the underlying communications mechanism is paramount. Again, we find that the dual nature of clusters asserts itself. Somehow, we must achieve optimal communications among processors within a node (intraserver) as well as across multiple nodes (interserver). OnLine XPS uses shared memory with pointer passing for intraserver communications, and message passing for interserver communications. By providing these two types of communication, OnLine XPS is able efficiently to exploit the parallel resources of clusters. OnLine XPS also provides SQL extensions that can reduce the communications traffic between processors and, more important, between nodes. For example, the "FIRST n" clause allows the user to request only a few records of interest (say, the top 10 best-selling products); the rest may simply be discarded along the way.

Although cooperating co-servers could be used to manage separate processors within a single SMP node, doing so would not be efficient. We would be unnecessarily duplicating code and data structures that are easily held in common in the shared memory of a node. Instead, OnLine XPS uses the concept of virtual processors and threads to manage the processing resources of a node. *Threads* are "lightweight" processes in the sense that they consume fewer resources (CPU and memory) when manipulated than do regular "heavyweight" Unix processes (recall the discussion in Section 1.3). Multiple threads are easily spawned and assigned to available hardware processors to perform any needed function, such as processing the I/O requests associated with a scan. Threads are owned and managed by *virtual processors* in the DBMS software rather than by the operating system. Besides fulfilling the parental role of keeping track of threads, virtual processes provide a convenient mechanism for managing the resources of the machine. For example, the number of virtual processes can be configured through parameters of OnLine XPS to control the resources consumed by various functions of the DBMS, or by the DBMS as a whole. The latter is particularly useful if the DBMS must share the machine with other programs.

Data and Control Partitioning

We have already discussed how XPS supports query partitioning through the use of iterators. But effective parallelization of a query requires partitioning not only of query execution, but data and control as well. In Chapter 7 we discussed several data partitioning strategies, including *range partitioning, round-robin partitioning,* and *hash partitioning.* Online XPS supports all of these. In addition, OnLine XPS supports *expression partitioning.* This is similar to range partitioning, but the partitioning key need not be ordered. This allows, for example, partitioning on the state in which a customer is located. The partitioning expression is defined in the same way as the WHERE clause of an SQL query. Of particular interest for cluster architectures is *hybrid partitioning.* This allows different partitioning strategies to be used within a node and across nodes. For example, hash partitioning can be used to minimize data skew across nodes, while range partitioning can be used to optimize I/O efficiency within a node. This combination has proved to be effective in common decision support queries.

As mentioned earlier, each co-server in OnLine XPS runs its own services for logging, recovery, lock management, and buffer management. This partitioning of control is essential to fully exploit shared-nothing hardware architectures. Partitioned logging and recovery is the enabling mechanism for parallel backup and restore. Partitioned lock management is a natural outcome of a shared-nothing software architecture, and eliminates the potential bottleneck of a central lock manager. Partitioned buffer management is also a natural outcome of a shared-nothing software architecture, and allows each co-server to manage the memory resources on its node as it sees fit.

10.3 CONSIDERATIONS

In the next few paragraphs we revisit some of the implications of the cluster architecture as exemplified by a the HP 9000 EPS. Under the general heading of scalability, we will consider two issues: balance, and limitations at the upper end. That is, we say that an architecture is scalable if it is able to maintain *balance* between system performance measures over the range of its configurations. We also say that an architecture is scalable if it is able to sustain its performance up to very large configurations.

Under the heading of balanced architectures, we observe that a cluster architecture offers a great variety of configuration options. To illustrate this point, observe that a total of (say) 48 processors can be obtained in a variety of ways: four cabinets with 12 processors each; six cabinets with eight processors; eight cabinets with six processors; 12 cabinets with four processors; 16 cabinets with three processors. We cannot have more than 16 cabinets, since the Fibre Channel switch supports only 16 ports; and we cannot have fewer than four cabinets, since each cabinet will hold no more than 12 processors.

What are the relative strengths and weaknesses of these configurations? In terms of total computing power, more cabinets will tend to be better than fewer. First, each cabinet can be configured with its maximum memory and its maximum I/O capacity. Thus for a fixed number of processors, having fewer processors per cabinet and more cabinets increases the balance between the number of processors and (1) the amount of memory and (2) both storage capacity and I/O bandwidth. The same is true of total network bandwidth: Since each cabinet has its own port into the switch, increasing the number of cabinets automatically increases the amount of network bandwidth.

To summarize this phenomenon briefly, five important system parameters—memory, memory bandwidth, storage capacity, disk I/O bandwidth, and network bandwidth—scale with the cabinet count (that is, the number of SMPs in the cluster) rather than with processor count. Keeping the number of cabinets constant and increasing the number of CPUs has no effect on these important measures. Thus in considering a cluster configuration for high-end DS applications, we will often be considering many sparsely populated cabinets, each configured for maximum memory, disk storage, and I/O bandwidth. In this way, effective balance among the components can be maintained.

In terms of top-end architecture limitations, the single shared resource in the cluster configuration is the 16-port Fibre Channel switch. Recent TPC-D benchmarks demonstrate effective scaling to 300-GB databases using 48 processors (using 12 SMP cabinets with four processors each). As the switch size increases (say, to 32 ports) and the speed of each link increases (say, from 25 MB/sec to 100 MB/sec), balanced configurations of a couple of hundred processors should be possible.

Beyond that there are two possible options. One is to increase the number of CPUs per cabinet but at the expense of maintaining overall balance among performance metrics. The other option is to scale the network to larger configurations. As described in Chapter 2, one approach to achieving this goal is to introduce a second (or third) level in the switching hierarchy. That is, instead of ports routing to SMP cabinets, some ports in each switch are used to route to other switches at higher levels in a multistage switch network (MSSN). Although this is possible *in theory*, it is not currently a supported product offering from HP, and the reason is clear. With a single switch, systems can be configured that handle very large databases easily. Only a small number of customers will need configurations beyond 3 or 4 TB (300 GB active data), already within the reach of the clustered HP approach. Thus, in the absence of market pressure, there appears to be no good reason to introduce the additional complexity and expense of multistage switches. For most data warehouses, a cluster of (say) 12 cabinets with four CPUs per cabinet will be more than adequate.

In the past (see, for example, the discussion in Chapter 1), clusters have been subject to the charge of inadequate network interconnection bandwidth. Clusters tended to use LAN technology and associated high-overhead, high-latency communication protocols. This, in turn, meant that a "LAN of SMPs" could not match the performance characteristics of a true DM architecture which included a high-bandwidth, low-latency interconnection network. Recently, however, this balance has changed dramatically. Commodity interconnection approachs (such as Fibre Channel, SCI, SSA, and ultra-SCSI) now offer off-the-shelf performance characteristics approaching those of custom implementations, but at a more attractive cost. The HP 9000 EPS of this example shows that, in effect, a high-performance DM architecture can be constructed using commodity parts. Just as microprocessors have, over the years, crept up on and even surpassed traditional mainframe technologies, so commodity networking is now encroaching from below on bandwidth and latency performance levels previously reserved for proprietary interconnection schemes.

The result is that it is now possible to build a supercomputer with reasonable balance between processing power, memory bandwidth, I/O bandwidth, and interconnection netowork latency and bandwidth from off-the-shelf components. The only thing missing from this mix is the software (file systems, compilers, libraries, profilers, and debuggers) that the traditional supercomputer market has demanded. As we have observed several times elsewhere, these facilities are also of great benefit to the development of high-performance custom data mining algorithms: Building a data warehouse on a platform that also has good code development facilities will facilitate the construction of powerful data mining and knowledge extraction algorithms not easily implemented directly from SQL.

When we consider the HP family, we see at the top end the Exemplar architecture. The Exemplar was developed by Convex Computers (now a wholly owned subsidiary of HP) and was originally targeted at the scientific computing market. The Exemplar is a true NUMA architecture (see Chapter 3), with directory-based cache coherence extending across multiple cabinets. To date, HP has elected not to port any of the large database products to the Exemplar. Even so, the Exemplar technologies (compilers, operating system, libraries, and so on) are now available at lower points in the product family line. Thus HP is well positioned to bring to market the kind of fully integrated data warehouse + data mining system that we have recommended.

The remaining missing piece in this hypothetical system is a fully parallelized interface between the RDBMS—in our present context, Informix-OnLine XPS—and the native parallel file system of the hardware platform. The absence of such an interface is not unique to Informix; it is a capability not currently supported by any of the large RDBMS suppliers, nor by any included in our set of examples. In the meantime, data mining will be limited either to operating on small data extracts or to living with the bottleneck of sequentialized output which is part of the SQL standard.

To summarize: For large data warehouses, scalability is a significant factor affecting market penetration. SMPs are now addressing the charge of lack of scalability by, in effect, turning themselves into DM machines through the use of commodity interconnection technologies. The levels of latency and bandwidth performance offered by these off-the-shelf network components is such that quite capable configurations can be assembled with a minumum of proprietary hardware. Nonrecurring engineering (NRE) costs are minimized, as is time-to-market. The resulting "cluster of SMPs" architecture, as exemplified by the HP 9000 EPS considered in this chapter, can achieve not only excellent *price* performance but also high *absolute* performance, enough to be a serious contender for large DS applications.

Standard parallel RDBMS products with a shared-nothing architecture, such as Informix-OnLine XPS considered here, can easily take full advantage of clusters because of their close architectural resemblance to DM machines. OnLine XPS has the added advantage that it is multithreaded, so it can effectively utilize the parallel hardware within each SMP node. The resulting HW/SW combination is a formidable entry in the lucrative and expanding data warehouse market.

Oracle 7 Executing on a Sun Starfire Ultra Enterprise 10000

Readers who, attracted perhaps by the celebrity of Oracle in the IT world, turned to this chapter first and thus are unacquainted with the preceding material will find that they have missed an interesting "plot line" that can only be appreciated by first becoming moderately familiar with the SMP-DM-NUMA hardware approaches discussed in Part I and the SE-SD-SN software approaches discussed primarily in Chapter 6. Although it may appear presumptuous to claim a plot line for a technical book such as this, there is genuine drama in what we are about to examine: a *real* technical problem, with an *ingenious* technical solution, and a large payoff hanging in the balance. For those who follow the high-tech world at all, this is better than a John D. MacDonald potboiler.

The technical problem was neatly summed up in Chapters 1 (on SMPs) and 2 (on DMs). SMPs (so the argument went) have a great programming model but are not scalable, due to the presence of a shared memory bus backplane that imposes architecturally inherent limits on achievable memory bandwidth. DMs address the scalability issue by providing nonshared memory bandwidth to each node in the parallel array; what they give up is the convenience of a shared memory programming style: They must rely, instead, on message passing. As we also saw (Chapter 3), attempts to marry these two approaches (DSM/NUMA architectures) have a kind of schizophrenia: True shared memory programming runs the (serious) risk of poor performance due to the nonuniform nature of the memory latency hierarchy. In Part II we saw how the various software architectures map onto these hardware architectures (at least at an abstract level), and concluded that the SE/SMP combination did not appear to be sufficiently scalable to serve as a platform for a data warehouse.

In this chapter we have to eat those words. Oracle (a shared-everything software architecture) executing on a Sun Starfire Ultra Enterprise 10000 (a uniform memory access SMP-style hardware platform) has demonstrated world-class performance on the TPC-D benchmark suite and (in our opinion) is worthy of serious consideration by any organization interested in large-scale decision support. In the remainder of this chapter we explore in some detail exactly how and why this dramatic reversal has taken place. We shall find that the hardware internals of the Starfire have enabled the machine to circumvent the memory bandwidth bottleneck characteristic of traditional bus-based SMP architectures. We shall also see how this hardware technology has been fully exploited by the Oracle shared-everything software approach. Let this, then, be an object lesson to anyone who thinks there is nothing new under the sun and that technology can't be full of surprises.

11.1 THE SUN STARFIRE ULTRA ENTERPRISE 10000

The Sun Starfire Ultra Enterprise 10000 (that is, the *Starfire*) is the flagship of the Sun line of servers. Fully binary compatible up and down the line (based on the SPARC instruction set and using SPARC processors), the Starfire gives Sun a credible entry at the enterprise server level of performance, reliability, and industrial-strength IT features. The history of the Starfire is interesting and permits some insight into how the architecture came into its present form. Most recently, the ancestor of the Starfire was a product of Cray Research (the Minneapolis-based supercomputer firm founded by the high-performance guru Seymour Cray). When Cray Research was acquired by Silicon Graphics in mid-1996, the Starfire was separated off and sold directly to Sun. Thus the Starfire has a hybrid heritage: the high-performance emphasis of Cray Research (that was then), and the business and commercial savvy and marketing clout of Sun (this is now). This has been good for both sides, and the Starfire is another example of a parallel processor which has shown that it can pay its way by providing real business value in commercial accounts.

An Architectural Detour

To appreciate the significance of the Sun Starfire Ultra Enterprise 10000, we must briefly revisit some architectural issues first addressed in Chapter 1. There, we observed two things (see Figure 1–3). First, we saw that bus and memory bandwidth are an inherent architecture limitation for backplane bus SMPs. Second, we saw that a shared bus, in particular, is essential to the standard snoopy protocol used for cache coherence. The significance of the Starfire is the way in which they have broken through this bottleneck to provide extremely high levels of uniform memory and disk I/O bandwidth.

By way of background, consider Figure 11–1. This shows a top-level block diagram of an architecture that has been around since the mid-1970's, the *dance hall architecture*. The motivation for the terminology is an old-style square dance, in which the men (processors?) line up opposite the women (memory banks?); the interconnection network is the dance floor, and the idea is that *any pairing of partners* is permitted. In technospeak, it is possible for any set of processors simultaneously to access any set of memory banks, provided only that no two processors access the same memory (that is, two gents can't both dance with the same lady at the same time).

Figure 11–1 Generic Dance Hall Architecture

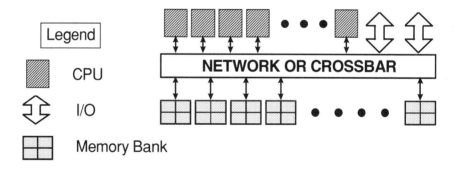

Some observations about this architecture. First, the notion of *memory banks* is important. While memory is logically a single extent, physically it has been broken into separate chunks each with a port into the network. This means that multiple memory banks can be active simultaneously, thereby increasing total available memory bandwidth. Although this structure is not shown in Figure 1–3 (which shows a single block of memory), in fact the physical implementation of memories in SMPs makes use of this concept. The logical memory address space is physically interleaved over many memory banks in exactly the same way that a single logical file can be striped across many disks.

What makes the dance hall architecture different from an ordinary SMP is that the processors are connected to the memory banks using the crossbar (or interconnection network). In a traditional SMP (like that shown in Figure 1–3), the system bus is used to connect the processors to the memories. Since only one processor can use the bus at a time, the bus bandwidth becomes a shared resource and hence a bottleneck setting a limit on scalability. The dance hall architecture does not have this restriction. As we saw in Chapter 2, interconnection networks are capable of scaling smoothly to very large configurations. While the latency to traverse the network (that is, the elapsed time for the address and data to move across the network) may increase with larger sizes, various techniques of latency hiding can be employed to mask this overhead. The result is an architecture with potentially unlimited scalability. Another feature of note regarding this architecture is that it is *UMA* (that is, *uniform memory access*). Every processor is equally far away from every memory bank. Hence the problems of data locality we encountered in the DSM/NUMA designs do not apply here.

The vector supercomputers traditional to Cray Research all employed this basic architecture, so it is not surprising that we encounter this technique in a machine with a strong Cray heritage. What *is* surprising is that it claims to be an SMP. What are missing in Figure 11–1 are local caches for the microprocessors and, concomitantly, a mechanism for cache coherence. To see what the problem is, consider Figure 11–2, which shows a *notional* dance hall architecture with local caches. Nobody to my knowledge has ever tried to build a machine that looked like this, and it is important to understand why. In this architecture *there is no obvious way to implement cache coherence.* When a bus is used to access memory, a snoopy protocol allows all processors to listen in on all bus traffic. A write to a variable held in cache results immediately in the variable being marked "dirty" by other caches. Subsequent references to the variable are then passed through to main memory, where the true value now resides. In Figure 11–2 there is no mechanism like the global shared bus to maintain cache coherence. A write by a processor to its local cache is invisible to other processors. Thus the memory structure shown in Figure 11–2 is not coherent, and it therefore becomes the programmer's responsibility to ensure that coherence is maintained. Although programming devices to implement software coherence have been explored, they have never been successful; resistance to programming for a noncoherent shared memory has been greater (if possible) than resistance to message passing for DM architectures.

Figure 11–2 Generic Dance Hall Architecture, with Local Caches

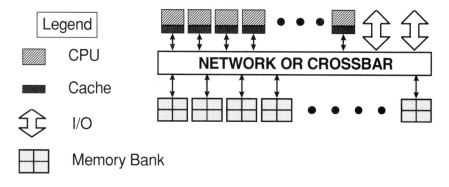

The answer proposed by the Starfire to this dilemma is a "best of both worlds" approach (see Figure 11–3). The machine has both a crossbar (to implement the scalable dance hall style memory architecture) and a separate bus (actually, a set of four buses) to implement the addressing and cache coherence. The presence of the crossbar permits extremely high memory bandwidths compared to conventional bus-based SMPs. The presence of the address buses permits use of a snoopy protocol and allows addresses to access memory banks at very high rates. It is the very clever combination of the two approaches—crossbars for moving data, and buses for moving addresses and cache coherence data—that allows the Sun Starfire Ultra Enterprise 10000 to break through the memory bandwidth bottleneck that is typical of traditional SMP approaches.

Figure 11–3 Using Address Buses for Cache Coherence in a Dance Hall Architecture

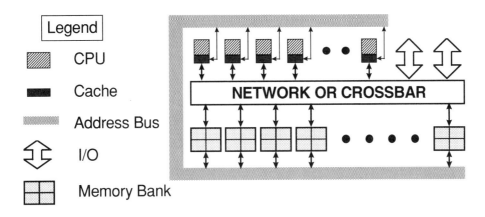

Details

With this background, we can turn to the specifics of the Starfire internals. The Cray heritage is also evident in the approach to packaging (for those new to this type of discussion, *packaging* refers to the way in which electronic components—chips, wires, power, and so on—are distributed across the two-dimensional world of boards and backplanes). The problem is how best to take the somewhat ungainly picture in Figure 11–3 and turn it into real, manufacturable hardware. The solution provided by the Starfire is elegant and instructive. At its simplest, we may consider two main components: (1) the system board (which houses the microprocessor, memory banks, I/O channels, and interfaces to both the crossbar and the address buses); and (2) an active center plane which is the electronic realization of the interconnection devices (both the crossbar and the address buses). We discuss each in turn and then consider the system as a whole.

Each system board (see Figure 11–4) contains a complete collection of functional units in balanced proportion. First, there are two sets of two microprocessors. These are UltraSPARC RISC chips; they are standard in the Sun product family and are state-of-the-art microprocessors. Each micro-pro-cessor has its own cache, and each set of two has its own set of interfaces to the four address buses. These buses are the mechanism by which systemwide cache coherence is maintained, and they extend across all system boards. Next, there are two I/O channels, each of which can support up to two disk controllers. These also have a separate interface into the set of address buses. Next, each system board contains a set of four memory banks, each with up to 1 GB of memory. These also interface to the set of four address buses. Finally, each

Figure 11–4 Top-Level Block Diagram of Starfire System Board

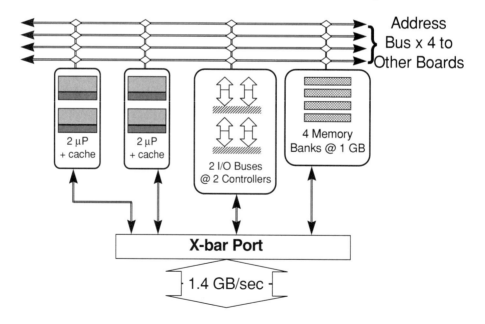

system board has a port into the high-performance crossbar switch. This port has an aggregate I/O capacity of 1.4 GB/sec per system board. The systemwide crossbar switch has been benchmarked at a sustained rate of 10.3 GB/sec.

While in some sense the system board looks like a stand-alone processing node, the desire to provide uniform access between all processors and all memory banks means that memory transfers must take place over the crossbar. This is very different from the NUMA architectures described in Chapter 3 (see, for example, Figure 3–1), where memory references to local banks have much better latency than memory references to remote memory banks. Thus co-location of processors and memory on the same system board does not provide any latency advantage; or put more positively, *non-co-location* of processors and memory does *not* impose any latency penalty! This is truly a *uniform memory access* system, and this is why Sun markets the Ultra Enterprise 10000 as an SMP. We have more to say about this terminology in Section 11.3.

This packaging approach has several advantages, of which we mention three. First, it is fundamental to the scalability of the system. The way in which the system grows in size—from as few as 1 to as many as 16—is by adding system boards. Because of the packaging strategy, adding a system board automatically adds memory, memory bandwidth, processing power, and I/O bandwidth in a balanced fashion. The system is *scalable* because all the major system performance parameters remain in the same ratio—the ratio as configured on a single system board—as the system size increases. In effect, one can compute the performance of a single system board and multiply by the number of boards to find the total system performance, up to the maximum configuration (16 boards ~ 64 μPs ~ 64 GB memory ~ 64 disk controllers ~ a full 16 × 16 crossbar at 1.4 GB/sec per switch port). This is in sharp contrast to bus-based SMP architectures, where (in particular) the total available memory and bus bandwidth are fixed in advance with a relatively low upper bound. The second advantage of this packaging strategy is that by decreasing the number of different types of board that must be engineered, it greatly simplifies manufacturing. Instead of using separate board types for processor, memory, and I/O (typical of SMP implementations), a single board type suffices for all. This, in turn, supports the third advantage: a uniform interface to the high-performance crossbar. There are not different board types using the bus for different things; rather, we have a single board type, with a single port interface, whose various on-board components share access to the available bandwidth provided by the port.

We turn now to the second major component of the system, the centerplane, which implements both the address buses and the crossbar. If we were to view the system from above (see Figure 11–5), we would see a central board (the *center plane*) running down the middle of the box, with up to 16 system boards and two center-plane support boards extending off each side. The center plane is a very aggressive piece of technology, and incorporates active devices to support the switching which implements the crossbar. Here, again, the high-performance heritage of the machine is in evidence.

Figure 11–5 View of the System Architecture from Above

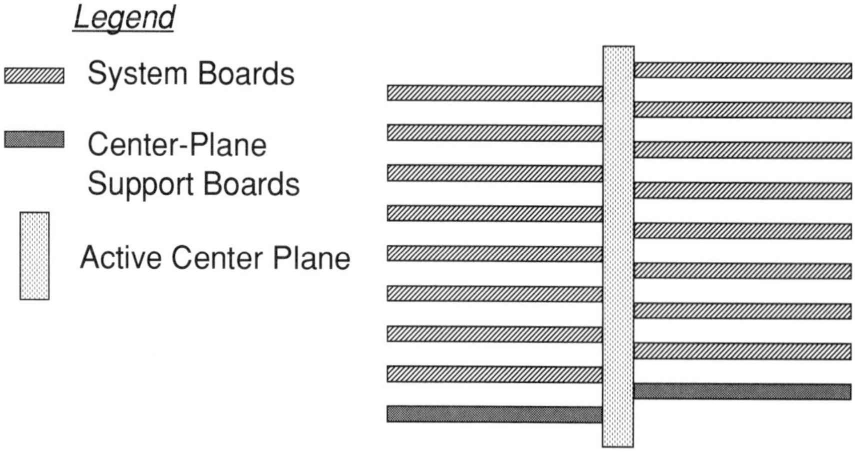

Legend

System Boards

Center-Plane
Support Boards

Active Center Plane

We turn next to the I/O architecture of the Starfire. As we have mentioned on several occasions, the key to good performance on large DSS-style queries is the ability to maintain very high bandwidth against single large tables. As we have seen, each system board provides two channels, each of which can support two disk controllers. The Starfire supports fast/wide SCSI, Ultra SCSI, and Fibre Channel. In a recent announcement, Fibre Channel Arbitrated Loops (FC-AL) will soon be supported. In a typical configuration, the controllers might be SCSI fast and wide devices with (say) seven disks per controller. With up to 64 controllers available (16 boards with two channels, each with two controllers), and assuming 20 MB/sec per controller, a theoretical peak of 3 GB/sec might be obtained (with higher rates on the way). In fact, with a less aggressive configuration the Starfire has been able to *sustain* 1.4-GB/sec I/O bandwidth to single tables, a very impressive achievement from an SMP-style architecture. RAID 5 is supported for all channel types, either in the controller or in software (using the Veritas volume manager). A bit of simple arithmetic (controllers × disks × storage per disk) will show that very large amounts of disk storage and I/O bandwidth can be supported by the system. Interested readers can also contact Sun directly for impressive I/O benchmark performance numbers.

A capability that is expected in large commercial IT shops, but which is not available from other Unix platforms, is the ability to partition the system into completely independent operational domains, executing separate operating systems and providing absolute assurance that failures in one partition cannot affect any other. This capability, provided by the Sun Starfire Ultra Enterprise 10000, is an example of the type of industrial-strength features that makes the machine a legitimate contender as an enterprise server. Similarly, "hot swap" of system boards is supported. The operating system "drains" the failed board of all activity by migrating memory pages and processes to other boards. At that point, the failed board can be powered down and a new board inserted while processing continues on the rest of the system. The newly installed board can then be powered up and automatically integrated by the operating system back into its domain.

A number of features are provided by the operating system (*Solaris* is Sun's implementation of Unix) to ensure that memory hot spots are avoided (see the discussion in Chapter 1) and that all the available memory bandwidth is utilized. The key is to ensure that active pages of memory are spread evenly across all memory banks. For example, a single page of memory is always interleaved by cache lines over four co-located memory banks. Pages, on the other hand, are interleaved across separate memory boards. Thus references to separate pages are spread evenly over the banks on separate boards. Similarly, when I/O operations occur, there is no preference by the OS for the memory banks local to the board on which the I/O controller is located. The I/O stream flows directly over the crossbar from the controller to the destination memory bank, wherever it may be located in the system. Thus I/O bandwidth is also uniform in the expected SMP manner.

Summary

At the heart of the Sun Starfire Ultra Enterprise 10000 is a high-performance crossbar switch. Using a classic scalable dance hall style of architecture, very high memory bandwidth is provided from all processors uniformly to all memory banks. To also achieve cache coherence, a set of four independent address buses supplements the crossbar using a snoopy protocol. By implementing all major components on a single system board (processors, memory, I/O, and network bandwidth), adding system boards automatically maintains balanced performance across all system performance measures. This scalability allows the system to grow smoothly to large configurations suitable for data warehouse implementations.

11.2 Implementation of Oracle 7

At the outset, it is important to say what the following discussion is *not*. It is not, and could not pretend to be, a comprehensive discussion of the Oracle RDBMS. For that purpose, the reader is referred to the excellent *Oracle Press* series published by Osborne/McGraw-Hill. These texts, reviewed by, and often authored by, Oracle professionals, deal in detail with practical implementation issues. Our purpose is much different—to illustrate by specific examples the general hardware and software architectural issues introduced in Parts I and II. For that purpose it is not necessary to discuss low-level implementation details (which are beyond both the scope of the book and the competence of its authors). Rather, we wish to show at a more general level how the architectural strengths of the Sun Starfire Ultra Enterprise 10000 hardware (discussed in Section 11.1) can be exploited effectively by the general software architectural approach taken by Oracle. Readers who want detailed implementation and optimization advice will have to look elsewhere.

Oracle 7 executes on many different machines and many different parallel architectures. For example, we noted how it is able to execute on the SP2, a DM machine, by using the virtual shared disk (VSD) facility. It is also able to execute on SMPs, on clusters of SMPs, on non-Unix platforms—in fact, as Larry Elison (the founder and CEO of Oracle) once said, "We're willing to get into bed with anyone." This universality is one of Oracle's market strengths, since it means that applications using Oracle as the database subsystem have a very broad base into which to market. That having been said, it is nonetheless true that the heritage of Oracle—the background out of which it developed, which is still reflected in many architectural features—is a shared memory, shared disk system. When Oracle executes outside that environment, software is required that hides the hardware details is such a way that software abstractions used by Oracle to parallelize the workload can be utilized.

In this context, the Starfire is a nearly ideal fit for the Oracle software architecture. It does provide multithreading capabilities, uniform shared memory access, and uniform shared disk I/O bandwidth. The "abstractions" used by Oracle are hardware and OS reality for this machine, so that there is no need for constructing or interposing additional layers of software to implement the software-to-hardware mapping. In the following paragraphs, we discuss three specific ways in which this helps not just Oracle, but any shared-everything RDBMS executing large DSS queries: load balancing, achieving high I/O bandwidth, and use of address arithmetic.

Load Balancing

In Chapter 6 we discussed one of the main advantages of a shared-everything approach: the ability to coordinate many small independent tasks. The model was a manager of a work queue, with independent processes "reporting in" to find out what work is left to do, getting their next assignment, and proceeding to execute. This model has great advantages in terms of balancing the workload. First, as long as there is something left in the work queue, all processors are always busy. Second, as long as the individual tasks are not very large, a nice upper bound is placed on the maximum delay that can be incurred: the time of the longest job. A shared memory hardware architecture is the ideal mechanism to implement such an approach, since the "work queue" can be a shared data structure equally accessible to all active processes, managed by a "queue manager" process that updates the queue periodically and monitors its status.

This model is particularly relevant to OTLP, where the workload consists of the independent queries being submitted. It turns out, however, that the same model can be used for large DSS-style queries by decomposing a single complex query into a large number of smaller subqueries. We consider ways to accomplish this decomposition shortly. Now, however, we want to observe that such a strategy has the potential to exploit many features originally developed for an OLTP environment.

In a shared-nothing environment, the *workload* must be divided among processors. Typically, this means that the *data* must be divided, one "bucket" of data for each processor, with attention paid to ensuring that no bucket is significantly larger than any other (otherwise, one processor will have more work to do and the load will become unbalanced). The Oracle approach to load balancing is to spawn off many small tasks, many more than the number of processors that are available. During execution of the query, any particular CPU in the system might find itself executing several of these smaller tasks. In fact, because Unix is a time-sharing system, multiple smaller tasks will be "active" (that is, in the midst of execution) for each CPU. This time-sharing approach also supports overlapping I/O (processes waiting for an I/O to complete can be swapped out while others utilize the CPU resource). By decomposing the single large query into many small subqueries, and by allowing the operating system to assign CPU resources using its dispatch algorithms, Oracle is able to achieve an effective approach to load balancing. A critical role is played by the shared memory, since our assumption is that the work queue will take the form of a shared data structure.

The specific form that this general concept takes in Oracle is the use of a query coordinator and multiple query servers. These are Unix processes that are not bound to any single CPU. Rather, utilizing the Unix model, the processes are assigned to CPUs by priority and as available. The query coordinator manages the query execution as determined by query optimization software. It decomposes the large query into multiple small queries, at which point each query server can get to work on its piece of the problem. It is not necessary that the number of query servers match the number of physical CPUs. The exact number of query servers is a tuning parameter, and Oracle can also take into account other information (for example, hints in the SQL, statistics about table size) in selecting the best number of query servers to use at run time. For large DSS applications on the Starfire the optimal ratio turns out to be between 2 and 4:1—that is, considerably more query server processes active than there are CPUs in the system.

Achieving High I/O Bandwidth

A major theme of this book has been the need to achieve very high I/O bandwidth to single tables. The basic strategy (see Chapter 4) was simple: Spread the table out over many disks and have all the disks active in parallel. The total bandwidth to the table then becomes the sum of the bandwidths of the individual disks. In practice, however, the issue arises of how to split the table and distribute it across the multiple disks. In shared-nothing systems on DM machines, the approach involved the application of some sort of partitioning scheme: hashing, range partitioning, round robin, and so on. Each processor was then thought of as having private, nonshared access to the portion of the table that has been sent its way. Many individual processors, each accessing its private disks in parallel, achieved high aggregate bandwidth.

The situation on the Sun Starfire Ultra Enterprise 10000 is very different. The table is thought of as being a single large flat file, and parallel I/O is achieved by simple striping. That is, the file is broken into blocks and spread across the disks *independent of row structure or key values*. When a query server wishes to access some part of the table, it is simply given a file pointer into the large file that holds the data. Since many file pointers can be active on the same file, the model is one in which each of the active query servers (more query servers, we observed, than there are CPUs) simultaneously reads its assigned subset of the large file holding the table. Since the table has been striped across all the available disks, and since many query servers are active, a very large number of I/Os can and will be occurring at any given moment. That translates directly into high sustained I/O bandwidth *without* the need for explicit table partitioning.

We noted in Section 11.1 that a fully configured Starfire has slots available for up to 64 disk controllers. Pegging the fast/wide SCSI controllers at about 20 MB/sec, a single controller could sustain about four disks at 5 MB/sec. If we suppose that 32 controllers are active (two per system board), we should expect to be able to sustain over 600-MB/sec bandwidth in this middle-of-the road configuration. This is world-class bandwidth by anybody's standards, and as we noted above, the Starfire has sustained even higher rates directly from Oracle.

Volume Manager software is used to implement the striping (Sun has typically used Veritas in its benchmark runs), and Oracle need not be directly involved in the block-by-block striping or disk management. The key is to spread the data as evenly as possible over all the disks and let the randomness of the access patterns take care of the rest. As we noted, this has proven to be a highly successful strategy for large DSS queries. In an actual implementation, Oracle may choose to break a single large file into smaller ones to speed recovery (it is quicker and easier to recover a small file—the one that happened to fail—than a single large file). However, this subdivision is not based on key values or partitioning schemes; it is simply a technique for improving availability. Also, our discussion has not taken RAID into account. Sun supports RAID level 5, the preferred disk arrangement for large data warehouse implementations.

Address Arithmetic

Anyone who ever took a class in database algorithms knows that the "right" way to implement most data manipulation algorithms is through *pointers* (that is, manipulate the *address* of the data rather than physically move the data itself). Unfortunately, this approach breaks down in a distributed memory architecture because every processor has its own nonshared memory space. An "address" of data in one processor's memory is no good at all to another processor, since it has no means of referencing that data using the address. To get at the data, a *copy* of the data must be moved from the memory of one processor (the one that has the data) into the memory of the other processor (the one that wants it). It is the equivalent of a memory copy operation in a conventional shared memory. However, the shared memory architecture has another arrow in its bow: Pass the *address* of the data rather than the data itself; the processor wanting the data can then reference it directly using the address.

Linked lists are the most commonly used mechanism that rely on address arithmetic. Logically, the list is implemented using forward and backward pointers; physically, the data can be spread hither and yon across the large shared memory. In a DM machine, however, linked lists can only be utilized within the address space of a single processor. This is precisely why the data redistribution phases are required (see Figure 5–6). The rows from tables to be joined must be *co-located* in the local memory of the processor that will do the work. In a shared memory, however, such physical relocation of the data can be avoided. Any CPU can directly access any row, wherever that row may happen to be in the system, simply by issuing its address.

Consider, for example, the implementation of a hash join (one of the join algorithm options considered by the Oracle query optimizer in constructing the query execution plan). Recall that in a shared-nothing system, the rows of each table are *hashed to the address of a processor*. In a shared memory system, however, no such restriction is required. The data can be hashed to a *logical "bucket,"* and as many or few such buckets can be used as is deemed desirable. Query servers can then be assigned to process these buckets independently. The beauty is that *no data need be physically moved at all*!

There are, in fact, many ways to implement (say) a join using shared memory techniques, and Oracle software engineers will have considered and highly optimized the best of these. From our point of view, the specific details of the algorithm are less important than the fact that the uniformly accessible large shared memory of the Starfire offers to Oracle a set of algorithmic options that are not available in a distributed memory or NUMA setting.

Summary

The "natural" environment for Oracle is a shared memory, shared disk machine. It wants to spawn logical processes, independent of the number of CPUs, and allow them to have multiple file pointers open to single large flat files. It wants to achieve high disk I/O and load balancing by partitioning the *problem* up into lots of small subqueries rather than by partitioning the *data* up into separate files. Although software abstractions can be built that allow Oracle to treat other parallel architectures in this way, a uniformly accessible large shared memory and shared disk I/O is its preferred setting. The Sun Starfire Ultra Enterprise 10000, then, appears to be ideally suited as an Oracle engine for large DSS applications. This conclusion, based on abstract architectural considerations, has been confirmed empirically by a number of benchmark results.

11.3 CONSIDERATIONS

Scalability Reconsidered

Our discussion of the Starfire and its ability to break through the memory bandwidth bottleneck ordinarily associated with backplane SMPs shows that some care needs to be exercised when using loosely defined terms such as scalability. In our previous discussion (see Chapter 2) we stressed the importance of balance: All the important performance characteristics of the system—memory size and bandwidth, processing power, I/O bandwidth, interconnection bandwidth—should be able to maintain the same ratio (that is, remain in balance) over the entire range of system configurations. In this sense the Starfire is scalable, since (as we saw) adding system boards automatically increases all these performance characteristics in proportion.

Traditional backplane SMPs cannot make that claim. It has been repeatedly demonstrated that the limitation of the system bus as the memory access mechanism imposes an upper bound beyond which the system loses the necessary balance. For a time in the early 1990s this became a *cause célèbre*, because some vendors offered SMP configurations with large numbers of CPUs that ran out of steam long before all slots were full. In this context, the charge that the system was "not scalable" meant that the largest configurations available on the price sheet were not able to deliver proportionate levels of performance. The Starfire does *not* fall in this category. Throughout its entire space of configuration options, adding more hardware delivers proportionately more performance in all relevant measures. This in itself is a remarkable technical achievement.

In what sense, then, might we say that the ES10000 architecture is not scalable? Here we would have to use the term *scalable* in a somewhat different sense, but one that is common in the parallel processing community: the ability to "scale up" to the very highest levels of processing power (today, this might mean 50-TB or larger databases and 100K MIPs). In that specialized sense, the Starfire is not scalable, since it has a hard upper limit of 64 processors. This upper limit, in turn, is largely driven by the decision (a good one, in our opinion) to implement the crossbar and address bus using a single center plane. The architectural upper bound is set by the number of slots into this center plane.

The discriminating reader should, at this point, be asking the question: So what? Customers do not buy scalability; they buy solutions to real problems. The configuration range of the ES10000 is, by any reasonable standard, very large, certainly large enough to support data warehouses of interest to most organizations. If a customer only needs (say) a 3-TB data warehouse, the fact that somebody else may want to build a 50-TB warehouse is irrelevant. Indeed, the term *data warehouse* is used by some vendors to refer to databases as small as 2 or 3 GB, so that in the real world of commercial decision support, the Starfire is able to "scale up" to configurations that cover almost all real requirements.

Saying that the Starfire is scalable over its large performance range is not the same as saying that SMP architectures, in general, are scalable. In Chapter 1 we used an irreverent metaphor to characterize the memory bandwidth issues with backplane SMPs. We referred to hogs (the microprocessors) gathered around a trough (the available memory bandwidth). By using a crossbar, the Starfire has, in effect, provided a much larger trough than that of its backplane competitors. But it is still a trough, and the metaphor still applies.

The reason the Sun Starfire Ultra Enterprise 10000 likes to refer to itself as an SMP is because it supports the widely utilized SMP programming model. As we have seen, at the heart of this programming model is the notion of *uniform memory access* (UMA). Our concern with NUMA architectures (see Chapter 3) was precisely that by failing to provide an underlying UMA hardware basis for the UMA (= SMP) software model, the potential exists for serious performance difficulties. (To reiterate this important point: The software abstraction no longer matches the underlying hardware reality.) The Starfire is not susceptible to this charge, since it truly provides a hardware UMA basis that exactly matches the SMP software model.

It may be that we are in need of new terminology, and the author respectfully submits for consideration the term *scalable uniform memory access (SUMA)*. Such an architecture, of which the Starfire is an excellent example, provides the twin benefits of scalability to very large configurations (if not the largest possible) while maintaining a true UMA hardware model. Under this proposed taxonomy, the term *SMP* would be reserved for traditional backplane architectures that are UMA but not scalable (per Chapter 1); and the term *NUMA* would be used to refer to highly scalable architectures that support an SMP-like programming model, but with hardware locality-of-reference latency effects lurking in the background.

Range Partitioning for Shared-Everything Databases

In the next few paragraphs, we wish to speculate about the potential utility of some level of data partitioning, especially range partitioning, for shared-everything RDBMS software architectures such as Oracle. The issue at stake is easily understood. Whenever it is possible to eliminate large numbers of rows from consideration immediately, the rows need not be fetched from disk, and the I/O part of the query (which often dominates in large complex queries) can be greatly reduced. Indexes are the most common implementation of this idea. If the query is highly selective (that is, only one or a few rows will participate in the result), the index permits location of those rows using a logarithmic search on the sorted key values. With queries that have low selectivity, however, the use of indexes will not be of benefit. Briefly, the overhead of index retrieval and subsequent "random" disk access will equal or exceed the brute-force approach of full table scans.

One approach to achieving some degree of selectivity is to clump the data into blocks based on a commonly used retrieval key (such as *date*). When a query is submitted that restricts based on this key, only the rows within the affected clumps need be retrieved and examined. Since the assignment of a row to a clump is based on key value, this amounts to a kind of range partitioning, and thus it is directly applicable in a shared-disk or shared-nothing setting. For a shared-everything architecture, there are also benefits, since even a query with low selectivity can benefit if a large fraction of the fact table can be eliminated from consideration.

There are work-arounds available in the current product. For example, if it is desired to clump data based on date, separate tables can be defined for separate time periods: weeks, or months, or quarters. These tables, in effect, become the clumps. However, the application software issuing the SQL must be aware of this structure and must UNION the appropriate tables when queries arrive that span multiple time intervals. One difficulty with this approach is the TPC-D benchmarks, which explicitly disallow such table redefinition at the top level of the schema. Further, it is likely that the applications used by some organizations do not recognize such a structure and would prefer to select against time intervals directly rather than indirectly using separate tables. Such applications, however, could benefit from an "under the covers" partitioning ability at a coarse level that can eliminate a significant amount of I/O for commonly submitted retrieval conditions. We also remind the reader that even coarse range partitioning provides no benefit if the query does not select based on the partitioning key.

Those who have read Chapter 8 will know the importance the author attaches to sorting and will see in the notion of coarse range partitioning the first step toward the ability to physically sort a large table on a significant key. After all, if the data has already been clumped by key value, a physical sort of each clump independently results in a completely sorted table. On the other hand, recall that range partitioning runs the risk of load imbalance due to data skew in the key space. All of these are interesting and demanding technical challenges, but the potential payoff (elimination of indexes is one that comes to mind) seems to be considerable.

Interface to Data Mining Algorithms

A theme that we have touched on at several points and discuss again in Chapter 14 is the current difficulty in interfacing data mining algorithms to parallel RDBMSs. Many data mining algorithms are not easily expressible in SQL, and the serialized nature of the SQL output model imposes a sequential bottleneck that can greatly hinder overall performance. Further, it would be very nice to have the customized data mining algorithms execute in parallel on the same hardware platform as the parallel RDBMS. This, in turn, means that the platform ought to support such features (long standard in the HPC community) as powerful compilers, libraries, file systems, and software development tools.

The Sun Starfire Ultra Enterprise 10000 is currently marketed primarily as an Enterprise server, but the potential attractiveness of the product to the HPC market has not escaped notice. Given the Cray Research heritage, a dual-pronged strategy for the machine appears to make sense, and Sun has indicated as much by committing to such HPC essentials as HiPPI. All this is also good news for data warehouses, since it means that the capability will be in place to develop and execute custom parallelized data mining codes on the Starfire. The only missing link (and we had the same comment about DB2/PE on the SP2) is a fully parallelized interface between the RDBMS (say, Oracle) and the native parallel file system.

Chapter 12

White Cross Systems

In this chapter we turn to a type of closely coupled hardware/software architecture that is quite different from the examples we have seen previously. In our other examples, the database system is an *application* that has been developed and is purchased separately from the hardware platform on which it executes. Other applications may also execute on the processor array, and typically the software package is developed so that it can execute on more than one type of hardware. White Cross Systems provides an example of a different approach. Here, the hardware and software are purchased as a single entity, sometimes referred to as a *database machine*. The software has been optimized to the target hardware in a way not possible in systems that are intended to be independent of the hardware on which they execute. Similarly, hardware features are incorporated in this design specifically to assist in database execution. Because the hardware is only intended to execute the associated database software, it can avoid "general-purpose" features needed in a computer that must execute many different types of application.

Considerable ink has been spilled over the years discussing the relative merits of "open" systems, on the one hand, and "special-purpose" hardware and software, on the other. The reader will no doubt have his or her own experience and preferences. The trade space is fairly clear and well understood. By focusing on a single problem, special-purpose hardware and software can achieve both absolute performance and price performance gains not possible for systems targeting a wide range of applications. Since an RDBMS is so widely used, and for so many purposes, it is perhaps a bit misleading to characterize a database engine as special purpose. It can do all the things a general-purpose database can do, and it meets the external SQL interface standard. What is given up includes (1) the ability to execute or develop other applications on the hardware, and (2) the ability to switch hardware platforms (so that the customer is tied to the vendor for both hardware and software). Mitigating against the importance of each of these is the recent popularity of *client–server* architectures. Here, many different vendors may participate, with each server dedicated to a specific function and with open standards facilitating the connectivity among many different platforms. Each organization will have to make the trade for itself. In the authors' opinion, there is no "one size fits all" answer to this trade. For many organizations the advantages of general-purpose hardware and software will carry the day. For others, particularly those faced with computational demands that stretch or exceed the capabilities of conventional approaches, a more narrowly focused solution may well be right. The success of systems such as TeraData (another database machine) and White Cross Systems indicates that there is plenty of room in the market for both types of approach.

A bit of background on the company may be in order. White Cross Systems was founded in 1991 in the United Kingdom by a small group of former TeraData engineers and marketers. The key idea was to exploit parallelism, via the Transputer microprocessor, to achieve very high in-RAM single-table scan rates. Because scans of very large tables are an important element in many decision support and data warehouse environments, it was felt that blazing performance on this operation would provide a sufficient advantage for many customers to outweigh the potential disadvantages of a special-purpose implementation. As we progress through the discussion of the hardware (Section 12.1) and software (Section 12.2) design, we shall see many specific decisions made with this fundamental objective in mind. In Section 12.3 we discuss types of applications that appear to be able to exploit the specific performance advantage offered by White Cross Systems. Because of its unique capabilities, the concept of operations for a White Cross Systems installation may be different—perhaps *very* different—from a traditional approach. It would not be unreasonable for a reader to turn briefly first to the material in Section 12.3. Seeing how fast scans can be *used* for decision support is a useful motivation prior to understanding how they can be *achieved technically.*

The material presented here has been reviewed for accuracy Dan Holle and Doug Heying, both of whom have been with White Cross Systems since its inception and provide senior technical direction for the product. White Cross Systems is located in Bracknell, UK, a western suburb of London. For surfers, a web site is available at *www.whitecross.com.*

12.1 THE HARDWARE PLATFORM

As we noted in the Introduction, the hardware and software of the White Cross Systems (WX) machine are closely coupled. As a result, at many points in the design a "hardware versus software" option was available to WX that is not available to less closely coupled systems. One example (among many others) is implementation of RAID. Another concerns how much of standard "operating systems" functionality to place in hardware. Thus the division line between hardware and software on a WX system is less sharply drawn than in traditional approaches. Hopefully between Sections 12.1 and 12.2 all the important topics will be covered, even if they do not show up exactly where a conventional taxonomy might place them.

A top-level block diagram for a WX system is shown in Figures 12–1 and 12–2. Ignoring low-level packaging considerations, we may think of the system as comprising three basic components. A *RAM-Store node* consists of a processor, local memory, and an interface to the high-performance interconnection network. In a typical WX operational scenario, a table will be constructed (including joins, if required) and brought into the memory of the RAM-Store nodes. At that point, and until the table is removed from RAM, subsequent queries and scan operations against this table will proceed at speeds dictated by RAM retrieval rates, not by disk retrieval rates. This is how a WX system achieves ultrafast scan rates: The tables against which it operates are "pinned in memory" for the duration of an interactive query session. The second type of component is a *Disk-Store node*. Here is where the persistent version of a base table resides. Disk-Store nodes participate in data loading and retrieval, but they do not participate in RAM-based scan operations. Like the RAM-Store nodes, each Disk-Store node has an interface to the high-performance interconnection network. Finally, there are a small number of *communications processors*. Their function is to provide the user and/or application interface. WX systems have been validated against SQL-89 (so-called SQL-1), and in a typical configuration MicroSoft's ODBC protocol will be used. What with an ongoing process of extension and enhancement, SQL-2 is a more accurate characterization of the level of capability provided (the NIST test for SQL-92 is used internally for test and validation). Thus applications that meet these industry standard interfaces can use WX systems without modification in the standard client–server model. Only a few (or even

one) communications processors are usually required, since a
high-performance microprocessor is used that is able to support many external connections simultaneously. The reader
will recognize this as a classic example of the *distributed memory* architecture discussed in Chapter 2.

Figure 12–1   Types of Hardware Components

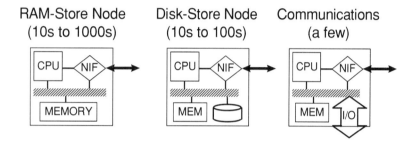

Figure 12–2   Typical White Cross Configuration

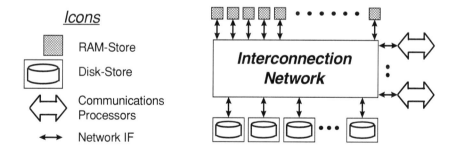

We turn now to the lower-level details of how this architecture has been implemented. It is important to distinguish
between the current first-generation implementation, which is
nearing the end of its components' design life, and the future
second-generation version which is currently under development. Our discussion focuses on the current version, but we
provide a brief peek at future plans.

In the WX system the interconnection network is closely tied to the microprocessor on each node. The reason is that the microprocessor used by White Cross is a Transputer (the T425), a design in which interprocessor communication facilities are supported directly in hardware on the microprocessor. Figure 12–3 shows a top-level block diagram of the Transputer microprocessor chip. The interesting thing to note about this design is that it supports four direct external *links*. As shown in Figure 12–4, links between Transputers can be connected to form very large interconnection networks. The four links naturally support an N-S-E-W two-dimensional grid (shown in Figure 12–4), but other interconnection topologies can also be built. In the WX systems, a ring-of-rings approach is used to generate potentially very large configurations.

Returning briefly to Figure 12–2, we note that all system components have a network interface to the interconnection network. In the current generation, this means that every system component has a Transputer whose links are connected into the larger grid. This means that every component can talk to every other component, using intermediate Transputers as "store and forward" relays along the route (see the discussion of routing in point-to-point networks in Chapter 2). We also note that the physical realization of the point-to-point links between the Transputers is made using a combination of copper wire (within a subrack) and fiber optics (between subracks). The use of fiber optics for "long-distance" connectivity has advantages in increased speed, lower latency, and reduced cabling complexity.

The Transputer also has packaging advantages. Although it is now older technology, its speed matches well the retrieval rate of commodity DRAM. This means that cache is not required, and it permits very dense on-board packaging. A typical processor board for a WX system contains six Transputers, each with its own private 16 MB of error detection/error correction DRAM. This packaging density is made possible by the tight integration of the interconnection network directly into the microprocessor.

Figure 12–3   Top-Level Block Diagram (Chip) of a T425
Microprocessor

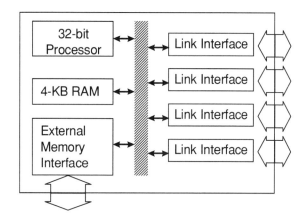

Figure 12–4   Interconnection Networks Using Transputers

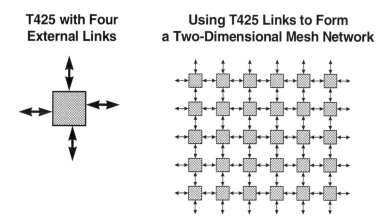

The approach to disks in a WX system is interesting and
unique. Standard commodity Winchester disks are used (currently at 2 or 4 GB capacity), and each disk is controlled by a
single dedicated Transputer (see again the block diagram for a
Disk-Store node in Figure 12–1). This one-to-one ratio of disk
to processor again reflects the relatively slower clock speed of

the Transputer. However, in the processing flow, the CPU at a Disk-Store node is doing much more than controlling its disk. It is also helping to implement query processing—for example, by eliminating rows using SELECT criteria prior to routing table data out to the RAM-Store nodes for further processing. Here we see an advantage of the tight HW/SW coupling in the WX design. The disk controller does not need to be fully general purpose as in a conventional design. Hence WX can incorporate at the disk controller substantial query processing logic. Such tight integration would not be possible if the hardware and software were developed independently.

The WX implementation of RAID is also unique. Current industry practice is to implement RAID within the logic of a single disk controller. In the WX implementation, multiple Disk-Store nodes coordinate their individual disks *using the interconnection network* as the mechanism for distribution of parity data. This is illustrated in Figure 12–5, which shows a group of four Disk-Store nodes logically aggregated as a single RAID unit. Both RAID levels 3 and 5 are both supported; if Disk-Store nodes are paired (that is, groups of two rather than four), an effective mirroring scheme can be implemented.

Figure 12–5   Implementing RAID Using the Interconnection
Network

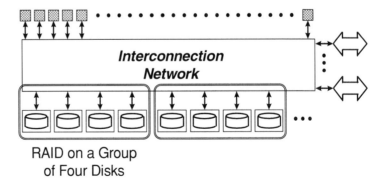

RAID on a Group
of Four Disks

Turning now to packaging, the model WX9020 is the version appropriate for large (that is, data warehouse sized) implementations. A subrack (that is, a cage) contains processor and/or disk cards on which are mounted (respectively) RAM-Store and/or Disk-Store nodes. In addition, two (redundant) network link cards provide connectivity between multiple subracks using a ring-of-rings network topology. Basically, the nodes within a subrack are connected to each other and to their local network link cards; and network link cards are connected to each other across the entire system. A single subrack fully populated with processor cards (at six nodes per card) would contain 114 processors and 1.8 GB of RAM. A subrack devoted to disk storage would contain 32 processors (24 for RAM-Store and 8 for Disk-Store), 384 MB of RAM, and 11.6 GB of usable RAID level 3 or 5 storage on four disks (up to 40 GB if hardware-supported compression is utilized). Subracks are stacked four to a cabinet, with multiple cabinets connected using fiber optic cables as the realization of the high-performance interconnection network. All components are air-cooled, but at 750 W per subrack (3 KW per cabinet), a raised-floor data center environment would be appropriate. Power supplies are $(N + 1)$ redundant. As a point of reference, suppose that the 24 subracks in six cabinets were allocated as follows: 10 disk subracks, 12 processor subracks, and two controller/communications subracks. The resulting configuration would contain 26.5 GB of RAM-Store, 120 GB of Disk-Store, and about 20,000 MIPS of RAM-Store computational power.

The description above is based on the current generation of hardware, which, as we noted earlier, is nearing the end of its product cycle. What trends can be discerned for the next generation? Although the following is speculative, it takes into account probable changes based on the current state of the art and trends in microprocessor, disk, and interconnect technologies. First, it seems inevitable that the Transputer will no longer be used. It has not received the broad industry support of other microprocessors and hence has not been able to sustain the industry's exponential rate of performance growth. Thus we would expect White Cross to move to one of the many available commodity microprocessors (Sparc, Intel, MIPS, Alpha, and so on). Because the current interconnect is closely tied to the Transputer's on-chip links, another interconnection strategy must be provided. The simplest approach would involve a multistage switched network (commodity switch chips to implement this are available), but a point-to-point routing scheme using two- or three-dimensional routing devices is also possible. In any case, compared to current store-and-forward routing used by the Transputer, we would expect roughly a 100-fold improvement in *both* latency and bandwidth. Memory, currently based on 16-MB DRAM technology, will move to 64-MB and 256-MB SDRAM—a 4- or 16-fold improvement in memory board density. Current 4-GB disks will move to 9-GB and 16-GB disks as they become commodity items.

Taking this speculative design point (which is certainly achievable in several ways with today's technology), let us compare it with the six-cabinet version described above. For about the same price, we would expect 200 GB of RAM-Store, 1 TB of Disk-Store, and about 200 GIPS (giga-instructions per second) of RAM-Store computational power. Technology marches on!

12.2 SOFTWARE ARCHITECTURE

We divide the discussion on software into three topics: the use of in-RAM tables, special features and techniques, and system administration and utilities. Each is considered in turn.

In-RAM Tables

To understand the unique approach taken by White Cross Systems, it is important to grasp a fundamental distinction in the flow of control as a query is being processed. This is illustrated in Figure 12–6. The processing flow begins as the query is received from the client, parsed, and a query execution plan devised. At the center of the diagram we see a decision point and a branching of control. The explicit recognition of the significance of this decision is at the heart of the WX strategy for achieving very high scan rates. The decision resolves around whether or not the table (or tables) needed to resolve the query *have already been loaded into RAM*. If they have, the query can execute to completion without the need for disk access. Since disk access is several orders of magnitude slower than RAM access, whenever the query can complete by following the "straight line" flow across the top of Figure 12–6, substantial performance advantage results. The very high scan rate numbers quoted by WX are based on the assumption that this in-RAM processing flow is being taken.

Figure 12–6   Top-Level Flow for Query Processing

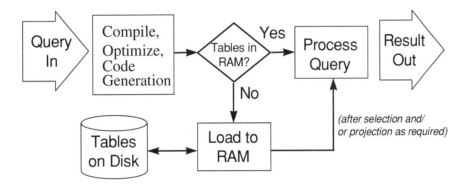

How does this approach differ from conventional approaches? In most commercial RDBMS systems, the distinction is not between "on disk versus in RAM" but between "on disk versus in buffer." That is, as a consequence of previous retrievals, the system may discover, as it traces its way down the tree of pointers to the data, that the data happens to be in a local memory buffer already. When that occurs, a disk retrieval is not needed; however, the decision concerning whether a disk retrieval is required can only be made fairly deep in the fetch calling tree. In the WX system, this crucial piece of information is forced up to the top level.

To pursue the question a little further, the WX system views the data not one row at a time (using "get next row" semantics), but as a single long array that is in memory and whose memory location is known. This permits the WX software effectively to bypass much of the data location and retrieval code required by other approaches. In this context the operative metric is "operations per row." The WX approach enables it to better standard industry practice by as much as two orders of magnitude for long in-RAM table scans.

The mechanism used by WX to force RAM residence is an extension to SQL called CREATE TABLE IMAGE. The significance of "IMAGE" in this construct is that the table created by this call resides completely in RAM, so that the upper flow across Figure 12–6 can occur. Considerable flexibility is available in the corresponding syntax for this construct. For example, columns not needed for selectivity can be omitted, thereby reducing the size of the table as it sits in RAM (that is, the table in RAM need not be identical to its parent table on disk). JOINs can be precomputed, and the resulting additional columns appended (that is, the table can be *denormalized*). Such operators as DISTINCT and GROUP BY can be preapplied. The end result, then, is a table residing in RAM against which subsequent queries can proceed very rapidly.

Of course, a table created in this way must be partitioned across the RAM-Store nodes (see Section 12.1 for the meaning of RAM-Store nodes, particularly Figures 12–1 and 12–2). As would be expected, this is done by hashing (or replication of small tables), and the user may specify the hashing key(s). The data as it resides on disk is always partitioned round-robin (see the following discussion), but independent calls to CREATE TABLE IMAGE can specify different hashing schemes more appropriate to the retrieval patterns of current interest. Thus more flexibility in hash partitioning is provided than the "once for all" approach that must be used when hashing is applied at the time of data loading. In Section 12.3, we discuss the implications of the use of CREATE TABLE IMAGE on a concept of operations for the WX system.

If the table(s) needed for the query are *not* in RAM, the second (lower) branch of the execution path must be taken. In effect, this causes execution of the code that would have been executed had a prior CREATE TABLE IMAGE operation been specified. That is, data is retrieved from disk, local predicates are applied at the Disk-Store nodes (see Section 12.1), and JOINs are accomplished using hash-join or broadcast techniques (see Section 7.2). Using coarse bitmapped indexes (see the discussion below), unnecessary disk reads can often be avoided. Further, because the processing of disk-based tables utilizes the same highly optimized scan and join algorithms developed for in-RAM tables, significant performance advantages accrue. Thus, even for the second (not-in-RAM) path of execution, the WX system provides significant optimizations. While the full power of the machine is most evident for in-RAM scans, disk-resident access performance is fully competitive with conventional alternatives.

Special Features and Techniques

At an internal level, the fact that the hardware and software are so tightly coupled provides many opportunities for optimization that are not available to more conventional approaches. For example, there is no "operating system" in the ordinary sense (note, however, that the communications server interfacing to the client executes a full-up commercial version of Unix and can interface to other industry standard operating systems, including Windows NT). Such matters as memory management, process initiation, process-to-processor assignment, and message passing are all handled directly either by WX application code or by hardware in the Transputer itself. Only the few services directly required by the application are provided (as opposed to a full general-purpose suite of services). This keeps the code small and tight, with corresponding benefits in small code image footprint and rapid execution. As we discussed previously, this in turn results in a significant performance enhancement by greatly (as much as 100-fold) reducing the number of operations per row executed in full-table scans.

An associated benefit of not being machine-independent is that all major operations are compiled to object level prior to query execution. That is, the code generator for the query actually produces an object module that is distributed to and executed by the processors in the array. Since the query is always compiled (never interpreted), significant performance gains result. This includes, for example, the sorting algorithms used to complete local JOIN operations. The code is able to test the local size of both tables to be JOINed and make the more optimal inner–outer table choice at run time. This choice can differ from node to node based on the actual distribution of the tables resulting from hash partitioning.

We mentioned in passing that the WX system always partitions data across disks using a round-robin technique. This has a number of advantages. First, the data on every table is always spread over all the disks, thus maximizing I/O bandwidth (see Chapter 4 for details). Second, because no assumptions about hashing are made, the problem of reorganizing the data when additional disks are added (that is, reconfiguration and scaling) is easy: In fact, it doesn't matter to which Disk-Store node the data is assigned. To help with data retrieval, a very simple but effective "bit index" can be constructed on selected fields. In this index, each bit corresponds to an entire disk block and is set if any row in that block has a value corresponding to the index. A good example is time-ordered data. Typical data warehouse operations update data periodically in large load blocks. Thus the data is naturally (and coarsely) arranged on disk in time order. If bit masks (say, based on week, or month, or quarter) have been built, large portions of a table on disk can be eliminated when the query involves a SELECT using time as a retrieval condition. By ANDing these bit masks together, even greater selectivity can be achieved. These compressed indexes are kept in RAM at the Disk-Store nodes. When they can be used, they accelerate performance by greatly reducing the number of disk reads that must be performed.

A particular strength of the WX system is its use of *journaling* techniques in the file system. Specifically, an UPDATE to a record results in a separate time-tagged copy of the record rather than a physical change to the data in the prior row. This use of time tags permits the use of *snapshots* of the data (that is, data current and internally consistent at a given time). This gives the user an internally consistent view of committed data and avoids the difficulties of "dirty reads." It also supports a more rapid commit process and agrees with the point of view strongly recommended in this book, that decision support should be characterized by static (read-only) data updated periodically and infrequently in large blocks.

During data redistribution (for example, to support JOIN operations), large amounts of data are transferred around the network. Generally, it is preferable to have fewer and larger messages, since the latency overhead is reduced (fewer total messages) and amortized over a larger base (the individual messages are larger). The WX system achieves this by buffering data locally until a large enough message has been generated to trigger a "send." All "send" messages require an explicit acknowledgment of receipt, and time-outs are used to detect the possibility of internal hardware or software failures.

The query optimizer uses a cost-based model to minimize execution time. Alternate JOIN sequences and intermediate table realizations are considered, and the cost of data redistribution using the interconnection network is explicitly modeled. The costing model is fully parameterized so that little modification should be required when the software moves to the new hardware platform. Both hash and broadcast JOINs are supported (see the discussion in Section 7.2), and the optimizer considers these options as well as the hashing used during a CREATE TABLE IMAGE operation. Thus, if the user knows something about the current query pattern of interest, a "good" hashing key can be used during CREATE TABLE IMAGE to accelerate common queries, and the query optimizer will be able to take advantage of that knowledge.

The WX implementation provides all the standard services characteristic of a full SQL implementation: lock management (to enforce sequential semantics), referential integrity, and the capability to provide several levels of audit detail (at the user's discretion). The philosophy on detection and correction of faults reflects typical decision support requirements. Detection of a fault results in (usually automatic) system reconfiguration around the faulty component. White Cross refers to this as *fault resilience*. The focus is on bringing the system very rapidly back to a fully functional state rather than on "nonstop," 100% availability.

System Administration and Utilities

Users should find installation and operation of a White Cross system fairly painless. First, integration into an existing hardware suite is eased by adherence to connectivity standards (SQL, ODBC, operating system interfaces, network interfaces, and so on). A system console provides direct visibility into all aspects of the current state of the system: disk and RAM capacity, user activity, health and status, and environmental monitoring. The WX system uses its own relational model to maintain internal tables with this information, and these tables are accessed using SQL. It is for maintenance of these tables that lock management and updating are most heavily used.

White Cross supports a fully parallelized bulk data update facility. Because tables are partitioned round-robin, the parallelization strategy is simple, robust, and effective. Once local Disk-Store nodes have received row data for appending, they can proceed independently and in parallel (except, of course, for groups of four associated with RAID parity processing). Bulk deletes and reclaiming of disk space are also fully independent and parallelized, easing the task of disk storage management, a perennial DBA headache.

Considerable flexibility is provided in configuring the software→hardware mapping. Starting from a sound initial default, users can tune performance by assigning specific functionality to specific RAM-Store nodes. The idea is that some functionality—parsing of SQL, query optimization, and code generation—might better be "pinned" to specific RAM-Store nodes. Dedicating functionality to specific nodes permits more even load balancing (due to symmetry) among nodes sharing a task. In particular, when a table is distributed across a group of RAM-store nodes, we'd like all of them to have (roughly) the same amount of memory and processing power available. To address this tuning issue, the White Cross console enables the system administrator to designate groups of nodes as exclusively assigned to particular functions. Significant performance advantages can result from proper attention to this functional partitioning. As mentioned, WX engineers will provide a good initial default configuration.

12.3. CONSIDERATIONS

Special-Purpose versus General-Purpose Redux

We began this chapter with some brief comments on the relative strengths and weaknesses of special-purpose and general-purpose machines. Let's reexamine those issues now that we have the details of the White Cross Systems machine before us. First, it is clear that in many respects the White Cross Systems 9020 *is* a general-purpose database server. A client application interfacing to a WX system using standard SQL should be able to execute without modification. The shared-nothing, distributed memory architecture is scalable over a very large range of configurations, from datamart size (a few tens of GBs) up to quite large data warehouses (hundreds of GBs). Utilities are provided to support the kind of "heavy lifting" operations (bulk loads and deletes, disk storage management, configuration tuning) needed for large data warehouse operations in the enterprise data center.

Further, as we have seen, the close coupling of hardware and software made possible by a unified design permits a number of performance optimizations not easily implemented when the software is intended to be hardware independent. For very computationally demanding operations, the operating system can impose a high overhead in address resolution and buffer management that the White Cross design circumvents. The strategy of White Cross Systems is to exploit this "gap" in the design space to deliver systems with very attractive price performance characteristics.

This said, it is also true that, to date, most White Cross accounts have had as their primary goal the desire to exploit the ultrahigh scan rates made possible by an in-RAM scan. The general-purpose features we enumerated above significantly ease the tasks of integration and interface to legacy systems and applications. Beyond those basic capabilties, however, the White Cross design provides additional business value in the special-purpose performance characteristics of the CREATE TABLE IMAGE extension.

One difficulty that faces White Cross is that many applications are *tuned* to the performance characteristics of the more broadly based RDBMS vendors. That is, instead of exploiting the benefits of in-RAM very fast scans, these applications (and here, we are thinking of a number of OLAP and data mining products) make certain assumptions about server performance and tune their schemas and GUIs appropriately. As a result, both the schema and query structure is often chosen so as to avoid exactly the areas of strength that White Cross provides. Such tuning for conventional databases comes, however, with implicit consequences. Truly ad hoc queries, which cannot be addressed adequately by precomputed aggregates and data cubes characteristic of schemas for these applications, are simply avoided entirely in the user interface. Only a sophisticated user would even be aware of this "under the covers" performance limitation. This mismatch between applications and White Cross capabilities has worked against broad market acceptance of the White Cross paradigm.

A Concept of Operations

How, then, can the unique strengths of a White Cross database machine best be exploited? The company's logo, *Data Exploration*, gives a hint of the right direction. For one thing, we see that with a WX system, the choice of schema and construction of indexes will have little impact on scan performance! The reason is that once the table is in the correct form in RAM, it does not matter how the data was initially laid out in the underlying base tables. As a result, the WX system is superbly fitted for very rapid quick-hit analysis of very large data sets. Rather than thinking of the system as a large fixed monolithic mass of data—a typical way of conceiving of a data warehouse—the WX systems permits the detailed design of the database schema to be decoupled from the use of the system in extracting useful information. One no longer need wait for an elaborate detailed database design to get useful results from the data.

The ability of the WX system to bypass (or, at least, drastically to shortcut) the design process is an unexpected and welcome by-product of its ability to do fast in-RAM scans. Whatever the system may give up in general-purpose applicability it returns in flexibility and support for rapid prototyping and a quick-hit data analysis capability.

In many settings, the CREATE TABLE IMAGE capability will be exercised by the DBA as part of system initialization.

Ordinary users need not be aware, and simply gain the benefits of rapid full-table scans in improved response time. The general-purpose nature of the system is the key here; the WX system fits easily into traditional IT operations while offering a turbocharge to the most demanding queries.

Alternatively, we can also consider another type of application and user able to take full advantage of the unique capabilities of the machine. We envisage a sophisticated user community anxious to "explore data" in unusual ways not provided directly by off-the-shelf applications. The key phrases include *rapid prototyping, proof of concept,* and the ability to try out new ideas rapidly on large data sets without incurring the expense of a large development effort. This user community is accustomed to development of applications using SQL and will think of the WX systems as a query engine to explore data mining and knowledge extraction algorithms on realistically sized files. The ability to exploit the CREATE TABLE IMAGE feature of the WX system will be seen as a dynamic tool to accelerate individual queries—not a static, one-time setting imposed by the DBA.

Of course, most users of RDBMSs system are not directly aware of any of these issues. Their preferred interface is a slick GUI that cans the SQL queries and returns results in an intuitive form; the RDBMS is never directly a matter of interest. While WX supports this traditional setting, it also provides a unique capability that can be of great benefit to users who value ultrafast scans on large tables. This means a relatively technically sophisticated user community, able to work without the need for elaborate GUI tools, and with the imagination to envision problems now accessible that were unthinkable previously. Training is only part of the problem; what is really wanted is imagination, flexibility, and the willingness to experiment. In such an environment, the WX system will be viewed as the perfect tool for the job.

Summary

This brings us to the end of Part III. We have seen several examples of commercial practice on a variety of hardware platforms. Based on this survey, we now feel justified in asserting that, indeed, parallel processing has come of age. What was cutting edge and unworkably cumbersome 10 years ago has, through the efforts of both hardware vendors and software developers, become a genuinely useful business tool. The systems we have examined are proof that the power of parallel processing can be "tamed" and applied to problems with real business value.

Earlier we spoke of the data warehouse as an application domain nearly perfectly suited to a large parallel implementation. We are now, I think, in a position to see more clearly why that is so. The key to the issue is *scalability*. The mere size of the data, and the complexity of computations against it in a decision support setting, demand high levels of performance from both hardware and software. For their part, parallel machines need large problems with high payoff to fully exploit their capabilities (see Chapter 1 for a discussion of Amdahl's law). In a data warehouse, we have the requisite combination of factors: (1) a *big problem* with (2) a *big business value* providing a need and justification for (3) a *big machine*. The discussion in previous chapters has shown how hardware and software vendors have been able to exploit the market potential of this need, to bring parallel processing into the mainstream of commercial computing. For those of us who have watched parallel processing struggle on the periphery of computing for the past dozen years, it is both a vindication and a realization of a dream long postponed.

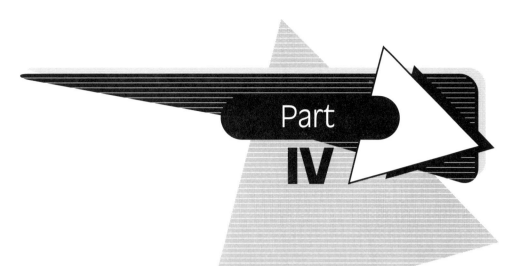

Applications and Implementation

In Part IV, attention turns to the role played by parallel hardware and software in the major application domains associated with the data warehouse. In Chapter 13 we consider on-line analytical processing (OLAP), probably the most common use of decision support systems. In Chapter 14 we turn to one of the major subthemes of the book, the use of data mining and knowledge extraction algorithms to detect significant patterns and relationships in large volumes of data that would otherwise go unnoticed. The computational complexity of these algorithms makes them ideal candidates for parallel implementation, but the interface to the parallel RDBMS presents difficulties. In Chapter 15, an emerging technology— object-relational databases—is considered. The ability to include user-defined operations (*methods*, in the object-

291

oriented argot) within the relational model is a powerful idea, and parallelism significantly broadens the areas of potential applicability. Finally, in Chapter 16 we consider issues affecting procurement and implementation. Benchmarking and development strategies are discussed, and in a final section we ask twenty embarrassing questions that ought to be considered before taking the plunge into a parallel decision support infrastructure.

On-Line Analytical Processing

In this chapter we explore the way in which most users currently work with the data warehouse—on-line analytical processing (OLAP). We begin with a brief functional overview of OLAP in Section 13.1. In Section 13.2 we examine in some detail how parallel processing in the data warehouse makes OLAP practical. Finally, in Section 13.3, we explore the limits of parallelism for OLAP and additional techniques being employed to meet the performance expectations of users.

13.1 BASIC CONCEPTS

On-line analytical processing (OLAP) refers to the interactive analysis of multidimensional information. In its most common form, OLAP involves three basic activities:

- Applying mathematical operators to various measures

293

(for example, revenue and expense) to create other measures (for example, profit).

- Reorganizing (pivoting) measures along a variety of dimensions such as time, organizational unit, or expense type (for example, pivoting data to view first expenses by year, then expenses by department).

- Aggregating measures (drill up) and decomposing aggregates (drill down) to different hierarchical levels within a dimension (for example, drilling down from expenses by year to expenses by quarter).

Figure 13–1 illustrates a typical OLAP session. The user starts with a high-level summary by vehicle type. Next, the user drills down on revenue to display yearly detail. Finally, the user pivots the data to see totals by year instead of totals by vehicle type. In contrast to OLTP, which is used primarily to support the *operations* of an enterprise, OLAP is used primarily to support *decision making* within an enterprise. The current interest in OLAP is driven by several related factors. First, increasing competition and shrinking budgets have driven many organizations to seek new ways to improve the speed and quality of their decision-making processes. The key to achieving this improvement is the use of *facts*, not guesses, as the basis for decision making. Second, most large organizations have OLTP systems that, running day in and day out, have amassed precisely the facts needed to provide an objective basis for critical decisions. Unfortunately, they are usually not organized in a way that easily supports the sort of ad hoc navigation through the data characteristic of decision support. Finally, as we will soon see, parallel systems for data warehousing now make it feasible in many cases to analyze that mass of data on-line (that is, interactively) to pursue answers to questions about the business. It is important to remember that for many users, the primary purpose of a data warehouse is to provide needed data rapidly to the user's favorite OLAP tools (see Figure 13–2).

Figure 13–1 Typical OLAP Session

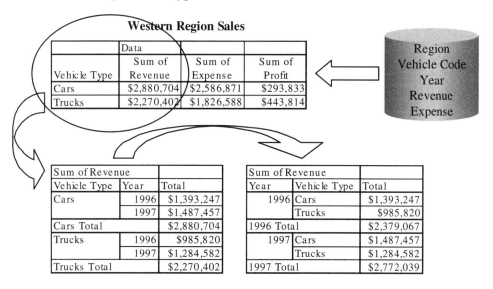

Figure 13–2 OLAP and Parallel Databases

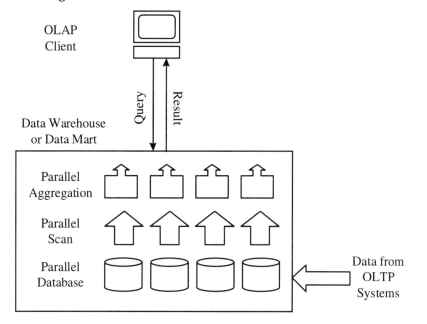

From the perspective of the data warehouse, OLAP queries differ from OLTP queries in three respects. First, OLAP queries tend to reference a much broader set of the available data in the database. Whereas for operations (OLTP) we may want to enter the dollar amount for a single sale, for decision support (OLAP) we are likely to want the total revenue from *all* sales. Second, OLAP queries tend to be more varied and unpredictable than OLTP queries. The queries in an OLTP system are typically predetermined (at least in their general structure) by an application such as an order-entry system. The rules of the business naturally limit the types of queries that can be issued. By contrast, OLAP is driven directly by an end user, and the types of queries issued are thus relatively unpredictable. Finally, OLAP queries tend to be much more complex than OLTP queries. This is because the information and analysis needed to support even simple business decisions are generally much more complex than that needed, say, to check the status of an order.

What OLAP *does* share in common with OLTP is that the queries are time sensitive. Ideally, an answer should be returned within seconds to avoid disrupting the train of thought of the users performing interactive analyses. It is this time constraint, and the broad scope, variability, and complexity of the queries, that are the primary drivers of the need for parallel systems for OLAP. The need for interactive response times in OLAP has resulted in a variety of approaches all geared toward improving performance. One approach is to use a *data mart*, which contains a subset or summary of data in the warehouse that is tailored to the specific needs of a department or business area (see Figure 13–3). There are several advantages to this arrangement. First, each department has the tools and data tailored to its function. The data warehouse is dedicated to the "heavy lifting" operations of very large databases, and the data mart can offload many specialized queries from the central server. In the most extreme example of this, individual users at workstations may have their own highly customized set of tools accessing local databases that have been downloaded from the data warehouse. Another advantage is that the data mart can be optimized to the access patterns of a specific user group. For example, a data mart for a marketing department can have prebuilt aggregates for dimensions of most interest to marketing, such as "customer" or "region." In that case, commonly used aggregates can be precomputed during database load and update; they do not need to be recomputed for every query using full-table scans. The OLAP tool can be configured to recognize and take advantage of these prebuilt aggregates and to bound the universe of possible queries into a more predictable set.

Figure 13–3 Data Marts and OLAP

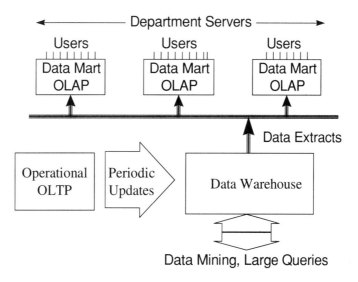

When deployed in this way, OLAP need not be particularly computationally burdensome. Nonetheless, this approach and others are eventually limited in their ability to provide interactive response time for OLAP. The possible dimensions and levels of a drill hierarchy are generally too numerous for all aggregates to be prebuilt. Eventually, users will drill through an aggregate to the detail data anyway. Only parallel processing can deliver interactive response times when the queries are complex, truly ad hoc, or involve the detail data. Thus the primary focus of this chapter is on parallelism and how it can provide the response times needed for decision support, even when querying the entire data warehouse.

13.2 INTRAQUERY PARALLELISM FOR OLAP

As discussed in Chapter 5, the need to process large, complex queries interactively makes *intraquery* parallelism much more important for decision support (and hence OLAP) than it is for OLTP. That is, it is no longer sufficient simply to execute more that one query in parallel. Rather, a single large query must now be broken up into smaller components that themselves can be executed in parallel. As discussed in Section 5.1, executing independent processes in parallel is useful but relatively simple. It is putting multiple processors to work on a single task that is the real challenge, and OLAP certainly has raised this challenge for the parallel DBMS vendors.

Recall that large queries can be broken down into smaller components for parallel execution in two ways. In the context of query processing, we'll call these *pipeline* parallelism and *partitioned* parallelism (see Figure 13–4). Pipeline parallelism refers to running multiple operations of a query (such as scan, join, and sort) in parallel, one on each processor. Each operation in the pipeline is started as soon as enough data from the preceding operation is available. Partitioned parallelism refers to splitting a single query operation (such as a sort) into multiple independent parallel processes, each handling some subset of the data.

Figure 13–4 Pipeline and Partitioned Parallelism in OLAP Queries

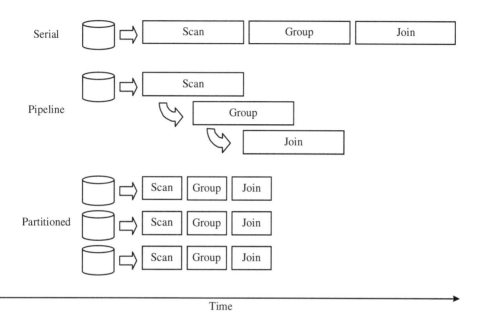

Pipeline parallelism is limited in its effectiveness for par-allelizing OLAP queries because there are only a handful of operations to be pipelined in any given query, and because some operations (for example, sort) may have to be completed in full before any data can be sent to the next operation in the pipeline. Partitioned parallelism, on the other hand, can (at least in theory) achieve any degree of parallelism desired, simply by dividing the data into as many subsets as there are available hardware processors. There are practical limits, however, because there is a cost to combining the results from each processor (especially for the *group* operation) into a sin-gle answer. At some point, the contribution of an additional processor will not be worth the overhead required to get its results and combine them with those from the rest of the pro-cessors. Anyone who has worked with a large team of people is likely to have experienced this phenomenon of diminishing returns due to coordination overhead, communication overhead, and resource conflict.

The overhead of combining the results from each processor depends primarily on two factors: the size of the individual results, and the speed and latency of the interprocessor communication links. What makes OLAP particularly amenable to parallel processing is that it generally involves *aggregation*. As depicted in Figure 13–2, the raw data processed may be very large (for example, millions of individual sales records), but the results may be very small, perhaps only a single number (for example, total sales). This is a natural outcome of the fact that the person driving the OLAP session wants a small amount of useful information, not large volumes of data. In such cases, the overhead of combining intermediate results is insignificant, and adding processors can result in near-linear speed-up.

What does this mean to an analyst or manager performing an OLAP query? With linear speed-up, a typical parallel database system with 10 to 100 processors will perform an OLAP query 10 to 100 times faster than will a uniprocessor system. This provides the capability to reduce query execution time from hours to minutes, or from minutes to seconds, and thereby enables the change from batch reporting to interactive analysis. Sometimes, however, the intermediate results are not small in relation to the raw data processed, and the speed and latency of the interprocessor communication links becomes much more important. A principal goal of both data modeling and query optimization is to reduce the amount of data that must be exchanged among processors. The primary obstacle to reaching this goal is that we never know which attribute the user will choose to aggregate on, not only because the selection of attributes is subject to the whim of the user, but because drill-down and pivoting change the aggregates needed moment to moment. Consider, for example, what happens if data is partitioned across nodes by region and the user requests total sales by vehicle type (rather than by region). In this case, partial sums for all vehicle types will have to be collected from each node and added together, rather than just collecting complete, nonoverlapping sums for each region. We do, however, have allies in our quest for performance. The first of these is the natural constraint of the decision support domain. We can predict, for example, that an OLAP system for financial analysts would often aggregate by time (for example, fiscal quarter and fiscal year). And if we can predict it, we can optimize it. Another ally is the client OLAP tool, which can be configured to impose a uniform view of the data that also makes the queries more predictable.

Because partitioned parallelism relies on dividing the data into subsets to be handled by each available hardware processor, it is important to be able to feed data to each processor fast enough to keep it busy. Whether provided by the DBMS or the OS file system, parallel I/O is essential to enabling horizontal parallelism. Even with parallel I/O, however, it may be difficult to get data off disk and to the processors fast enough to realize our goal of interactive analysis. As we shall see, OLAP queries pose a unique challenge that has prompted some interesting solutions.

13.3 SPECIAL OPTIMIZATIONS FOR OLAP AND DATA WAREHOUSING

Consider the analysis depicted in Figure 13–1. This analysis exhibits several characteristics typical of OLAP:

- Conditional selection based on a field with a small number of possible values: in this case, only sales in the western region.

- Aggregation of detail data: in this case, a sum of revenue and expenses by vehicle type.

- A join of a large table containing detail data with a small table containing code definitions: for example, to look up and display the vehicle type given the vehicle code in the sales record.

- Application of a mathematical function: in this case, a simple difference of revenue and expenses to calculate profit.

Let's consider the implications of each of these characteristics.

Full-Table Scans: Keeping the "On-Line" in OLAP

A conditional selection on a field with relatively few possible values results in a low selectivity of the query. Selectivity is defined as the percentage of the total rows in a table returned by a query, where a lower percentage indicates a higher selectivity. If there are, say, only four valid values for "region" in our example database, the selectivity of our example query for western regional sales will probably be around 25%. That is, for any value we specify for region, 25% of the records will, on average, contain that value. In such cases, an index is of little use, because it will be simpler and faster simply to check each record to see if it qualifies than it would be to maintain and use an index. Reading all the records in a table is known as a *full-table scan*. Although unusual in OLTP systems, full-table scans are common in OLAP systems. This is because users often perform analyses against fields like "region" with low selectivity.

Another reason that full-table scans are common in OLAP systems is that OLAP often involves exploring the data in an unpredictable manner. Unlike batch reporting, where (by definition) questions are predefined, we never really know what an OLAP user is going to do. Indeed, it is this flexibility that makes OLAP so attractive. But not being able to predict the user's questions makes it more difficult to build useful indexes. We could build indexes against every field, to cover all possible questions that a user might ask. But indexes can require as much or more storage space as the data itself, and they take time to build and maintain, so there is a cost to doing this. And, as noted previously, it is quite possible that such an index might never be used, due to low selectivity. The bottom line is that one cannot completely avoid full-table scans in OLAP systems (see Figure 13–5).

Figure 13–5 Parallelizing Full-Table Scans

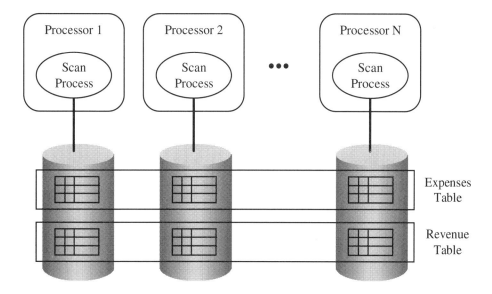

This leaves us with a problem: full-table scans can be very time consuming. For example, scanning a 10-GB table serially at 10 MB/sec (typical SCSI disk speeds) would take more than 15 minutes. Clearly, our interactive OLAP user is not going to find this satisfactory. To reduce this time, parallel I/O is essential. Parallel (RAID) disks can help some (perhaps by a factor of 5), but parallel I/O across tens or hundreds of disks is needed to really make an appreciable difference in scan time. It is important to remember that additional I/O channels and disks are not enough. In the Unix environment, processors are often intimately involved in I/O; they are responsible for managing I/O buffers in memory, moving the data to and from the user's address space, and so on. It is not unusual for the I/O from two fast SCSI disks to cause a typical processor to become 100% utilized during a simple scan (but hardware assists may offload some of this from the processor onto a controller; see Chapter 4).

The good news is that it is relatively easy to achieve efficient parallel scans. The key is to partition the data across multiple disks (see Chapter 7 for a discussion of partitioning schemes). The scan process itself requires no coordination among the processors: They each simply read the data on their assigned disks into memory as fast as they are able. Correspondingly, one can add as many disks and processors as needed to obtain the desired throughput. Assume that we wanted to scan the previously mentioned 10-GB table fast enough for an interactive user, say 5 seconds instead of 15 minutes. This requires a total system throughput of 2 GB/sec. Using the same disks and processors as before, this would require perhaps a couple of hundred disks and a hundred processors. Interestingly enough, even this moderate-sized problem requires a level of throughput that exceeds the memory and system bus bandwidth of most current SMP processors. With contemporary data warehouses ranging from hundreds of gigabytes to several terabytes, the reason for the rising popularity of MPP machines becomes clear. (However, see Chapters 10 and 11 for commercial examples of how SMP ideas can be scaled to data warehouse-sized configurations.)

These issues are illustrated in Figure 13–6, which shows typical throughputs for a variety of system components, and the throughput required to complete a full-table scan within 10 seconds as a function of database size. Note that both scales are logarithmic. Sometimes, achieving sufficient improvement in scan times through brute-force parallelism is not affordable. The only alternatives in that case are to reduce the volume of data to be scanned or to avoid the scan altogether. One common technique used in OLAP systems is to precalculate and store the most commonly used aggregates.

Because the aggregates require relatively little storage space and the underlying data was typically updated much less often than the aggregates are referenced, this can result in huge reductions in query times at the cost of some additional storage. (Note that this assumption is typically valid for OLAP systems, although it is typically not true of OLTP systems.) Aggregates can be calculated once (perhaps overnight), then used repeatedly by many users over many OLAP sessions. Of course, because we never know what query an OLAP user might generate, there are times when stored aggregates will not help.

Figure 13–6 Database Size versus Required Throughput

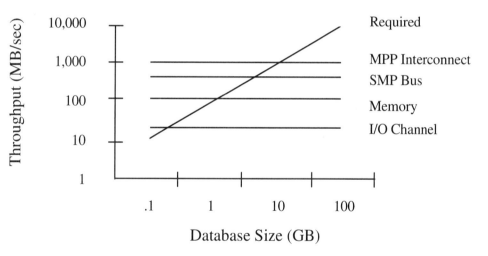

Another approach is to use bitmap indexes. A bitmap index consists of arrays of bits, with each array containing one bit for each record in the database. There is one array for each possible value of a field, as depicted in Figure 13–7. If all we need is, say, the count of vehicles sold in the western region, we need count only the bits in the corresponding index. This is easy to do quickly, and avoids the need to access the table with the raw data entirely. But bitmap indexes have other uses as well. The process of drilling down through aggregates focuses on a subset of the available data and has the effect of adding additional conditions to a query. The combination of conditions can quickly raise the selectivity of the query to the point where indexed access can be used instead of a full-table scan. To identify the records corresponding to males in the western region, we need only logically "and" the corresponding bitmap indexes together. All contemporary processors are able to do this efficiently, either 32 or 64 bits (corresponding to 32 or 64 records) at a time.

Figure 13–7 Example of Bitmap Indexes

Invoice Number	Truck	Western Region	Eastern Region	Truck and Western Region (Calculated)
1001	1	1	0	1
1002	0	1	0	0
1003	1	0	1	0
1004	0	0	1	0
.				
.				
.				

Aggregation and Multidimensional Databases

In our example, after the raw records have been scanned and selected, aggregation is performed to sum expenses by vehicle type. For OLAP, the ability to perform aggregation quickly is clearly important. Parallel aggregation is discussed further in Chapter 5. The importance of aggregation in OLAP has led to the development of *multidimensional* DBMSs specifically designed to do this quickly. A multidimensional database stores measures in "data cubes" specifically designed to enable fast aggregation along any dimension of the cube.

They also typically use custom query languages that support operators commonly needed in OLAP, such as moving averages. There are many considerations involved in choosing to do OLAP with a multidimensional database (MOLAP) versus a relational database (ROLAP), but the primary trade-off is between speed and analytical functionality (in favor of MOLAP), versus flexibility, standards compliance, and the ability to drill all the way down to detail data (in favor of ROLAP). Opinions vary, but one can expect that the major relational DBMS vendors will continue to improve the performance and analytical capabilities of their products for OLAP, and that the multidimensional DBMS vendors will continue to add flexibility and support for standards to their interfaces. In the near term, OLAP architectures combining both multidimensional DBMSs (for summary data) and relational DBMSs (for detail data) are likely to be common.

Joins in OLAP

Following aggregation, a join is performed to look up the vehicle type based on the vehicle code. Parallel joins are discussed in detail in Chapter 7. In this case, as is often the case in OLAP, the second table being joined is relatively small, consisting of only tens of hundreds of records. In an SMP architecture, this presents no unique problem, because once read into memory, the table is available equally to all the processors performing the join. However, in an MPP architecture, such a small table is likely to be stored on only one node, causing every other node to wait until the table can be distributed across the interprocessor communication fabric. This is not much different from having one waiter to serve everyone in a large restaurant, and is likely to result in similarly unacceptable delays. One solution to this is to replicate these small tables on every node or, even better, cache them in memory on every node. Such optimizations are being added to parallel RDBMSs to better ensure that massive parallelism does not get stalled by small serializations.

Analytical Operators and Functions

In our example, the last step is to calculate profit based on revenue and expense. The mathematical operators and analytical functions available in OLAP tools range from the simple (for example, variance) to the complex (for example, net present value or 10-day moving average). Any financial or statistical function commonly found in a spreadsheet is likely to be useful in OLAP. There are two issues here. First, relatively few such functions are specified in the current SQL standard. Second, when they are provided by a relational DBMS, they are not necessarily implemented in "parallel aware" algorithms. It is likely, however, that the current movement of the major relational DBMSs to an object-relational model will improve the variety of analytical functions available to support OLAP. Meanwhile, multidimensional DBMSs typically provide a much richer set of analytical functions.

A brief note of caution is warranted here. Our focus on parallelism in the data warehouse necessarily focuses us on shared parallel platforms. However, we should not forget that another form of parallelism, *distributed processing*, can also be exploited for OLAP. If there are a hundred OLAP users, there are likely to be a hundred fast workstations on the desktop. Given that, one must consider whether it is prudent to concentrate analytical operations on a shared server. Distributing the analytical load to the client machine can improve scalability (adding users automatically adds analytical processing capacity) and may reduce network load (only base measures, not derived measures, need be sent from the OLAP server to the user). Like the shared data in the warehouse, analytical processing in the warehouse should have some value. This value may be to provide measures that must be derived from the detail data (for example, min, max). In the near term, there may also be value in the ability to deliver OLAP to "thin" Web clients. The important point is not to recreate in another guise the very problem we are trying to solve with parallelism.

Chapter
14

Data Mining on
Parallel Systems

In this chapter we explore data mining, one of the fastest-growing and most intriguing applications of parallel processing. We begin in Section 14.1 with an overview of the business problems that drive the need for data mining and discuss the various techniques that have emerged to address those problems. In Section 14.2 we explore the characteristics of data mining algorithms and how parallel processing has enabled data mining to make the transition from academic research to commercial applications. We also examine the capabilities and limitations of parallel relational databases relative to the demands of data mining. Finally, in Section 14.3, we discuss specific examples of how data mining is currently being used.

14.1 BACKGROUND

The process of divining information and insight from large bodies of data has traditionally been performed by a person, with limited assistance from analytical tools. The purpose of reports, ad hoc queries, OLAP, statistical analysis, and even visualization is simply to present data and calculated measures in a form that allows the *user* to identify important facts, relationships, or trends. With these tools, the user is responsible for forming a hypothesis and directing the search for an answer. This works well but has some limitations. As the volume and complexity of the data increase, it becomes difficult or impossible for a human to formulate every question that might be asked about the data or to examine the detailed data for all possible relationships. Instead, users must limit their analyses to a small subset of the possible questions (selected based on prior experience and reasonable guesses) and rely on summaries and samples of the data rather than on examining the data itself. In doing so, the possibility exists of overlooking information hidden in the data. As an example, the sum of revenue for all products will remain unchanged even when there is a significant shift in revenue from one product to another. Examination of summary aggregates could miss a significant underlying relationship. What is needed are tools that will perform the drudgery of examining the detailed data for us, and that can point out potentially significant facts, relationships, and trends for further analysis.

Advanced data mining consists of a set of techniques that automatically identify patterns in data. With data mining tools, the data itself, not the user, guides formation of hypotheses and the search for patterns. Automation of the search process means that thousands or millions of questions about the data can be formed and explored exhaustively. Sometimes the results can be used directly. Other times, it is preferable to have the data mining tool rank the patterns found by their significance. The most interesting patterns can then be further explored by the user through traditional means. In short, traditional analysis can help find answers, but data mining can help find the right questions.

Data mining techniques are based on the results of research in artificial intelligence and machine learning. Most of the popular techniques are relatively mature and well understood by those in the field. What has prevented these techniques from being applied until recently is that they are extremely demanding in terms of both computation and I/O. Exploring the relationships between *every possible value* of *every field* results in a geometric explosion that can overwhelm even the most powerful machines. This complexity is driven both by the large set of combinations and by the large size of the underlying database to be searched. Only the recent combination of aggressively optimized data mining algorithms and parallel processing makes attacking such large problems possible. With this convergence of technique and technology, data mining is rapidly moving from an academic curiosity to a mainstream business tool.

Of particular interest from the standpoint of this book is the need to perform data mining on very large amounts of data. Commercial applications of data mining are vastly different from tinkering in a research lab. For example, mining information from phone customer records or insurance claims can routinely require processing millions of records totaling hundreds of gigabytes of data. And techniques to reduce the data volume, particularly sampling and summarization, can hide the most valuable information. Consider, for example, data mining to detect fraudulent insurance claims. Hopefully, these claims are a relatively small percentage of the total number of claims. As a result, sparse samples are likely to miss the very records of most interest. Again, we find that parallel processing is necessary to have even a hope of processing the volumes of data involved.

There are a large number of data mining techniques, and a detailed discussion of each is beyond the scope of this book. Commonly used data mining techniques include the following:

- *Symbolic segmentation, association, and rule induction.* These search for statistically significant patterns in the combinations of symbolic or numeric values. Decision trees, including classification and regression trees (CART) and chi-square automatic interaction detection

(CHAID), fall into this category. CHAID works on symbolic values, while CART works on either symbolic or numeric values. Rule induction is a particularly popular technique because the results are typically expressed in if–then rules that can be read and evaluated by users.

- *Cluster analysis.* This covers a number of techniques for clustering records into related groups. *K*-nearest neighbor is one of the more popular search techniques useful for cluster analysis. It works by treating each attribute of a set of records as an axis in a multidimensional space, projecting the records into that space, examining a user-specified number (*K*) of records nearest to a given record in that space, and adjusting the weight (or scale) of each axis to reduce the distance between neighbors.

- *Neural networks.* Modeled after the human brain, these consist of networks of interconnected nodes (neurons), where each node is represented by a formula that takes a weighted combination of inputs (from source data or other nodes) and produces a response. The response may be passed on to other nodes, or may be an output that indicates some property of interest, such as the likelihood of default on a loan application.

- *Genetic algorithms.* Modeled after evolution in biological organisms, these take a user-specified set of formulas and parameters, randomly recombine them as if they were pieces of DNA, and keep the ones that best describe the data in terms of some objective. This technique exploits randomness in the search process to prevent settling into a false local minimum.

- *Link analysis.* This covers a number of techniques for tracing and examining the links between entities (for example, financial transactions between accounts). It takes as a starting point a weighted graph reflecting degrees of connection between the entities of interest.

As we saw in Chapter 8, constructing this graph may require a full self-join of the central fact table against itself and hence be very computationally demanding.

For our purposes it is not necessary to understand these techniques in any great detail. The point of the foregoing is simply that there are a large number of techniques, some of which are fairly complicated. What *is* important is that all these techniques are (unfortunately) extremely demanding in terms of processing and I/O, but also are (fortunately) inherently parallel:

- In rule induction, many candidate rules can be pursued in parallel.

- In cluster analysis (*K*-nearest neighbors), analysis of different "neighborhoods" can be conducted in parallel.

- In neural networks, the responses for different nodes can be calculated in parallel.

- In genetic algorithms, the performance of "individuals" can be calculated and evaluated in parallel, or whole "species" can be evolved in parallel.

- In link analysis, searches of all links for reference to a specific node can be performed in parallel.

In the next section we explore some of these algorithms in a bit more detail to reveal some of the opportunities and problems that arise when one tries to implement parallel data mining algorithms in a data warehouse.

14.2 OPPORTUNITITES FOR PARALLELISM IN DATA MINING ALGORITHMS

To understand the use of parallel systems for data mining, it is helpful to understand at a high level how data mining algorithms process data. We will see that parallel I/O plays a very important role in making data mining possible, and that relational databases currently have several limitations in their ability to support data mining. In the following discussion we consider algorithms for two popular data mining techniques: neural networks and rule induction.

Artificial Neural Networks

As mentioned previously, these consist of networks of interconnected nodes (neurons), where each node is represented by a formula that takes a weighted combination of inputs (from source data or other nodes) and produces a response. A typical neural network is depicted in Figure 14–1. Neurons appear as nodes and represent computations. The interactions between neurons appear as arrows and represent data flow in the neural network. For the mathematically inclined reader, a typical node is depicted in Figure 14–2. Each input is multiplied by a weight that determines the sensitivity of a neuron to that input. The sum of all the weighted inputs is the *activation*, which represents the magnitude of the total stimulus of the neuron. The activation is used in turn in a calculation to determine the magnitude of the output.

Neural networks generally must be trained before they can be used. *Training* a neural network to recognize patterns requires sequentially reading a training data set over and over, incrementally changing the weights of the internal connections until the network converges on a solution. Training the neural network using examples of data that represent the pattern to be recognized is the most computationally demanding aspect of the process. Both true (positive) and false (negative) examples must be provided, and these must be chosen to be representative of the actual data to which the neural network will eventually be applied. Even so, it is not likely that the neural network will be able to achieve perfect accuracy. The selection of appropriate weights for the neural connections is, itself, an approximation. However, the accuracy of the neural network can be greatly improved by using a large and robust set of training data. This, in turn, significantly increases the computational complexity of the training process.

Figure 14–1 Typical Neural Network

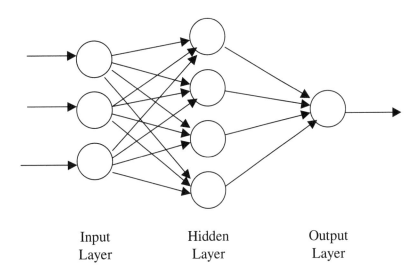

| Input Layer | Hidden Layer | Output Layer |

Figure 14–2 Mathematical Form of a Neuron

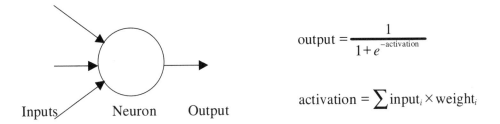

Inputs   Neuron   Output

$$output = \frac{1}{1 + e^{-activation}}$$

$$activation = \sum input_i \times weight_i$$

Once the neural network has been trained, it can now be *used* by applying it to a single record and using the result to classify the record. That is, the record is submitted as an input stimulus to the network, and the response of the network to this stimulus is computed using the weights determined during training. Thus neural networks characteristically involve a large number of sequential scans during training and a single sequential scan during use. The number of nodes and interconnections in a neural network is typically modest, on the order of tens or hundreds. Consequently, there are typically tens or hundreds of calculations for each record processed during either training or use. Although the calculations and I/O access characteristics are relatively simple, it can take many iterations during training for a neural network to converge on a solution. It is not unusual, for example, for training to take several hours on even modest amounts of data. As the size of the input training set increases, the computational burden rapidly becomes intractable without the computational horsepower provided by parallel processing.

Parallel systems can provide dramatic reductions in training time by exploiting parallelism inherent in the structure of the neural network. Consider, for example, a parallel implementation of a neural network that simply assigns each node to a separate processor (see Figure 14–3). This solution exhibits two kinds of parallelism discussed in Chapter 5. Within a layer, the solution is *embarrassingly parallel*, because all the nodes within a layer are independent of each other and thus can perform their respective calculations simultaneously. Between layers, however, the solution is *pipeline parallel*, because each layer depends on results from the preceding layer.

Figure 14–3 Parallelizing a Neural Network

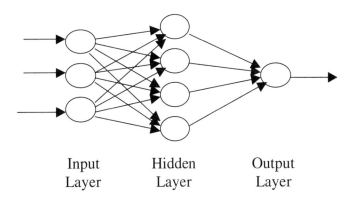

Input
Layer

Hidden
Layer

Output
Layer

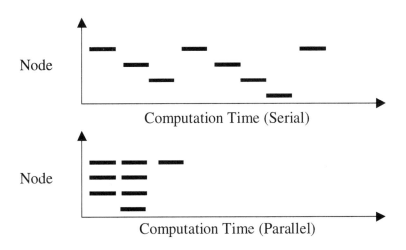

Node

Computation Time (Serial)

Node

Computation Time (Parallel)

At the input layer, the diagram suggests that parallel I/O could be used, but we will find this more difficult than we might first think. Each input to a network node represents a single attribute of a record, so the granularity of the input is very fine. Further, a node in the hidden layer must wait for the result of *every* input node that is connected to it before it can calculate its own result. Thus the opportunity for *skew* is rather high: If all the fields of an input record are not available to the input nodes simultaneously, we will have a lot of nodes (processors) sitting around idle, waiting for input. We can see that this is particularly true if we have assigned the input nodes of our network to different physical nodes in an MPP machine. Some parallel file systems provide facilities to store a single record over many disks on different nodes and provide synchronized retrieval, but we are likely to find it more practical to put entire records on a single disk, and read separate records in parallel. The individual fields of any given input record must be distributed to the input nodes in the same way that the results produced by the hidden layer are distributed to the output layer.

The discussion above assumes that we have complete flexibility in how we map the neural network to the machine. What happens, though, when the data to be processed by the neural network is in a data warehouse based on a parallel RDBMS? We will find first that standard SQL does not provide the mathematical operators needed to define the function of each node defined in Figure 14–2. Next, we will find that the network itself (that is, the node interconnections) cannot be expressed in a uniform fashion, but must, instead, be coded into a formula manually. Finally, we find that SQL does not support the concepts of nonpersistent working storage or sequential processes; we would need one or both of these to implement the connections between layers without having to write the intermediate results to disk.

The outcome of all this is that the neural network must be implemented as an application that only uses the RDBMS for data access. But recall that the characteristic data access pattern of neural networks is a series of sequential scans. While RDBMSs can certainly support this type of access, just storing the data in files is likely to be simpler, faster, and cheaper. In fact, if we look at this situation a little closer, we will see a performance bottleneck lurking. Note that the query interface to an RDBMS returns the final query results through the single processor controlling the query, as depicted in Figure 14–4. Even if both our RDBMS and our application are fully parallel, this serialization point will force all query results through a single processor. In the case of our sequential scan for the neural network, we are not selecting out any records, and thus we must pump the entire database through this single processor. Not only is the RDBMS not doing any significant work, it is introducing a serious performance problem. This is not to say the RDBMS provides no value at all, even in this situation. It may be the case, for example, that the data to be analyzed must be updated or otherwise managed as part of a larger operational picture. The RDBMS, in that case, provides value for data management even if it is not providing significant value for data analysis.

Finally, we observe that parallelizing the training function for a neural network may take an unexpected form. The problem can be cast as a straightforward optimization problem—choose the activation weights so as to optimize the ability to classify correctly on the training data. Traditionally, this optimization has been accomplished using a highly sequential technique known as back propagation (for the cognoscenti, a form of gradient search). However, there are many other and more effective parallel optimization algorithms that are more immune to the dangers of settling too readily into a false local minima. Thus, parallelism can not only accelerate the search process; it can also produce a better final result.

Figure 14–4 Serial Interface between the RDBMS and the Data Mining Algorithm

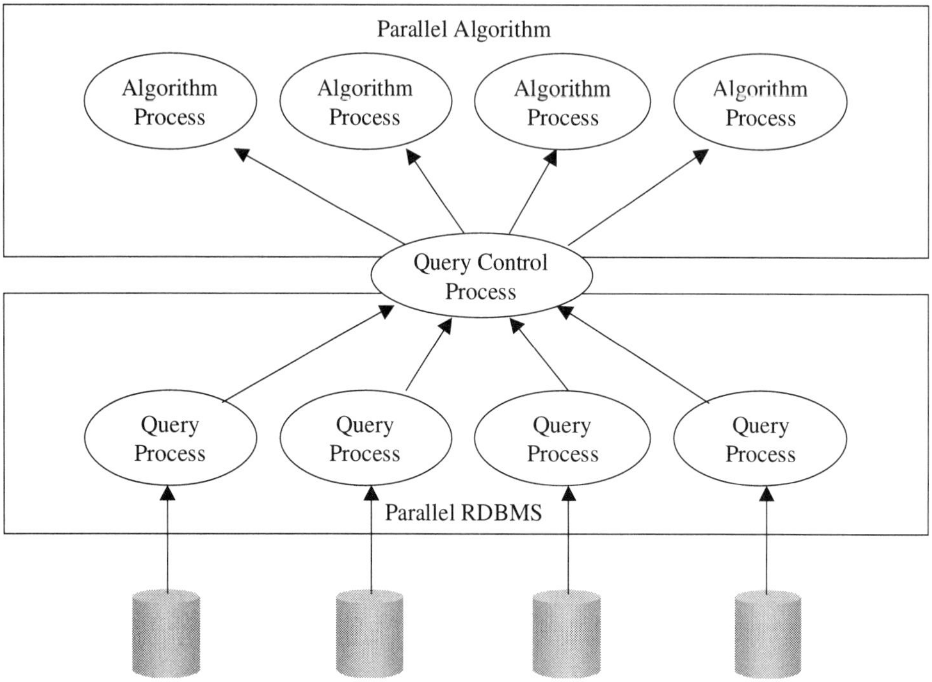

Rule Induction

Our discussion of neural nets showed that it is an example of pattern recognition using training data: The training data encapsulate the pattern to be matched, and the algorithm trains itself against that data so that it can then be applied to data it has not seen. A typical example is response to a mail solicitation. Many examples of "respondent" are known based on the experience of previous mailings. The net can be trained using these examples and can then be applied to a new mailing list to try to cull out nonresponders and reduce the mailing cost without thereby reducing the number of respondents.

There are many instances, however, in which the pattern to be recognized (or, more formally, the information to be extracted) is *not known in advance*. The job here is to take the raw data and "let it speak for itself" by finding hidden relationships among the fields and values. As opposed to pattern recognition based on training, such algorithms are *bootstrap* algorithms, since they do not require preknowledge of the patterns to be recognized.

Rule induction algorithms are an important example of bootstrapping. They rely on determining and ranking the probabilities of different values of attributes occurring alone and together. For example, consider the simple set of records of telephone customers shown in Figure 14–5.

Figure 14–5 Example of Rule Induction Data

Customer	Phone Use	Second Line	Call Waiting
1	High	Yes	No
2	Low	No	No
3	High	No	Yes
4	Low	Yes	No

In a data set this small, it is easy to find something potentially significant just by looking at the data. For example, we can induce the following rule from this data: "Customers who have high phone use and no second line have call waiting." This rule is useful if, for example, we want to find other customers who might like to buy call waiting. What makes this rule "significant" is that while call waiting is "yes" in only 25% of the records, it is "yes" 100% of the time when phone use is "high" and second line is "no." It is essentially this measure of significance that rule induction algorithms use to identify and rank rules. In a sense, these algorithms automatically drill-down through the data along multiple dimensions to find significant correlations.

This simple example certainly does not require sophisticated rule induction software and parallel systems to mine this rule from the data. The story is somewhat different, however, with real databases containing millions of customer records, with dozens or hundreds of attributes that can take on many different values. The core issue is one of scaling: The problem quickly becomes much harder as the number of attributes and the number of values those attributes can assume increases. Let's take a more careful look at the algorithm we used to identify the rule of interest discussed previously.

First, we need to determine the frequency of occurrence of every value of every attribute. In our example, this requires three histograms: one for phone use, one for second line, and one for call waiting. Next, we need to determine the frequency of occurrence for the various combinations of attributes. This requires four histograms: (1) phone use and number of lines, (2) phone use and call waiting, (3) number of lines and call waiting, and (4) phone use and number of lines and call waiting. Using these histograms, we can then calculate the probability of occurrence of each value of each attribute alone and in combination, and use the difference between the two to identify good rules. This requires 16 comparisons: four for two values of phone use in combination with two values of call waiting, and so on. As the number of attributes increases, the number of histograms required increases geometrically. And as the number of values of each attribute increases, the size of the histograms and the number of comparisons increases geometrically. For real-world problems, the histograms generally cannot fit into the memory of even the largest machines, and the comparisons can take hours on the fastest processors. Smart algorithms that prune the problem space to avoid unproductive comparisons can reduce the computational load to a manageable level. We must then rely on parallel processing and parallel I/O to bring the total time down to something that end users will find acceptable.

In contrast to our examination of neural networks, we will find rule induction more compatible with the capabilities and strengths of parallel relational databases. The histograms required for rule induction are simply counts of the unique values (or combinations of values) for the attributes and are easily created using the COUNT(*) function and GROUP BY clause of SQL. For example, we could create a histogram of the values of phone use with the following query:

```
SELECT phone_usage, COUNT(*)
FROM customer_data
GROUP BY phone_usage;
```

Here we see in concrete terms the importance of counting (and, by implication, sorting) discussed in Chapter 8. This query is easily decomposed by a parallel DBMS and makes effective use of the resources of a parallel machine. In an MPP machine, for example, each node can independently compute counts on the records it owns, then the counts across all nodes are consolidated. Note that the GROUP BY clause may be implemented by sorting or hashing, so the quality of the implementation of parallel sorting and hashing has a significant effect on the performance of this query.

The probability calculations needed to measure the "significance" of different rules are simply ratios of the counts in the histograms and are also easily handled by SQL. Typically, we will want to measure the significance of many candidate rules and rank them to find the best. The set-oriented structure of SQL fits this requirement well. It is conceivable, then, that rule induction could be implemented using the capabilities of a data warehouse based on a parallel RDBMS. In fact, this has been done in a research environment, and several commercial products that use this approach have recently emerged.

There is one problem that can cause an implementation of rule induction using SQL to perform poorly relative to an implementation in a procedural language. The structure of SQL is such that a separate query is required to create each histogram, and thus the data must be read multiple times. This can be a problem, not only because the underlying data set is typically large (reading it once is painful enough), but also because the number of histograms needed can also be large (so we must read it again and again). Note that our previous simple example already requires seven histograms. In general, if we choose M attributes at a time from N available attributes we will need $N! / [M! \times (N-M)!]$ histograms. A real-world problem might evaluate at least three attributes at a time from a data set with 15 attributes and would require $(15 \times 14 \times 13 \times \ldots \times 1) / [(3 \times 2 \times 1) \times (12 \times 11 \times \ldots \times 1)] = 455$ histograms and thus require reading the data 455 times. By contrast, procedural programs can create all the required histograms in a single pass through the data (although they don't necessarily do so).

It is possible that changes to current RDBMSs and the current SQL language could enable data mining to be performed efficiently without relying on procedural programming. For example, interquery optimization could enable a single data scan to serve simultaneously multiple queries that need the data, such as our previous histogram queries. Or SQL could be extended with a function to build all the histograms at once. Coincidentally, histograms of attribute values are also useful for optimizing queries. So makers of DBMSs, facing the same efficiency problems described previously, have specialized commands (for example, UPDATE STATISTICS) that allow multiple histograms to be created at once. Unfortunately, the results of this command are not made available for user queries.

What we'd like to be able to say is something like the following:

```
SELECT INDUCE_RULES(phone_usage, second_line, call_waiting)
FROM data;
```

where the function INDUCE_RULES is provided by a commercial "plug-in" data mining package for a commercial DBMS. As we will see in Chapter 15, emerging object-relational DBMSs may soon provide the ability to extend relational databases to more efficiently implement data mining within the DBMS.

There is still considerable algorithmic work needed to realize the full potential of rule induction. Primary difficulties revolve around the tension between the specificity of the rule and its accuracy. Highly accurate rules tend to have many clauses and to apply only to a small subset of the data (in the most extreme case, a single record). By giving up some degree of accuracy (that is, by being willing to accept some false negatives and false positives), we can obtain rules that are far more general (that is, that can be applied to a much greater percentage of the data). Thus there is inherent tension between the competing goals of accuracy (always being right) and generality (being applicable to many records). To date, the techniques available for reconciling these competing goals are largely heuristic and involve a "person in the loop." In an interactive session, the system will produce a proposed rule and will display its accuracy and generality against the sample data. The user must then decide whether the trade is good enough, and if not, suggest to the device the direction in which it should attempt to move (greater accuracy, or greater generality). Thus far, attempts to automate this aspect of rule induction have been unsuccessful. However, by greatly improving response time and by enabling much larger and more representative sample data sets to be used, parallel processing can accelerate this interactive process and improve the quality of the results.

14.3 DATA MINING USES AND SUCCESS STORIES

The use of data mining has been driven by organizations with both large volumes of data and the potential for large payoffs from understanding that data better. The payoff has been most evident in the financial, retail, and insurance industries. As a result, these industries have been leaders in commercial uses of data mining. However, the federal government is also making significant investments in data mining because of important defense, intelligence, and scientific applications.

From the user's perspective, the goal of data mining is typically one of the following:

- To explicitly identify important facts, relationships, and trends that are implicit in the data. A key fact might be anomalous credit card use which indicates that the card has been stolen. A key relationship might be similar characteristics of defective products that point to a specific problem in a manufacturing process. A key trend might be a shift in revenue from one product to another.

- To form predictive models from historical data: for example, to predict future stock prices from past prices.

These two goals are generally complementary. For example, if we can identify an important relationship in the current data (such as common characteristics of customers who purchased a product), we can probably build a predictive model that is useful (characteristics of potential customers for that product). Not all data mining techniques are equal in both tasks, however. In particular, some techniques (notably neural networks) build predictive models that cannot be interpreted by a user and thus are less suited to the first goal above than they are the second goal.

Potentially, data mining can be applied any time there is a question to be asked and data that might hold a clue to the answer. Probable functional uses of data mining include the following:

Use	Typical Questions
Market segmentation	Who is a likely customer of a product or service?
Market basket analysis	What products are often purchased together?
Resource management	What products should be stocked in each store in different regions?
Customer management	Which customers are likely to cancel their service? Which customers are using the wrong set of services?
Product evaluation	What are the effects of a new drug under various conditions of use?
Quality assurance	What are the likely causes of various manufacturing defects?
Fraud detection	Which insurance claims are likely to be fraudulent? What patterns indicate that a cellular phone number has been stolen?
Risk assessment	What is the risk of default on a given loan?
Image analysis	What spectral characteristics differentiate various types of land cover?
Sequence analysis	What other stocks have the same behavior as a given stock?

The industries in which data mining is currently being used also cover a broad range. Some of them are summarized in the following list.

Industry	Use of Data Mining
Manufacturing	Quality/defect management
Retail sales and marketing	Market segmentation Market basket analysis Inventory management
Finance (banking, credit cards, stocks)	Customer management Loan risk assessment Stock price prediction Fraud detection
Telecommunications	Cellular fraud detection Customer management
Insurance	Fraud detection Product design
Health care	Treatment evaluation
Environmental science	Land-cover classification
Defense	Land-cover classification Target recognition
Law enforcement	Fraud detection

While the possible uses of data mining are clearly numerous, we would not want to fall victim to the same hype and dashed hopes that afflicted artificial intelligence a decade ago. To this end, the following paragraphs provide specific real examples of applications where data mining has been used successfully.

Targeted Marketing with CART

Direct-mail marketing campaigns are a useful way to find new customers. However, the relatively low response rate to direct mailings (typically, a few percent) means that most of the cost of a direct mailing is spent sending information to people who don't want it. Thinking Machines Corp. used classification and regression trees (CART) to identify 60% of the potential responders in only 5% of the general population for a direct mailing campaign. This reduced the cost of the direct mailing campaign by a factor of 20 and improved the response rate sixfold.

Customer Retention with CHAID

Credit card providers are constantly faced with the problem of customer attrition. Losing good customers to another card provider translates directly into a loss of revenue and profit. The question is: What characteristics of customers and their credit card use can be used to predict that a customer is likely to leave, so that something can be done about it before it happens? Epsilon Data Management used their db-Quest suite of tools, including chi-square automatic interaction detection (CHAID), to create more than 20 predictive models of customer attrition. Data mining allowed these models to be created in about two months by two analysts rather than the much longer time typically required for manual hypothesis generation and validation. These models are currently being used to help reduce customer attrition.

Health Insurance Fraud Detection with Affinity Analysis

The Health Insurance Commission (HIC) is an agency of the Australian federal government in charge of processing claims for several Australian health-care benefit programs. Every year, HIC conducts over 300 million transactions and pays out $8 billion in benefits. The HIC data warehouse, implemented using IBM mainframes, contains approximately 1.3 TB of data. HIC has implemented checks discovered through data mining to detect fraudulent or erroneous claims. For example, using affinity analysis and neural network tools from IBM, HIC discovered an "upcoding" of pathology tests that was costing $1 million yearly in extra pathology charges. HIC was able to implement a check in the claim processing system to eliminate this practice.

Land-Cover Classification with Genetic Algorithms

Maps of land cover are useful for scientific, political, and defense purposes. They can be used to answer a broad variety of questions. What is the rate of deforestation in the Amazon? How much land in a country is being used for agriculture? Can a peacekeeping force cross the terrain between the landing area and the city? It is possible to use imagery from satellites to classify the land cover in a given area (urban, forest, agricultural, and so on), but it is difficult to find the equations that result in the best classification with the least error. In addition, with millions of pixels in an image and thousands of images to process, classification can take a very long time. MRJ Technology Solutions used genetic algorithms to evolve a basic set of functions (threshold, difference, ratio, and so on) into a land-cover classification algorithm. The resulting algorithm has about the same classification accuracy as those developed by traditional statistical means, but the genetic algorithm identifies the minimum data and the minimum processing required to do the job. For example, in 210-band hyperspectral satellite imagery, the genetic algorithm identified as few as six bands essential to land-cover classification. This selectivity, combined with the efficiency of the basic functions, has led to an improvement in total processing time of several orders of magnitude.

NBA Player Analysis with Attribute Focusing

Basketball is a game that moves at a blistering pace. It calls for fast moves not just by the players but by the coaches, too. Under the constant pressure of competition and the clock, coaches must make split-second decisions on plays, post-ups, match-ups, substitutes, and myriad other calls. IBM has developed a prototype system called "Advanced Scout" to help National Basketball Association (NBA) coaches and league officials to organize and interpret the mountains of data amassed at every game. Advanced Scout is based on a symbolic rule induction algorithm called "Attribute Focusing," developed by Inderpal Bhandari at IBM. It can detect interesting facts and patterns in the data so that a coach can know exactly which plays are most effective with which players and under what circumstances. For example, analysis of the data from a game played between the New York Knicks and the Charlotte Hornets revealed that when "Glenn Rice played the shooting guard position, he shot 5/6 (83%) on jump shots." In this case, Advanced Scout identified a specific player, position, and type of shot that is interesting because it differs considerably from the average shooting percentage of 54% for the Charlotte Hornets during that game. Patterns found by Advanced Scout are regularly posted on the NBA Website, and are the basis of the in-depth analysis of player and team match-ups presented on ESPN's broadcasts of "NBA Match-ups Presented by IBM."

Object-Relational DBMSs

In Chapters 13 and 14 we discussed the use of parallel DBMSs for (respectively) OLAP and data mining. A theme in both those chapters, and indeed throughout the book, is that the interface between the parallel RDBMS, on the one hand, and the application, on the other, can become a bottleneck. In the case of OLAP, performing analytical functions in the application can necessitate pulling large volumes of data across the (serial) application–DBMS interface. In the case of data mining, having the application request each needed histogram separately results in large numbers of full-table scans. What we would like to do is to lower the barrier between the application and the DBMS so that the parallelism provided by the DBMS is more easily accessible. In this chapter we explore briefly an emerging technology, the object-relational DBMS, and suggest how it can help lower this barrier.

Background

Current relational DBMSs provide a limited number of data types and a limited number of functions and operators that work on those data types. For example, the SQL-92 standard defines only five basic data types (character string, integer, floating-point, numeric/decimal, and day-time/interval) and a handful of functions that can be performed on them. These limitations are not inherent to the relational model per se. Rather, they are largely a reflection of the difficulty of standardizing a larger set of data types and functions, and of implementing them on a large number of platforms.

Although the number of data types and functions available in SQL has remained relatively constant over the last 10 years, application programming languages have made great advances in their support of application-defined *abstract data types*. These allow an application programmer to construct new data types from existing ones (for example, to construct a *point* as the composite of two integers for *x* and *y*) and to define operations on the new data type (for example, an operation that calculates the distance between two points). Programs written in object-oriented languages such as Smalltalk and C++ routinely make use of this capability. Although it is possible in theory to store any data in a relational database using binary large objects (or *BLOBs*), the data in a BLOB is a meaningless string of bytes to the DBMS and cannot effectively be queried or operated on. The growing mismatch between the data structures in application programs and those supported by SQL was one of the main factors that fueled the development and introduction of commercial object-oriented DBMSs (such as ObjectStore and Ontos) in the late 1980s and early 1990s. These DBMSs largely discarded the relational model and, consequently, support for SQL. At about the same time, however, products based on a hybrid approach emerged. These products (such as UniSQL and Illustra) supported abstract data types, or *objects*, but retained the relational model and hence were called *object-relational* DBMSs. When they were first introduced, object-relational DBMSs were mostly of interest for specialized applications that require complex data types, such as oil exploration map applications that require the ability to store and query points, lines, and polygons. The explosion of multimedia applications, however, has increased the general demand for complex data types such as images, graphics, and sound. The recent acquisition of Illustra by Informix signaled the entry of object-relational databases into the mainstream and set off announcements of so-called "universal server" products from the major DBMS vendors. From the perspective of this book, our interest is not so much on the support for abstract data types per se in object-relational DBMSs, as it is on the implications for parallelism. By revisiting our OLAP and data mining discussion, we will see how object-relational DBMSs can help exploit parallelism in the underlying platform.

Parallelism and Object-Relational DBMSs

Whenever large amounts of data must pass between the parallel RDBMS and the application—as must occur, for example, when the algorithm employed by the application is not easily expressed in SQL—a potential problem exists. The standard SQL interface is inherently sequential, which imposes a serial bottleneck. We have mentioned on several occasions the desirability, for example, of a direct interface between the RDBMS and the high-performance parallel file system resident on the parallel platform. However, the object relational model provides another means for addressing this concern. By extending SQL to include a much richer collection of operators, it may be possible to move functions back into the RDBMS that currently must be implemented in the application. In the following discussion we consider both possible approaches to dealing with the application/RDBMS bottleneck: (1) improving the parallel interface, and (2) improving RDBMS functionality.

The first approach is to provide a parallel interface between the application and the DBMS. Our parallel application could then retrieve the data from the DBMS in parallel. Some commercial parallel DBMSs (including IBM DB2/PE and Informix-OnLine XPS) provide the ability to restrict a query to the data local to a processing node; if the application itself can partition the query, it can then issue separate queries on each node in parallel. This solves the problem partially but does not address the fact that the DBMS, in this case, still doesn't really contribute much to the solution. As we have noted several times elsewhere in the book, the RDBMS-to-file system interface is still not a broadly supported capability.

The second approach is to push our algorithm down into the DBMS, where it can be executed directly in parallel using the same mechanisms that the DBMS uses for all its processing. Consider, for example, the following sample SQL that requests a neural network to classify the land cover in all the cloud-free images stored in a table:

```
SELECT classify(image)
FROM landsat_images
WHERE cloudiness(image) < 20%;
```

This query is easily parallelized, because each processing node can independently retrieve images, independently identify those where cloudiness is less than 20%, and then independently classify each qualifying image. The only problem, of course, is that this is not valid SQL. It requires an application-defined data type (image) and two application-defined functions (classify and cloudiness). As we noted previously, this is exactly the capability that object-relational DBMSs are intended to provide.

By virtue of its ability to let application programmers define new data types and functions, an object-relational DBMS allows us to push down into the DBMS functions needed specifically by the application. Once a new function is defined in the DBMS, it can, at least theoretically, be executed in parallel by the DBMS just like any of its predefined functions. In practice, most object-relational DBMSs are not yet parallel (and, conversely, most parallel DBMSs are not yet object-relational). The stage is set, however, for parallel object-relational DBMS implementations to emerge within the year from the major vendors. The point here is that a good data warehousing strategy must take this emerging technology into account. As one important example, traditional approaches to data aggregation utilized by multidimensional databases may need to give way as these new capabilities become broadly available.

The usefulness of parallel object-relational DBMSs is not, of course, limited to data mining with neural networks. In general, we will find that this capability will be useful anytime we have a need to store and process a data type that is not one of the standard SQL data types. These might include the following:

- *Time-series data.* These are fundamental to many financial analyses.

- *Spatial data, including points, lines, and polygons.* These are needed to efficiently store maps and to retrieve features of interest, such as all roadways and airports within an area of interest.

- *Multimedia data, including images, graphics, sound, and video.* These are useful in a broad variety of applications.

In practice, most organizations are not likely to write their own custom software to implement these functions. Rather, "third-party" vendors will utilize object-relational extensions to provide the increased functionality. As another example, recall our discussion on rule induction in Chapter 14. Our desired query appears to fit well into an object-relational model:

```
SELECT induce_rules(phone_use, second_line, call_waiting)
FROM data;
```

This query returns a set of rows, where each row represents a rule. For example, the row "high, yes, yes" would mean "if phone_use = high and second_line = yes, then call_waiting = yes." We would probably also want induce_rules to return additional information about each rule, such as the confidence in the rule or the number of records conforming to the rule. Still, all we need in this query is one application-defined function (induce_rules). There aren't even any application-defined data types. In fact, this query can be implemented in current-relational DBMSs by defining induce_rules as a stored procedure, because the arguments of the function, as well as the return values, are valid SQL data types. From this perspective, object-relational DBMSs are only a modest step beyond stored procedures. There are, however, some differences in the details. Typically, stored procedures are written in a proprietary interpreted language provided by the DBMS vendor. By contrast, object-relational DBMSs typically allow functions to be written in standard compiled languages (such as C). The performance and portability advantages of the latter can be significant.

As a final example, consider the previous discussion of OLAP in Chapter 13. We noted that multidimensional DBMSs have two features that make them attractive for OLAP: specialized data structures for fast aggregation, and specialized operators such as moving averages. In the authors' opinion, it is preferable to use fast aggregation in a parallel relational DBMSs with standard SQL interfaces rather than to use specialized DBMSs with proprietary interfaces. Too often, organizations have locked themselves into proprietary software solutions for short-term performance gains that are quickly solved by tomorrow's faster hardware. We have seen that aggregation, in particular, is the *forte* of parallel relational DBMSs, because both data partitioning and independence of processing are easy to achieve. In addition, aggregation *by definition* reduces the amount of data that must flow between nodes in a shared-nothing database architecture, making highly scalable solutions possible.

Object-relational DBMSs extend this natural advantage by providing the ability to define specialized data structures and access methods analogous to those in multidimensional DBMSs. The difference is that unlike multidimensional DBMSs, object-relational DBMS provides this capability without discarding the relational model altogether. This makes it possible, so to speak, to have your cake and eat it too.

Object-relational databases also support the use of specialized OLAP operators. As we mentioned previously, standard SQL defines only a handful of functions, while we are likely to need many others for OLAP. Note, for example, that a typical spreadsheet package supports well over 100 mathematical, financial, and statistical functions. The simplicity of a solution using an object-relational DBMS is thus attractive in itself. For example, it is possible using current products to store daily stock prices in a time-series data type, and to request the 10-day moving average as of today with a single statement as follows:

```
SELECT stock_name, moving_average(price_time_series,10, today() )
FROM daily_stock_prices;
```

The advantage, from our perspective, is that the opportunity for parallelism has been increased. Because the function moving_average is essentially an aggregation function, it can efficiently be distributed to different nodes of a parallel machine, and only the aggregate need be returned to the application. The alternative, retrieving the detail data through the serial application–DBMS interface and performing the calculations and aggregation in the application, will not perform nearly as well. In that case, as in our example on neural networks, the parallel DBMS does little more than act as a high-priced file server, and most of the parallel capability of the machine is wasted.

Numerous vendors are already writing plug-in modules for object-relational DBMSs to provide functions ranging from image processing to full-text search. We also know that the major DBMS vendors are integrating object-relational capabilities into their mainstream product lines. We fully expect to see in the near future parallel object-relational DBMSs with the capabilities needed to better support OLAP and data mining directly in the data warehouse.

Chapter

16

Benchmarking and Implementation

In this chapter the discussion turns to some of the practical issues facing an organization considering a parallel implementation of a data warehouse. As with previous chapters, our point of view will be on large decision support environments, and this will constrain and focus the discussion in a number of ways. The operational concept, the types of requirements, the relative priority of evaluation criteria, and the best approach to system development and deployment are all affected.

We begin (Section 16.1) with a discussion of the TPC-D benchmark suite published and administered by the Transaction Processing Council. This benchmark is capable of scaling to very large database sizes, and it exercises exactly the type of ad hoc complex queries typical of data warehouse implementations. Our discussion will provide a brief overview of the benchmarks, with some comments and suggestions about their use. In Section 16.2 we turn to a discussion of development and implementation. Parallel hardware and software is able to scale over several orders of magnitude of performance, and the development plan ought to take this into account and use it to advantage. This will also permit us to revisit for a final time a major theme of the book—the interface between the RDBMS, on the one hand, and high-performance data mining algorithms, on the other.

In Section 16.3, we summarize by providing *20 embarrassing questions* that ought to be asked when considering a parallel implementation of a data warehouse. Some of these are generic and are part of the more general planning and design process leading up to any data warehouse. Others are quite specific, and focus on the technical implications associated with parallel processing and parallel RDBMS software. This will also provide an opportunity to review what we feel are the key points made in the previous pages—a fitting conclusion summarizing and emphasizing salient ideas and recommendations.

16.1 BENCHMARKS AND PERFORMANCE ESTIMATION

Common Benchmark Metrics

Benchmarks are useful for a number of purposes. For example, if the benchmark accurately reflects the intended application and workload, it can help in *sizing*: How much storage, memory, and processing power are needed to meet the project's performance requirements? Benchmarking can also be used as a means of *comparison*: Given a certain size job, which of a set of competing products can do the job faster, or for a better price? If the job is somewhat like the intended application, then (it is felt) the machine that performs best on the benchmark also ought to perform best on the intended application.

It is the second of these uses—comparison of products—that tends to receive the most attention. The question of "which" software/hardware offering to purchase (comparison) is separated out from the question of "how large" a machine will be required (sizing). The foremost concern of most vendors is with the "which machine?" question, and only secondarily with the "how much machine?" question. Obtaining good results on recognized benchmarks is thus a major goal.

All this must be taken with a grain of salt. Ultimately, the "right" choice of machine for a given project will depend on a complex combination of evaluation criteria, only some of which are tied directly to timed execution on a fixed problem. These other criteria—functionality, reliability, security, interfacing to legacy hardware and software, and so on—are independent of, and can compete against, raw performance and cost/performance.

One important area, which we have stressed repeatedly, and which may be the most important of all in the long run, is *scalability*. The hardware and software must be able to grow over time smoothly to meet changing levels of use. There are a number of dimensions along which this scaling can occur: size of the database, number of users, complexity of queries, complexity of applications, need for improved response time. Changing requirements in any of these areas can push both hardware and software to more demanding levels of performance. The goal, then, is to be able to evolve the underlying system along any of these dimensions with as little disruption and as much flexibility as possible. In particular, the architecture must have *no inherent upper limit* that would prevent future requirements from being satisfied.

There are a number of techniques for taking scalability into account in constructing good parallel benchmarks. Most important (see Figure 16–1), the benchmark should be executed over a range of problem sizes and machine sizes. In the chart we envision measuring execution time for varying combinations of *both* the machine size and the problem size. The reader might envision a spreadsheet, with rows labeled by problem size, columns labeled by machine size, and the value in the cell recording the associated time to execute.

Figure 16–1 Three Types of Benchmark Measures

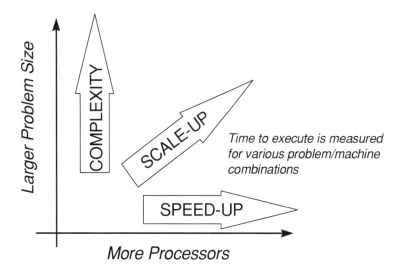

Three "directions" along the chart are possible. Moving *horizontally*, we hold problem size constant and increase the number of processing nodes in the machine. What we hope to see is that the performance increases linearly with machine size: Doubling (say) the number of processors should halve the execution time. This results in a speed-up curve (recall the discussion in Chapter 1), which is subject to Amdahl's law: If the problem size is held constant, eventually the sequential component of the problem dominates and a point is reached at which adding more nodes no longer improves performance. Second, we may move *vertically* across the array: that is, hold the machine size constant and measure performance (= time to execute) on a set of problems of varying sizes. Here we obtain a *complexity* curve, since many problems (such as sorting) scale superlinearly as a function of their size. Nevertheless, in this dimension Amdahl's law works *in favor* of large machines. The reason is (as we observed in Chapter 1) that machine efficiency will tend to improve as problem size increases. Thus a large percentage of the available power in the machine can usefully be put to work if the problem is large. As we observed in Chapter 1, large machines need large problems to be used efficiently. The third direction—and in some ways the most interesting—is to move *diagonally* up and to the right. Here we obtain what may be called the *scale-up curve*. The idea is to increase *both* the problem *and* the machine size together, a larger problem executing on a larger machine. Ideally, we hope to observe that the execution time holds constant: Doubling both the problem size and the machine size should result in no change in execution time.

A new type of benchmark has emerged in response to the need for this kind of analysis. Basically, the vendor is asked to determine how large a problem can be worked in a fixed amount of time—say, 1 minute. An example of such a benchmark for a parallel RDBMS might be: How many rows (of a fixed row size) can your machine scan in a minute? Here, both time and machine size are held constant and the problem size is allowed to vary (see Figure 16–2). We again obtain a speed-up curve, but this time displayed in a different form. For various machine sizes (the vertical axis), we see displayed the maximum problem size (horizontal axis) that can be solved in (say) 1 minute. We might call this the *fixed-time speed-up curve*, and it is a particularly good way of judging scalability over a large range of machine and problem sizes.

We have also discussed at some length the difference between *throughput* (a processing rate—how many independent instances of a problem can be solved per unit time?) and *latency* (how fast can a single problem be solved, dedicating all the machine resources to it?). Here, we meet our old friends interquery parallelism and intraquery parallelism in a different form. For example, to measure throughput, a benchmark might be designed to increase the rate at which queries are submitted (*à la* OLTP measures of performance) until the machine can no longer keep up. The typical "transactions per second" metric for OLTP benchmarks is of this sort, and it emphasizes interquery parallelism. In this book, however, we have stressed intraquery parallelism: How fast can the machine perform a single large complex query if all the machine's resources are dedicated to that problem? This appears to be a more appropriate measure for decision support and data warehouse applications, where a single query on a large machine might execute for tens or hundreds of seconds.

Figure 16–2   New Type of Scale-up Measure

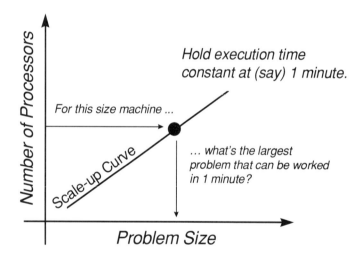

Transaction Processing Performance Council
TPC-D Benchmarks

The Transaction Processing Performance Council (TPC) has been established by industry vendors as an "honest broker" for defining and auditing query performance for RDBMS systems. Early benchmarks focused on OLTP, but a recent benchmark, TPC-D, focuses on complex queries for decision support. A complete specification of the benchmark, including schema, data set sizes, and SQL listings for the queries, can be downloaded from the TPC Web site: http://www.tpc.org. The following paragraphs, then, will serve solely as a brief introduction; detailed information is best obtained directly from the specification document itself. Also available are published results of audited benchmark performance for vendors who have completed successfully all phases of the benchmark. These results can also be used in advertising and promotional literature.

The heart of the benchmark are 17 complex queries that stress various aspects of the hardware–software combination, including full-table scans, complex joins, deeply nested SELECTs, and a variety of aggregation functions (SUM, COUNT, AVERAGE) on complex GROUP BY conditions. Each query is in the form of a template, with user-supplied parameters left undefined until run time. These "blanks" are then filled in at run time "at random" (that is, using a pseudo-random-number generator to select actual parameter values from a specified set or range of values). Thus vendors cannot "tune" the machine to specific queries, since the specific form of the query can vary greatly depending on how the template is filled in.

None of the 17 queries performs any update function. To deal with loads and deletes, two additional "queries" are included: one that performs a bulk load operation, and one that performs a bulk delete operation. Benchmark times include the time to execute these operations, although (in the throughput measure discussed later) the update function can (at the vendor's discretion) be implemented in a "trickle" fashion concurrently with ongoing query processing.

To complete the entire benchmark successfully, the vendor must not only execute the queries and obtain timings, but must also execute queries that demonstrate the ACID properties (atomicity, consistency, isolation, and durability). Further, detailed rules are included for pricing estimates, including full disclosure and five-year cost of ownership. Thus price–performance calculations are based on publicly available and audited price lists.

A *scale factor* is included with the benchmark and may be thought of as the size, in gigabytes, of the database on which the queries are executed. These scale factors range from 1 up to 10,000 (~ 10 TB). Most vendors targeting large data warehouse implementations are current executing at the 300 level (~ 300 GB). Total disk storage on benchmark systems at this scale factor ranges from 1.5 to 3.5 TB (a ratio of physical to real of anywhere from 5:1 to 12:1). The TPC stresses that results at different scale factors should *not* be compared against each other. Only performances against the *same* scale factor are reasonably comparable.

Three top-level metrics are produced by TPC-D, in addition to a host of lower-level detailed data. These are:

- QppD@scale_factor. Units are in queries per hour. The entire benchmark suite of 17 queries plus two load/delete operations is executed, one at a time, in order. The full machine is available for every query (*no* interquery parallelism is allowed in this phase). The "time per query" is taken to be the geometric mean of the individual query times, and the reported value converts this to a rate. QppD is sometimes called the *power metric*.

- QthD@scale_factor. Units are in queries per hour. Multiple query streams can be executed concurrently, so that interquery parallelism is allowed. It is interesting to note that, as of this publication, no vendor at the 300-GB scale factor has chosen to execute multiple query streams. The "time per query" is taken as the *arithmetic* mean of the individual query times (taken as the total time to execute all of them). Since the geometric mean (used in QppD) tends to be smaller than the arithmetic mean (QthD), QppD values have tended to be higher than QthD numbers. QthD is sometimes called the *throughput metric*.

- $/QphD@scale_factor. The units are dollars per queries per hour. Cost is audited five-year cost of ownership. The "queries per hour" in the denominator is the geometric mean of QppD and QthD.

The TPC-D benchmarks are intended to measure performance on ad hoc queries. One consequence of this is that database design strategies that take extensive advantage of preknowledge of queries patterns are not permitted. To show the affect of this, note that such commonly used statistics as sums—either horizontally across organization components, or vertically over time—can be precomputed and stored in directly accessible tables as part of the data load and update process. If a query asks for this data, it can be retrieved "instantly" without the need to recompute the sum by referencing the raw underlying fact table. If it is known in advance that users will make queries for this information (say, because they are provided with an OLAP GUI that presents exactly such queries), it makes sense to have this data precomputed and on-line. This technique is used by so-called multidimensional databases. What they give up in flexibility (that is, truly ad hoc queries of indeterminate complexity) they gain in access time (since the data has been largely precomputed).

One example of this phenomena occurs in Query 1, which forces a full-table scan of the central fact table accumulating a variety of summary statistics. If it were known in advance that these statistics are needed, the query processing time could be reduced from many hundreds of seconds to "instantaneous." Ordinarily, the TPC is very strict about not permitting variants to the SQL-92 standard syntax in which its queries are written. Except for query 15, where a VIEW is CREATEd and later DELETEd, all queries are written as single SELECT statements (with possibly nested SELECTs in the FROM and WHERE clauses). For whatever reason, the TPC has permitted vendors to rewrite some of the queries extensively using CREATE TABLE and CREATE VIEW syntax. All variants from the standard syntax are noted in the published full benchmark results, but do not appear (for example) in summary promotional literature, which cites only the top-level results. At the scale factor of 300, we may note particularly variant b of query 17, where vendors have been permitted to define explicitly an intermediate table to hold AVERAGE results from an initial table scan. The query then scans the table a second time, looking for instances that fall below 20% of the AVERAGE in a number of categories. As originally written, the query nests the AVERAGE calculation deep within a WHERE clause, while the approved variant lifts the intermediate table out as an explicit entity. At scale factors other than 300, we find similar approved variants for several other queries (7 through 9 and 11 through 14).

The reason for bringing this up is that it appears that rewriting of complex queries, particularly instructions to the query optimizer for construction of intermediate VIEWs and TABLEs, appears to have substantial performance advantages. The conclusion, then, is that some care may be required not just in tuning the database, but in the writing of SQL. In our opinion, the SQL prepared by the TPC is "standard," and it seems to us reasonable to expect a query optimizer to be able to sort through this syntax.

Finally, we note that the TPC-D is *not* a sizing tool. It does allow different hardware and software products to be compared in a controlled and auditable way, but it does not support (nor is it intended to support) database design decisions or sizing estimates. In this connection it is particularly interesting to observe that vendors at the 300-GB scale factor *have not attempted to execute multiple independent query streams*. Thus the TPC-D benchmark results at the 300-GB level contain no data at all on how the system will respond when multiple users are accessing the data concurrently. In a way, this is surprising, since interquery parallelism is ordinarily thought to be easier and more cost-effective than intraquery parallelism. Is it likely that many organizations will purchase large data warehouses in excess of $5 million just to execute single queries one after another? It seems to these observers that some bridge needs to be built between the highly focused single-user versions of the benchmark currently being executed at the 300-GB level and the intended operational environment.

Other Benchmarks

The best benchmarks are those an organization executes against its own data, using its own schema, and reflecting its own desired query patterns. Many vendors maintain facilities to support such benchmarking efforts, and it is at this stage where sizing estimates (memory, storage, number of processors, I/O channels, and so on) can be made. There is another area of benchmarking that may be relevant in instances where database mining is to be implemented which does *not* make direct use of SQL. The data mining code will have an interface to the RDBMS for data extraction, but once extracted, the application code will execute independently of the RDBMS. The most interesting configuration is one in which both the RDBMS and the data mining application code share the same parallel platform. This has two advantages. First, it offers the possibility that the RDBMS can export data directly to a parallel file system (rather than having to sequentialize the output stream, which is the typical external interface). Second, it permits the data mining algorithm to take full advantage of the processing power offered by a large parallel machine.

In such a case, the TPC-D benchmarks do not offer much advantage. What is needed is a benchmark that reflects the (often complex) processing characteristic of data mining and knowledge extraction algorithms. A good example of such an algorithm is *sorting*. As we mentioned in Chapter 8, *there is no SQL statement than can force a parallel RDBMS to sort data physically across all the processing nodes of a parallel machine*. On the other hand, it is precisely such sorted data that many (most?) data mining algorithms need. Thus a physical sort of a large flat file is an excellent benchmark for non-SQL-based data mining applications. The sort should be an external sort (that is, the data being sorted should be several times as large as the physical memory of the machine), and separate timings should be produced for the portion of the time the machine spends in I/O, in interprocessor communications, and in CPU processing.

It turns out that generating a sorting benchmark is far easier than generating a full TPC-D benchmark. This is also a perfect opportunity for using the *fixed-time scale-up metric* described previously: How many records can the machine sort in (say) 1 minute? By executing this same benchmark for various numbers of nodes (16, 32, 48, 64, and so on), good scaling data can be obtained quickly. Even if the TPC-D results are available, it is still useful to execute a sorting benchmark as one piece of data to support the procurement and sizing process. In the authors' opinion, no data warehouse purchase should be made without knowing how well the machine will be able to sort a large flat file.

Another simple but very important benchmark concerns sustained I/O bandwidth to disk. In the TPC-D benchmarks, the numbers that are produced are composite: We do not know how much of the run time for any given query is due to processing, I/O, interprocessor communications, and so on. Thus we do not know how scaling independently along any of these dimensions will affect performance. The benchmark has an "all or nothing" quality that blurs such fine distinctions. One way to penetrate this fog is to ask for benchmark results that focus solely on sustained I/O bandwidth. These should be executed using the intended RAID configuration and should be performed using a resident parallel file system. The task is (first) to read and (then) to write a single large disk-resident flat file some number of times. Such matters as block size and arrangement on disk should be chosen to match the intended implementation, since these factors can dramatically affect achievable performance. As with sorting, the authors believe that no data warehouse procurement should be made without benchmark evidence of sustainable I/O bandwidth, for both read and write operations.

16.2 IMPLEMENTATION ISSUES

The process of planning, designing, and implementing a data warehouse is complex, and a complete discussion of all the relevant issues goes far beyond the scope of the present volume. An excellent introduction to the broader issues can be found in a companion volume of this series, *Planning and Designing the Data Warehouse* (R. Barquin and H. Edelstein, Prentice Hall, Upper Saddle River, N.J., 1997). Our focus in the next few pages will be to discern the specific ways in which the use of parallel technology can affect the more general planning, design, and implementation process.

The following four steps encapsulate, at a high level, the typical sequence of activities leading to deployment of a data warehouse. This "methodology" is widely used by DSS industry consultants.

1. An opportunity is identified with high potential business value.
2. A small proof-of-concept is then developed, leading to both a refined set of requirements and demonstration to management of the value in concrete terms.
3. The full-up buy/build phase is then entered.
4. Operations are transferred to customer personnel.

This is envisioned as an iterative process, with subsequent development efforts following potentially on the success of the initial version. It often occurs that once a customer has experience with the potential of decision support technology, new ideas and opportunities with high business payoff are quickly identified, and demand for them increases among the user community. Thus, second or third iterations can follow, as appropriate, building on and expanding the core infrastructure developed during the first cycle of the process. This is sometimes referred to as a *spiral* methodology, and it is illustrated in Figure 16–3.

Figure 16–3   Spiral Development Methodology Suitable for Data Warehouses

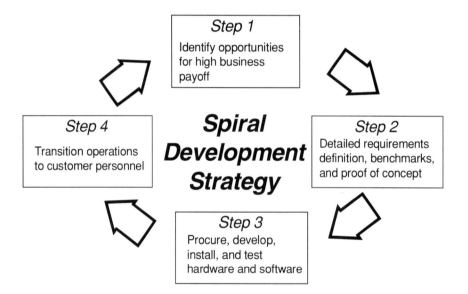

Whatever development methodology is selected, it should be able to take full advantage of the unique scalability features provided by parallel hardware and software. The key idea is that parallel architectures are capable of scaling, in small increments, from very small (prototype) configurations to very large (data warehouse) configurations with full reuse of the software. Thus there is no loss of investment as larger configurations become required. This enables a low-risk approach, which is particularly appropriate for organizations new to the technology or that are inherently risk-averse.

The same ideas can be exploited by any organization considering a parallel implementation of a decision support infrastructure. Small low-risk prototype implementations that demonstrate high business value are very appealing because they do not require a large up-front commitment of resources (both monetary and personnel). However, by selecting a scalable parallel platform (both hardware and software), all of the initial investment in the prototype can be recovered and migrated to a larger configuration. The prototype can also serve as an excellent means for in-house benchmarking, which in turn supports subsequent stages of detailed requirements definition. Long before the full-up multi-TB data warehouse rolls in the door, the tough questions about use patterns, data update cycles, backup and restore, and so on, will have been answered in a convincing way on real hardware.

Our experience has been that it is often preferable to do software and application development on small platforms, and then scale upward with full software reuse to large implementations. This approach works, and it avoids many pitfalls by working through the entire problem completely, once, in advance of final implementation. This low-risk "proof of concept" approach has proved itself repeatedly by avoiding pitfalls and demonstrating business value early in the development cycle.

There are other ways in which the use of parallel technology affects the plan–design–build process. One concerns facilities impact. A high-performance parallel platform requires a high-performance interconnection network (recall Chapter 2). This, in turn, often requires extensive cabling—connecting processor racks both to each other and to the disk storage units. A glance at some of the published TPC-D benchmarks will show the amount of cabling and its expense. For some organizations this may be a new experience, so a word to the wise is appropriate. Similarly, although parallel processors utilize air-cooled CMOS chip technology, the power dissipation of both microprocessors and interconnection components is increasing as clock speeds accelerate and transistor densities continue to improve. Thus thought must be given both to power supplies and to cooling. Although small configurations suitable, say, for data marts can exist in an office environment, raised-floor glass house facilities may well be required for larger assemblies. For most commercial hardware suppliers, aggressive packaging has not been a high priority.

The design of the schemas themselves can be affected by the choice of parallel implementations. As we have seen at some length in Part II, the key to high performance on large data warehouses is to maintain high I/O bandwidth to the major tables. This requires partitioning of the data; and this, in turn, must be kept in mind as the schemas are constructed. A fair amount of denormalization (that is, precomputed JOINs) may well be appropriate. Further, as we saw in the discussion of SQL variants of the TPC-D benchmarks, extensive use of explicitly constructed intermediate tables may be required for efficiency. Finally, the amount of working disk space must be reassessed in light of parallel implementations. A glance at the TPC-D benchmarks will show typical ratios of "live to required" data storage. A profile of the query workload can also help: Remember that not all queries in the TPC-D suite require the same amount of disk. If an organization does not need the most demanding types of query (or is willing to forgo them), disk storage savings can result.

Finally, some organization will find that an SQL interface to the database is not sufficient to implement their data mining algorithms. In that case, two immediate issues arise. First, the application code to implement the data mining application must be developed or procured, and this imposes its own sizing and benchmarking constraints. Second, an interface between the database (where the raw data resides) and the data mining code must be developed. At present, this interface is awkward: Most vendors still export data using a serial stream that can become a performance bottleneck on a large parallel system. In time, we fully expect to see direct interfaces between the parallel RDBMS and the parallel file system residing on the same parallel host. This will greatly facilitate this process, and we can envision a scenario in which the top-level application code freely migrates the data back and forth between the RDBMS and the data mining tools, allowing each to contribute in the area of its greatest strengths. Although this remains a future development, we have reason to believe that advantages inherent in this approach will drive the industry in this direction.

16.3 TWENTY EMBARRASSING QUESTIONS

In this final section we summarize many of the issues addressed throughout the book using the technique of introspection. What follows is a list of 20 embarrassing questions that anyone considering a data warehouse—particularly a data warehouse implemented using parallel technology—probably ought to be asking themselves as early in the process as possible. The questions span a considerable range, from quite general questions on purpose and scope to very specific questions relating to design and implementation. Having good answers to these questions is a strong indication of eventual success. Failure to answer a question indicates a chink in the armor and hence an area that probably needs to be addressed. Good luck with this quiz to assess your readiness to proceed with implementing a data warehouse!

1. Why do you want a data warehouse? What specific business questions do you intend to answer?

   Comment: Without clear business objectives, the project has a very much greater chance of failing. Data warehouses have recently achieved a patina of high-tech respectability that has many organizations scrambling. First things first. Identify the business need, then determine whether a decision support infrastructure is the right way to address that need.

2. How do you intend to measure return on investment for the data warehouse?

   Comment: A large data warehouse is a potential black hole for IT resources—monetary and personnel. What is the specific, measurable value it brings to the enterprise? How big is big enough? Note that with a scalable architecture, it is possible to start small and grow while retaining the full value of previous investment. The next increment of growth need not occur until the previous increment has proven its utility.

3. Concerning users: Who are they? What interface do they need? How many will need access to the data warehouse concurrently? What response time is acceptable?

   Comment: A clearly defined concept of operations is a key to success. How will the users access the data? Will OLAP tools be used, or are your users sophisticated SQL pros able to generate their own ad hoc queries? How many will be logged on at once? (See Question 8.)

4. Does the data warehouse directly support operations? What are the business consequences of unavailability?

   Comment: A realistic assessment of reliability and availability requirements is needed. Many decision support implementations do not require the kind of 24 × 7 availability numbers typical of OLTP. If not, savings are possible both for decreased storage (RAID 5 instead of mirroring) and software (no need to purchase the high-availability options of the software package).

5. What is your top-level architecture? Does your data warehouse service multiple local data marts?

   Comment: A typical and useful top-level architecture is for the central data warehouse to support (that is, supply data to) data marts targeted at specific user communities throughout the enterprise. In this case, the OLAP tools at the local sites match the users there, and the data warehouse is relieved of direct query processing other than bulk loads and occasional data extracts. In this business model, the TPC-D benchmarks are not particularly relevant since the data warehouse software will not be directly executing complex queries against its data. Further, OLAP structures at the local data marts can often achieve great efficiency since queries are precanned and can be prepared in advance.

6. What is the source of your data? How frequently will the data warehouse be updated/refreshed, and what is the likely size of these updates? How many weeks/months/years of data is the data warehouse expected to contain?

   Comment: A complete concept of operations includes the data update/refresh cycle. Often, data for the data warehouse comes from extracts from the OLTP operational data. Thus a coordinated interface to the OLTP function(s) is required. One common source of pressure for growth is the length of time covered by the accessible data. A typical scenario rolls out old data to make room for new data. If the data warehouse is larger, a longer time window for analysis can be supported.

7. Have you considered the possibility that your data sources contain "dirty" data? Are there format and definition conflicts among your data sources?

   Comment: A well-known problem in any data centralization effort is (1) reconciling data definitions that have grown up independently, and (2) cleaning the data. Unfortunately, this is a problem for which parallel processing offers no advantage.

8. Which is most important to your concept of operations: interquery parallelism (handling multiple independent queries concurrently), or intraquery parallelism (processing single complex queries as fast as possible)?

Comment: The answer to this question goes a long way toward determining the design of the database, particularly the degree of data partitioning and the operational setting. Note that OLAP tools are typically designed for interquery parallelism, and TPC-D benchmark results (at the 300-GB scale factor) focus on intraquery parallelism. It makes a difference which of these performance ranges your application is targeting, and it is hard to do both. The point of view taken in this book has been that OLAP should be run on smaller data marts located local to the organizations they support, and that the centralized data warehouse is where the very large ad hoc queries and data mining algorithms reside.

9. Have you considered the possibility of a small demonstration project to show proof-of-concept and demonstrate business value?

   Comment: The authors are firm believers in the point of view that says: (1) start small, (2) show business value, and (3) make sure that your architecture scales. Building a data warehouses is like revenge: It tastes better when eaten in small bites.

10. Where does scalability lie on your prioritized list of system requirements? What is the largest possible configuration that you can envision for the eventual system? Can you reach that goal without having to change hardware architecture and/or software database vendor?

    Comment: A consistent theme of this book has been the ability of parallel computers, particularly the variants of distributed memory architectures, to scale smoothly in small increments over a very large range of performance. Scalablility includes several dimensions: database size, number of users, complexity of queries, improved response time, and so on. By making the right choice at the beginning, a data warehouse implementation can ensure that there are no inherent architectural limitations to achieve what level of performance eventually is required. This consideration ought to be near the top of the list of considerations for prospective data warehouse projects.

11. Have you executed a sorting and a bulk data I/O benchmark on the intended platform?

   Comment: As mentioned in Section 16.1, we believe that a large out-of-core sort and a sustained I/O bandwidth benchmark should be part of any decision support procurement process.

12. Do you intend to execute non-SQL-based data mining algorithms? If so, what is the proposed interface to the data warehouse?

   Comment: A consistent theme of this book has been that many powerful data mining algorithms are not easily expressed in SQL. Thus an interface between the RDBMS and the data mining application is required—hopefully, one that does not become a serial I/O bottleneck. An ideal situation is when the data mining application executes on the same parallel platform as the RDBMS. We have expressed the hope that, over time, vendors will provide a way to exploit this potentiality.

13. Are the TPC-D benchmarks directly applicable to your project? Which of the TPC-D queries best reflect your intended use?

   Comment: The point of this question is to remind the reader that TPC-D benchmark results require interpretation. Some parts of the benchmark may be more appropriate than others, and there are some important performance issues for data warehouses that the benchmark does not address at all. Some thought and care regarding the benchmark can help prevent drawing unwarranted conclusions.

14. Does your intended schema match the suggested "star schema" pattern? If not, have you assessed the performance impact of your alternative?

   Comment: As discussed in Chapter 5, there are reasons behind the almost universal recommendation of the data warehouse industry in favor of a star schema. Readers should understand the reasons behind that recommendation and have good reasons of their own to depart from it. A very highly normalized schema requiring a large number of JOINs with low selectivity cannot be executed efficiently on *any* database.

15. What architecture type is your proposed hardware platform? (See Part I.) What architecture type is your proposed software RDBMS package? (See Part II.) Why did you select these approaches?

   Comment: An understanding of the architectural issues discussed in Parts I and II is essential for an informed decision about hardware and software implementations. We suggest that the reader be prepared to defend an HW/SW architecture choice in the terms presented there.

16. Do you expect complex ad hoc queries to form a large part of the workload? If not, can suitably constructed aggregation tables be constructed to speed execution of commonly asked "canned" queries and report generation?

   Comment: As discussed in the sections on OLAP and on TPC-D, if the query pattern can be prespecified into a known set of canned templates, there are a number of preaggregation strategies that can dramatically accelerate query performance. TPC-D, on the other hand, measures performance against ad hoc queries. This question is closely related to questions 3 and 8.

17. Is sorting—that is, full physical sorting of very large single tables—an important operation for your application? If so, how do you intend to implement it?

Comment: Yet another prod, reminding the reader that RDBMSs do not provide sorting of the kind described here and that sorting is a requirement for sophisticated data mining algorithms.

18. Have you seriously considered not using indexes for large table scans?

Comment: As discussed at some length in Chapters 5 and 6, there are many complex queries against large tables where indexes do not help. Indeed, the tendency among OLTP implementations to fully invert must be resisted, since indexes help only where the selectivity of the query is very high. Further, indexes require a large amount of additional storage, and they add substantial overhead during the load process. For large decision support applications, the default position should always be not to build an index unless there is some overriding reason to do so. The one exception to this rule (by which it is thereby proved) is the use of indexes on date, a very common retrieval parameter.

19. How much total storage will be required above and beyond the "live" data? What sizing methodology did you use to obtain that estimate?

Comment: Sizing of disk storage is not a topic that we have considered in any detail. TPC-D benchmark results show some examples of what vendors are suggesting, but it is not clear which of the queries drove the additional storage (ranging from factors of 5 upward) to their announced levels. Was it indexes? Was it temporary work space? Without a performance model indicating how and why the extra storage will be used, the buyer will be at the mercy of the system vendor in making these sizing decisions.

20. What will be your approach to data partitioning? What factors will you consider in making this decision?

Comment: A constant theme throughout the book has been the importance of data partitioning and redistribution techniques. This is the one piece of indispensable information needed by anybody considering implementing a parallel database. If this matter is not yet clear, a rereading of Chapters 4 (on parallel I/O), 5 (on general parallelization principles), and 6 (on major RDBMS architectures) would probably be appropriate. *Take heed:* Don't buy a parallel database unless you understand how and why data tables will be partitioned across the available disks!

References and Suggested Reading

Adriaans, P., and D. Zantinge, *Data Mining*, Addison-Wesley, Reading, Mass., 1996.

Agerwala, T., et al., "SP2 System Architecture," *IBM Systems Journal*, 1995, pp. 152–185.

Barquin, R., and H. Edelstein, *Planning and Designing the Data Warehouse*, Prentice Hall, Upper Saddle River, N.J., 1996.

Barquin, R. and H. Edelstein, *Building, Using, and Managing a Data Warehouse*, Prentice Hall, Upper Saddle River, N.J., 1995.

Baru, C. K., et al., "DB2 Parallel Edition," *IBM Systems Journal*, 1995, pp. 292–322.

Berry, M. A. J., and G. S. Linoff, *Data Mining Techniques for Marketing, Sales, and Customer Support*, Wiley, New York, 1997.

Braithwaite, K. S., *Systems Design in a Database Environment*, McGraw-Hill, New York, 1989.

Chen, P. M., et al., "RAID: High-Performance, Reliable Secondary Storage," Vol. 2, *ACM Computing Surveys*, 1994.

Corey, M., and M. Abbey, *Oracle Data Warehousing*, Osborne/McGraw-Hill, Berkeley, Calif., 1997.

Corey, J. C., et al., *Tuning Oracle* (in the *Oracle Press* series), Osborne/McGraw-Hill, Berkelely, Calif., 1995.

Date, C., *An Introduction to Database Systems,* Vol. I, Addison-Wesley, Reading, Mass., 1990.

Date, C. J., and H. Darwen, *A Guide to the SQL Standard, 3rd ed.*, Addison-Wesley, Reading, Mass., 1994.

DeWitt, D., and J. Gray, "Parallel Database Systems: The Future of High Performance Database Systems," in L. Hongjung et al., eds., *Query Processing in Parallel Relational Database Systems,* IEEE Press, New York, 1994, pp. 4–17.

Dhar, V., and R. Stein, *Seven Methods for Transforming Corporate Data into Business Intelligence*, Prentice Hall, Upper Saddle River, N.J., 1997.

Fayyad, U. M., et al., *Advances in Knowledge Discovery and Data Mining*, MIT Press, Cambridge, Mass., 1996.

Gill, H., and P. Rao, *The Official Client/Server Computing Guide to Data Warehousing*, Indianapolis, Ind., Que, 1996.

Hongjun, L., et al., eds., *Query Processing in Parallel Relational Database Systems*, IEEE Press, New York, 1994.

Informix, *INFORMIX-OnLine Dynamic Server: Performance Guide*, Informix Press, 1994.

Inmon, W., *Building the Data Warehouse*, Wiley, New York, 1993.

Inmon, W., and R. Hackathorn, *Using the Data Warehouse*, Wiley, New York, 1994.

Kelly, S., *Data Warehousing: The Route to Mass Customization*, Wiley, New York, 1994.

Kimball, R., *The Data Warehouse Toolkit*, Wiley, New York, 1996.

Mattison, R., *Data Warehousing: Strategies, Technologies, and Techniques*, McGraw-Hill, New York, 1996.

Miller, L. L., et al., *Parallel Architectures for Data/Knowledge-Based Systems*, IEEE Press, New York, 1994.

Morse, H. S., *Practical Parallel Computing*, Academic Press Professional, Chestnut Hill, Mass., 1994.

O'Neil, P., *Database Principles, Programming, Performance*, Morgan Kaufmann, San Francisco, 1994.

Piatetsky-Shapiro, G., and W. J. Frawley, *Knowledge Discovery in Databases*, MIT Press, Camridge, Mass., 1991.

Pirahesh, H., et al., "Parallelism in Relational Data Base Systems: Architectural Issues and Design Approaches," in L. Hongjung et al., *Query Processing in Parallel Relational Database Systems*, IEEE Press, New York, 1994, pp. 18–43.

Poe, XXX, *Building a Data Warehouse for Decision Support*, Prentice Hall, Upper Saddle River, N.J., 1996.

Spewak, S. H., *Enterprise Architecture Planning*, Wiley-QED, Somerset, N.J., 1992.

SSA Industry Association, *Serial Storage Architecture: A Technology Overview (V. 3.0)*, SSA, 1995.

Stonebraker, M., and D. Moore, *Object Relational DBMSs: The Next Great Wave*, Morgan Kaufmann, San Francisco, 1996.

Sun Microsystems, "The Ultra Enterprise 10000 Server," Technical White Paper, Sun, 1997.

Suaya and Birtwhistle, *VLSI and Parallel Computation*, Morgan Kaufman, San Francisco, 1990.

Tomasevic, M., *Cache-Coherence Problem in Shared-Memory Multiprocessors: Hardware Solutions*, IEEE Press, New York, 1993.

Transaction Processing Performance Council, *TPC Benchmark D Standard Specification 1.2.2*, TPPC, 1996.

Ullman, J. D., *Principles of Database Systems, 2nd ed*, Computer Science Press, New York, 1982.

Valduriez, P., "Parallel Database Systems: Open Problems and New Issues," *Distributed and Parallel Databases*, April 1993, pp. 137–166.

Acronyms and Glossary

ACID *Atomicity, consistency, isolation, durability*; four properties tested for by TPC benchmarks.

Amdahl's law The observation that the time taken to execute the sequential part of a problem is an upper bound to speed-up, no matter how many processors may be applied. Fortunately, the fraction of a problem that is sequential changes and becomes very small for very large problems. This is what enables massively parallel machines to achieve high efficiency on large problems.

associative retrieval Selection of rows based solely on key value. Range partitioning of tables can accelerate this type of operation, since partitions of the table that do not bracket the desired value can immediately be excluded from consideration.

atomicity One of the four ACID requirements in TPC benchmarks; ensures that all or none of the effects of query take place; partial updates are not permitted.

base table In the relational model, some tables are permanent or persistent and are used as input to the various relational operators to produce new tables as output. Usually, base tables are stored on disk.

bootstrap algorithm A data mining algorithm, such as rule induction, which does not depend on preexisting knowledge of the patterns to be recognized in the data.

bus sniffing Another name for *snoopy protocol.*

cache High-speed memory that sits between the microprocessor and main memory so as to better match the fast retrieval rate of the microprocessor. See also *cache coherence, DRAM,* and *SRAM.*

cache coherence In a shared memory architecture whose microprocessors use cache, it is possible for a single logical value to be physically instantiated in several caches. Cache coherence ensures the consistency of these instances in the face of possible modification of the variable by one of the processors.

CART *Classification and regression trees;* a data mining approach to rule induction that works well on both discrete (unordered) and continuous (ordered) data types.

CHAID *Chi-squared automatic interaction detection;* a data mining approach that finds significant correlation automatically among fields in the records of a database.

cluster A parallel architecture in which several independent SMPs are linked with a network, often using LAN technology, and applied to a single problem.

cluster analysis A data mining technique in which records of a database are treated as points in a multidimensional space and the distance between these points is used as a measure of similarity. By projecting onto different subspaces and adjusting the distance metric parameters, significant relationships among data can emerge. The *K*-nearest neighbors algorithm is one commonly encountered example of this technique.

consistency One of the four ACID requirements in TPC benchmarks; ensures that a query takes the database from one internally consistent state to another.

CPU *Central processing unit;* an archaic term now used to refer to a single microprocessor or processing node in a parallel machine.

cumulative distribution function See *histogram.*

dance hall architecture   A parallel computer architecture in which several processors are allowed uniform access to a set of memory banks using a crossbar switch or interconnection network.

DASD   *Direct access storage device*; in current parlance, the heavyweight counterpart to RAID storage devices. See also *SLED*.

database machine   A tightly integrated hardware/software system dedicated exclusively to database operations.

data mart   An imprecise term intended to convey the notion that similar decision support functionality is provided as in a data warehouse but on a smaller and more narrowly focused set of data. A data warehouse may provide periodic data loads to data marts servicing specific organizations within an enterprise. Data marts often use OLAP tools customized to their departmental needs.

data mining   Any of a number of algorithms used to identify patterns and extract "knowledge" from a large database. These algorithms may or may not be expressible in SQL, and often require physical sorting of large files or tables.

data partitioning   The mechanism by which a single logical table is split into groups of rows and spread across multiple disks. The reason for data partitioning is to increase I/O bandwidth to the table. See also *hash partitioning* and *range partitioning*.

data shipping   IBM's name for the shared disk parallel database architecture.

data skew   The state of affairs in which data is not evenly spread over the entire key space but is highly clumped into certain regions. Data skew can adversely affect load balancing in a parallel machine if a naive form of range partitioning is used to distribute the data in the table.

data warehouse A mechanism for delivering integrated business information to an organization.

deadlock An unfortunate situation that arises when two queries are each waiting for a lock to be released by the other. One function of a lock manager is to detect and correct such an occurrence.

decision support A type of database processing in which complex queries with low selectivity are serviced against a static database. Whereas OLTP systems are associated with ongoing operations, decision support is concerned with answering business questions about trends and patterns. Decision support systems typically have less severe RAS and responsiveness requirements than OLTP, and performance is measured by intraquery parallelism.

disk striping A technique in which a single logical data unit (a file or table) is spread across multiple disks so as to increase I/O bandwidth.

distributed memory One of the three major classes of parallel computer architecture; each node in the processor array has its private, nonshared memory, and data is communicated among processors by message passing over the interconnection network.

distributed shared memory One of the three major classes of parallel computer architecture, in which hardware and software implement cache coherence across a machine-wide address space. See also *NUMA*.

DM See *distributed memory.*

DRAM *Dynamic random access memory*; the VLSI technology of choice for implementing main memory (for reasons of cost, density, and low power dissipation).

DSM See *distributed shared memory.*

DSS *Decision support system.* See *decision support.*

durability One of the four ACID requirements in TPC benchmarks; concerns the ability of a database to recover an internally consistent and correct state in the face of system failure.

dynamic Rapidly changing over time (the opposite of static); typical of OLTP implementations, where individual queries frequently update the underlying data structures.

embarassingly parallel See *independent parallelism.*

external sort A sorting operation performed on data that is too large to fit entirely in main memory.

Fibre Channel A popular high-performance disk and peripheral connection technology using fiber optics as the data transfer backbone.

function shipping IBM's name for the shared-nothing parallel database architecture.

GUI *Graphical user interface*; for OLAP tools, this both facilitates user interaction (by providing a friendly means to access the data) and restricts user interaction (by providing only that subset of queries for which the tool and schema are optimized).

hashing A process in which values from one set (the domain) are mapped to another (the range) with the property that proximity (closeness) of values in the domain is not correlated to proximity in the range. In plain English, values that are close together can be hashed to widely separated destinations. In our case of interest, key values (the domain) are mapped to storage or processor nodes (the range). The hashing function is able to achieve load balancing by distributing the data evenly regardless of data skew. See also *hash partitioning*.

hash partitioning A technique of data partitioning in which a key from each row is hashed to the number of a disk or processing node. Hashing helps to support the goal of load balancing by spreading the data evenly over the disk and/or processor array, without regard to detailed knowledge of the distribution of keys.

histogram   A count of the number of occurrences falling within preselected bins. Histograms (and their sorted counterparts, cumulative distribution functions) are central to many data mining algorithms.

horizontal partitioning   The general technique of splitting a relational table up into groups of rows. The alternative, to split it up into groups of columns, is called vertical partitioning.

independent parallelism   It may happen that a process can be decomposed into separate tasks that do not depend on or need to communicate with each other. The ability of an algorithm to exploit such opportunities is called independent parallelism. A problem amenable to this approach is sometimes said to be embarrassingly parallel.

index   A data structure that allows search algorithms to treat a table as if it were sorted on a preselected key. This enables a logarithmic (high–low) search strategy and can greatly accelerate processing of queries with high selectivity against the key fields. A table with an index built using a certain key is said to be inverted on that key.

interconnection bandwidth   The rate at which data can be exchanged between processing nodes over the interconnection network. The typical units are megabytes per second (MB/sec) or gigabytes per second (GB/sec).

interconnection network   The means by which processing nodes are linked to each other and/or to memory using very high performance switch and routing technology. The interconnection network is the single most important component in a large parallel machine.

interleaving The technique by which a logical dataset is decomposed and spread across multiple disks and/or memory banks. The motivation behind interleaving is to improve bandwidth by parallelizing the I/O operations across many components. See also *striping*.

interquery parallelism Many independent queries are executed concurrently. The goal here is throughput—that is, executing as many queries as possible in a fixed time—and the proper measure is "queries per unit time." Interquery parallelism is characteristic of OLTP implementations.

intraquery parallelism Many (or all) processors are put to work on a single query so as to execute it as rapidly as possible. How to achieve intraquery parallelism is one of the main topics of this book and is what we mean when we speak of a parallel database. Intraquery parallelism is characteristic of complex ad hoc queries with low selectivity against large tables, typical of data warehouse implementations.

inverted table See *index*.

I/O bandwidth The rate at which data can be input to (or output from) the machine. In this book it refers primarily to disk bandwidth—that is, the rate at which data can be read from disk. The typical unit is megabytes per second (MB/sec).

isolation One of the four ACID requirements in TPC benchmarks; limits (in successively more stringent levels of requirement) the effects one transaction can have on another.

K-nearest neighbors algorithm A commonly encountered implementation of cluster analysis in data mining.

key An ordered set of column values taken from each row of a table.

latency The portion of a data transfer that is independent of the size of the message (sometimes called the time to transfer a zero-byte-long dataset). Sources of latency include software protocol overhead (for network traffic), data retrieval time (for memory and disk access), and the distance between source and destination.

load balancing The technique of ensuring that all processors in the parallel machine have about the same amount of work to do, so that all complete a task at about the same time. In databases, this is most often accomplished by partitioning the data evenly over the processors in the array.

lock manager The mechanism that prevents one query from accessing data until another query has finished modifying it. It is essential for managing interquery parallelism on a dynamic database characteristic of OLTP implementations.

memory bandwidth The rate at which data can be supplied from the main memory to the processor(s). The typical unit is megabytes per second (MB/sec).

memory bank In many memory architectures, the single logical address space is physically realized by using a number of independent units. When this is done, the separate units are referred to as memory banks. The idea is to increase memory bandwidth by having multiple banks active simultaneously.

message passing The natural programming paradigm for distributed memory machines, in which data is shared among processors by using explicit messages passed over the interconnection network.

microprocessor The well-known "computer on a chip"; all current parallel processors utilize microprocessors as their processing nodes.

MIMD *Multiple instruction multiple data*; any machine that is capable of executing more than one independent instruction stream concurrently.

MPP *Massively parallel processsing*; a general term for any parallel processor with a "large" number of nodes. It is also sometimes used to refer specifically to a distributed memory architecture.

MSSN   See *multistage switched network*.

multidimensional databases   See *OLAP*.

multistage switched network   One of the two major types of interconnection network for parallel machines, in which switches are linked into multiple levels or stages to provide interconnectivity between the processing nodes.

multithreaded application   Software that has been written to exploit the use of multiple threads in a shared memory parallel environment.

neural networks   A commonly used algorithm for pattern recognition. Using training data, a neural net can be constructed to recognize patterns similar to those for which it has been optimized.

NIST   *National Institute of Standards and Technology*; the implementers of the SQL-1 and SQL-2 language standards.

node   An imprecise term that generally designates a processor in a parallel processing array.

normalization   The technique of decomposing the database into independent tables, related by keys, so as to reduce data redundancy as much as possible. In a highly normalized database, updates will affect as few tables as possible.

NUMA   *Nonuniform memory access*; used interchangeably with *DSM*. The term *nonuniform* refers to the fact that memory references to local memory will complete more rapidly than references to memory held in remote nodes.

OLAP   *On-line analytical processing*; a type of decision support typified by "drill down" and "drill across" searches on aggregation fields (that is, exposing the lower component contributions to a top-level summary). Because the type of query (aggregation) is known in advance, data structures can be provided to precompute the desired data so that it is readily available. These are sometimes referred to as multidimensional databases. OLAP tools often have sophisticated graphical user interfaces to enable rapid point-and-click navigation through the database.

OLTP *Online transaction processing*; a type of database processing consisting of a continuous stream of many small queries with high selectivity from a large population of independent users. Many of these queries involve updates to the underlying data structures, so that the database is dynamic. OLTP systems often have stringent RAS and responsiveness requirements, and performance is measured by interquery parallelism.

parallel database See *intraquery parallelism.*

pipeline parallelism When a process consists of several successive stages, it may be possible for the "next" stage to get started before the "previous" stage has completed. (That is, partial outputs from one stage may be fed immediately to the next stage, before all outputs are complete.) In that case, both stages can be active at the same time. If this idea is repeated, it may even be possible for many stages of the process to be active simultaneously. The ability of an algorithm to exploit this opportunity is called pipeline parallelism. See also *independent parallelism.*

point-to-point network One of the two major types of interconnection networks for parallel machines, in which computing nodes have direct links to other computing nodes, their "neighbors" in the interconnection topology.

precomputed JOINs A technique of denormalizing data so as to reduce the number of JOIN operations required for query execution and thereby improve scan performance against large tables. See also *normalization.*

PTPN See *point-to-point network.*

RAID *Redundant array of inexpensive disks*; a technique in which disk striping is supplemented by additional error-correcting parity data to enable rapid recovery and high availability.

range partitioning A technique of data partitioning in which the key space is divided into subintervals or subsets, and rows are assigned to processors and/or disks, depending on which subset they belong to. A danger of range partitioning is data skew, which can adversely affect load balancing.

RAS *Reliability, availability, serviceability*; a generic term used to refer to properties of a system relating to its ability to be up and operational over extended periods of time.

RDBMS *Relational database management system*. See *relational model*.

relational model The formal set theoretical model, based on unordered tables, by which new tables can be generated from base tables using well-defined operators such as join, intersect, union, or project. This model is captured in the SQL syntax used to query an RDBMS.

round-robin partitioning When rows of the table are assigned to different storage bins without regard to key value, on a next-in-order basis. This achieves very uniform load balancing but does not permit optimizations based on key value.

rule induction A data mining algorithm that finds relationships among fields and values of the data in the form of logical assertions which are true (or mostly true) about the records under consideration. Rule induction is an example of a bootstrapping data mining algorithm.

scale-up A measure of improved performance when both the problem size and the number of processors are increased together. The hope is that by increasing machine size proportionately to problem size, execution time will not be affected. One useful approach to measuring scale-up is to hold the elapsed time constant and ask how large a problem can be executed for various machine sizes.

scalability   The property that enables a system to increase performance in any of a number of dimensions—number of processors, amount of memory, disk storage, number of users—smoothly and without requiring major hardware or software disruptions. Some parallel architectures are able to scale over three orders of magnitude without requiring modification of application software. A system fails to be scalable if there are hard upper bounds beyond which performance cannot be increased.

SCSI   *Small computer system interface*; the most widely used daisy-chain technology for access to disks and peripherals.

SDRAM   *Synchronous DRAM*; the most recent attempt to narrow the performance gap between microprocessors and the relative slow retrieval rate of DRAM.

selectivity   The percentage of the table(s) touched by the query. A query with high selectivity will touch only one or a few rows, and the use of indexes can greatly improve performance on this type of query (typical of OLTP implementations). A query with low selectivity will touch a large fraction of the table(s), and indexes do not help performance (typical of DSS implementations).

shared disk   One of the three major software architectures for parallel databases, in which processing nodes share access to all the disks but have private nonshared memory.

shared everything   One of the three major software architectures for parallel databases, in which both memory and disks are directly accessible by all nodes in the processor array.

shared memory   Any of a number of parallel architectures that provide a single global shared address space to all the processors in the machine. See also *DSM*, *NUMA*, and *SMP*.

shared nothing   One of the three major software architectures for parallel databases, in which each processing node has private, nonshared memory and disks. Data is exhanged among processors by message passing over the interconnection network. This is the software analog of the distributed memory hardware architecture.

single program, multiple data   A programming style for distributed memory architectures in which the same code executes, by replication, on all nodes of the processor array. With care, SPMD codes can also execute without modification on varying numbers of nodes.

SLED   *Single large expensive disk;* see also *DASD.*

SMP   See *symmetric multiprocessor.*

snoopy protocol   A method of implementing cache coherence in an SMP where all processors monitor the system bus looking for signals that cached data is no longer valid (as a result of modification).

sorting   The computational task of arranging all the rows of a table in order according to key values. Sorting is a major component of data mining algorithms.

speed-up   A measure of improved performance when the problem size is held constant and the number of processors applied to the problem is increased. It is the ratio of the time taken to execute the problem on one processor ($T1$) to the time taken to execute the problem on N processors (TN). Due to Amdahl's law, speed-up curves on small problems are poor [that is, $T1/TN) << N$], but speed-up curves on large problems can be very good [that is, $(T1/TN) \sim N$].

SPMD   See *single program, multiple data.*

SQL   *Structured query language;* an international standard syntax that implements the relational model and is used to query relational databases.

SRAM   *Static random access memory*; used to implement caches for microprocessors; faster than DRAM, but hotter, less dense, and more costly than DRAM.

SSA   *Serial storage architecture*; a disk and peripheral connection technology sponsored by IBM.

star schema   An approach to database design in which a large central fact table is "surrounded" by smaller dimension tables. Many-to-one join keys typically only run from the fact table out to the dimension tables, not between the dimension tables themselves. This may lead to a denormalized database, but it supports such DSS functions as rapid full-table scans.

static   Remaining constant over time (the opposite of *dynamic*); typical of DSS implementations in which updates occur (relatively) infrequently as bulk loads.

striping   The technique of decomposing a single file or data set into many small pieces, called *striping units*, and assigning these to a large number of disks in round-robin fashion. The disks can then retrieve the data in parallel, thereby dramatically improving I/O bandwidth to the dataset. See also *interleaving*.

symmetric multiprocessor   The most widely used form of shared memory parallel processing, in which cache coherence is implemented using a snoopy protocol on the system bus.

thread   In a shared memory parallel model, a thread is a lightweight, independent execution stream. Several threads may cooperate to accomplish a single task. Typically, each thread will be assigned to a separate CPU, and threads use the shared memory as the means to communciate and coordinate their activity.

throughput   The appropriate metric for performance on interquery parallelism; the ability of a machine to execute against a workload consisting of many independent tasks.

TLB *Translation look-aside buffer*; this is a rapid hardware scheme for mapping logical addresses to a physical location in main memory. Part of cache coherence involves maintaining consistency in the TLBs of multiple CPUs.

TPC *Transaction Processing Performance Council*; an independent organization that constructs and oversees benchmarks for database systems.

TPC-D The decision support benchmark recommended by the Transaction Processing Performance Council.

vertical partitioning Splitting up a relational table by columns instead of by rows; sometimes called *column splitting*. See also *horizontal partitioning*.

Index